The
⚜ Disastrous ⚜
Mrs. Weldon

*The Life,
Loves, and Lawsuits
of a
Legendary Victorian*

BRIAN
THOMPSON

The
❧ Disastrous ❧
Mrs. Weldon

Doubleday

New York   London   Toronto   Sydney   Auckland

PUBLISHED BY DOUBLEDAY
a division of Random House, Inc.
1540 Broadway, New York, New York 10036

DOUBLEDAY and the portrayal of an anchor with a dolphin
are trademarks of Doubleday, a division of Random House, Inc.

The Disastrous Mrs. Weldon: The Life, Loves, and Lawsuits of a Legendary Victorian
was originally published in the United Kingdom as
A Monkey Among Crocodiles: The Eccentric Life of Georgina Weldon
by HarperCollins Publishers UK.
The Doubleday edition is published by arrangement with HarperCollins Publishers UK.

BOOK DESIGN BY TERRY KARYDES

Library of Congress Cataloging-in-Publication Data
Thompson, Brian (Brian John William)
[Monkey among crocodiles]
The disastrous Mrs. Weldon: the life, loves, and lawsuits of a legendary Victorian /
Brian Thompson.— 1st ed.   p.   cm.
Originally published as: A monkey among crocodiles. 2000.
Includes bibliographical references and index.
1. Weldon, Georgina, 1837–1914. 2. Great Britain—Biography. I. Title.
CT788.W46 T48 2001
941.08'092—dc21
[B]   00-034032

ISBN 0-385-50090-4

FIRST EDITION IN THE UNITED STATES OF AMERICA
1   3   5   7   9   10   8   6   4   2

For Walter

Acknowledgments

I should like to thank some people for their help and wise comments. Mrs. Wendy Hill followed the London end of the story with a sharp eye for topographical detail. In Paris, Kay Dumas plunged into the Bibliothèque Nationale shortly after its removal to new premises and survived to tell the tale. I am grateful to the staff of the Bodleian Library, Oxford; Trinity College Cambridge Library; East Sussex County Records Office; and the staff of the Brighton Central Library. Elizabeth North gave me support and a novelist's insights into the central character and suffered her presence in the life we share with unfailing good humor. Finally, as every author knows, some works are happier to see through to a conclusion than others. This has been a happy book, for which I am indebted to David Miller and Rebecca Wilson, more than I can say here. And at the very last, my special gratitude goes to Arabella Pike and Amy Scheibe, two incomparable editors separated only by the steep Atlantic stream.

Contents

"I don't think there's ever been a human being put down on this earth afflicted by a temperament as shy and reclusive as mine. A shyness pushed to the point of suffering by a nervousness nothing could overcome. There's nothing more marvelous, nothing's ever happened that's more singular that I, among all the women in the world, find myself so to speak engulfed by the stormy existence that has been my lot since 1868."

—*My Orphanage*, 1877

"Look at Sarah Bernhardt—does she have my beauty, my voice, my worth, etc.? So from where does she get her fortune? Fame!"

—Georgina to her mother, 1877

"Quand on tombe, on tombe jamais bien."

—Dumas fils

The
❧ Disastrous ❧
Mrs. Weldon

One rainy evening in September 1889 the nuns of a small hospice in Gisors, France, on the north bank of the Seine, answered the night bell to find on their doorstep an Englishwoman called Mrs. Georgina Weldon. The luggage at her feet was modest—two pugs, some caged birds, and, peering from his wicker basket, a bedraggled monkey called Titileehee. Mrs. Weldon, who spoke rapid and idiomatic French, was not a woman to be argued with, and she was soon inside and shaking out her cape. The lateness of the hour was quickly explained. She had come hotfoot from London, her house stolen from under her by an accursed Frenchwoman she had considered to be a lifetime partner. In the background of the story was an estranged husband connected to the College of Arms, a man who was friend to princes. As she rattled on in her guileless, headlong fashion, the startled nuns learned how the less proximate cause of her ruin was the cowardice and ingratitude twenty years earlier of the celebrated composer Charles Gounod. That got their interest. Gounod was a revered national figure in his seventies, as much noted for his piety these days as for the operas he had composed in his golden years.

Over the next few days the garrulous Mrs. Weldon continued her catalogue of misfortunes. In her time, she had been falsely accused of lunacy, fought vigorous actions in the English courts in defense of her married rights, run an orphanage and several large choirs. She had served a prison sentence in Newgate for publishing "a false and scandalous libel," only to be cheered through the streets by her adoring public on her release. She served a second term in Holloway for an identical offense, and this time on her release her followers unshipped the horses from their shafts and dragged her carriage to Speakers' Corner in Hyde Park, from where she addressed a crowd estimated at 17,000.

The nuns grew nervous. This was many more than the population of Gisors. Ah yes, Mrs. Weldon went on, but it didn't end there—she was famous in so many ways! Her face had appeared in advertisements for Pear's soap on Clapham omnibuses, and as well as singing at the Paris Opéra, she had in more needy circumstances trod the boards of the London music halls. Nor was she in Gisors by chance. Twelve years previous she had found this selfsame hospice a haven and a blessing for a few months, as some of the older nuns might remember. And now here she was again at the mercy of the good sisters, seeking only calm and repose. A thought crossed her mind: had she mentioned she was once accused of going to look for Gounod with a loaded revolver?

The nuns admitted her out of charity and she stayed for twelve years, remaining more or less within the walls of the hospice all that time and seldom venturing outside. It was soon clear she was not there from considerations of piety. She was not a Catholic, nor was she very devout in any other direction, unless an alarming and scandalizing enthusiasm for summoning the spirits of the departed could be counted as such. Though her bills were paid more or less on time, there was much that was vexing about her behavior. She insisted on adopting the working dress of the hospice, which she wore with a theatrical dash quite contrary to the spirit of humility it signified. Her French was salted with Parisian slang, and she used it to command all those little things that were to her the necessities of life: stamps and writing paper, food for her pets. She played no part in the religious observances of the establishment but was not above the criticizing its management. (It was a matter of awe to some of the nuns that shortly after she arrived the cesspit was emptied at her insistence for the first time in thirty years.) She was fond of gardening and threw herself into the reorganization of the herb and vegetable plots, as well as designing and having built a better sort of cold greenhouse. She developed a passion for beekeeping and corresponded vigorously with local experts. Her peas, she asserted, were the admiration of all who saw them. You might travel by train to Paris without seeing better.

⚞ Georgina Weldon was fifty-two when she first entered the Hospice Orphelinat de St.-Thomas de Villeneuve. She was given rooms on the third floor, and one of her earliest acts was to hire a maid, a local girl called Charlotte. Since the other occupants of the building were elderly and alcoholic paupers, this caused a stir; but an even greater surprise came when the rest of her luggage arrived from England. Very quickly, two walls of her *salle de séjour* were lined out floor to ceiling with deed boxes. They accounted for only a fraction of the twenty-eight trunks of written and printed materials this strange Englishwoman had lugged across the Channel. The record of her life—if that was what all this paper indicated—was a staggering minuteness. As the French themselves say, God was in the details.

It became clear to the nuns that Mme Weldon's principal obsession was with herself. As well as the whiff of sulphur that seemed to rise from not one but dozens of court actions she had undertaken, there were in these papers the lighter fragrances of earlier and better times. The material for an autobiography had never been more assiduously gathered, and in addition to this massive chronofile, which included menus and theater programmes, *cartes de viste,* letters, sheet music, legal transcripts, and yellowing telegrams, were the handsomely bound diaries and journals she had commenced as a child, and a splendid visitor's book from a house in Tavistock Square that had once belonged to Dickens. She, who had once published her own newspaper, was setting up in Gisors with the intention of putting all this material into shape, not merely for her own pleasure but as a lesson for future generations. She was there to write her memoirs.

There was something artless about Mrs. Weldon, for all her protestations of genius. Gounod came into the story because—she claimed—she was, like him, a musician of the first rank, a singer and music educator such as the world had never before seen. His good opinion of her, which she freely embroidered now, had not stopped her in the past from demanding her husband horsewhip him on the steps of the Opéra. The more perceptive of the Sisters of St.-Thomas came to realize there was serious folly in her. She was more like a thwarted and disappointed child than the biblical Jeremiah she often invoked. However, if she was fool, she was a holy one. And there was one manner in her that was unchanging. Not very tall and no longer in possession of the beauty it was easy to see she had once owned, she nevertheless exuded a kind of upper-class English arrogance, a certainty that seemed to come from an aristocratic background only to be guessed at by the simple and pious folk in Gisors. This was the most cherished part of her persona. The nuns, with their blunt nails and chilblained feet, were left in no doubt they were dealing with a lady.

The memoirs she set about writing were to be vindication of all she had attempted in the name of art and love. She wrote in French, partly because she wished to address the work to her host nation, but much more plainly because any attempt to publish in English would most assuredly bring her before the courts again. The memoirs were a forest of libels directed against anyone who had ever dared to cross her will. She had already chosen this invocation, from Lamentations:

> *O vos omnes qui transitis per viam: attendite et videte si est dolor sicut dolor meus.*

And indeed, had anyone ever seen a misery such as hers? The prophetical Mrs. Weldon had suffered affliction in full biblical measure. However, unlike Jeremiah, she had not the slightest intention of taking it lying down. That had never been her way. Smoking cigarettes with a furious intensity, breaking off only to scold her maid or bully the gardeners, she roamed back over the turbulent events of her life. They grew to like her at Gisors. M. Robine, the lay administrator, felt he understood her. The narrow purpose of her efforts to expose the English system of justice was soon overwhelmed by her passion for digression. Robine knew enough about how the world wagged to see she was storing up trouble for herself with every page she wrote. One day she waved a letter in his face. London society ladies were preparing a tribute to Victoria on the occasion of the Queen's Diamond Jubilee. Mrs. Craigie had written: "No representative gathering of the women of England would be complete without Mrs. Weldon."

That might have been a good time to publish. Better still, it might have signaled peace and sent her home to England with her reputation restored. Instead, the galley proofs piled up in the offices of her long-suffering printers in Dijon while she hunted down letters she had sent a quarter of a century earlier. The Dreyfus Affair captured her attention for a while. Was she not the English Dreyfus, she asked her readers? A nephew met Oscar Wilde in Paris, and she wrote to him, sympathizing with his plight but deploring his crime. Wilde replied with courage and wit. She was much preoccupied with the legend of Louis XVI's son and his escape by substitution from the revolutionary terror. These matters and her peas and honey delayed completion of the great task she had set herself. In the end the *Mémoires* were not finally delivered from the printer until the new century. The work ran to fifteen hundred pages, bound up by the firm of Darantière in six volumes.

Even in French the *Mémoires* shriek. Georgina finally went back to England in 1901 to publicize them, and those few friends who remained in London persuaded her how dangerous and unwise she had been to have them printed at all. One of her principal targets in the work was her husband Harry, who was not only still alive but Acting Garter King of Arms, the most senior heraldic officer in the land. As such, he had stage-managed the funeral of Victoria and was now charged with the salvage of Edward's Coronation, postponed by the King's illness. Even Mrs. Weldon's most loyal supporters—and they were mostly women—were scandalized by the work. It was no good her telling them that the *Mémoires* were in print and on sale in France (though in fact she held most of the stock in boxes under her bed). Nothing good could come of promoting them in England, least of all their principal objective, her life vindicated at the bar of public opinion. In France itself they were not the sensation she had hoped and longed for over all those years of scribbling. She sent out presentation copies, sold a few sets of the work to unsuspecting customers, received no reviews. It was the bitterest blow. The whole enterprise sank like a stone into a lake. Was this to be the fate of what the medium Desbarolles had once assured her would be the most useful memoirs of her day and likely to last a century?

In 1996 a copy of the *Mémoires* bobbed to the surface in a French bookseller's catalogue. I read them with mounting incredulity in the garden of a house near Cognac, trying to fit a face to the name. Who was this engaging, maddening, self-deceiving Victorian? The work has little or no literary merit and is muddled, contradictory, and sometimes incoherent. The French in which it is written was a matter of wonder to my neighbors. The things it describes were far from their own concerns as small farmers and winegrowers. "Why are you bothering your head with this good woman?" the sardonic Mme Ayraud asked me over dinner one evening.

A short distance from where we ate, there is a village called Chez Audebert. At some time in the nineteen forties, in the garden of a house right on the main road, a simple man began making three-quarter-size statues in cement. He started with angels and children but gradually broadened his interests to include de Gaulle, Elvis, and Marilyn Monroe. There is a man who might or might not be Jean Gabin and another who resembles Danny Kaye. The sculptor of Audebert made dogs, most of them with impudent, knowing grins; birds—owls—and lions. There are nudes of young girls with their arms held out in innocent welcome; knock-kneed schoolchildren; and peasants like himself lurching home along a dusty track. Some of the people depicted carry briefcases and smoke jaunty pipes. Gradually his garden filled up with maybe a hundred statues all arranged higgledy-piggledy. When he died his widow left the gate open for anyone to visit, and so it stands today. Whenever two or more people are in the garden, the living are quickly trapped in the arms and legs, breasts and buttocks of this mysterious sculpture park. If they are motionless for a moment, it is sometimes difficult to separate them from the statues all around.

We don't know why the Audebert villager made these sculptures, and they are regarded with an embarrassed condescension by his neighbors. Mme Ayraud's comment is typical: "Pouf! He was not an artist, he was a poor man who had big ideas. That sort of thing never works." It is true that one Audebert figure on its own would be disappointing. A hundred are a different matter.

The great attraction of the *Mémoires Weldon* is a similar plenty. Georgina wrote as she spoke, pell-mell. The pages are crowded, noisy, exuberant, and give a view of the nineteenth century that is not often recorded. As to her purpose in writing, one of the striking things about Georgina Weldon's search for justice is the degree to which she incriminates herself. Many of the things that can be held against her—her highhandedness, her occasional cruelties, the want of a sense of humor that might have protected her from some of her disasters—come direct from her own narrative errors. The more she struggles, the deeper she sinks.

There is nevertheless great beauty in her story. "It's the faith in what is good, what is beautiful and just that has armed my natural convictions," she wrote. "Gounod always called me his Jeanne d'Arc—others have called me Madame Don Quixote, a visionary, a utopian." After all the flimflam and absurdity that dogged her has been discounted, these are the words that stick in the mind. How true they are is the subject of the present book.

Thomas

1

*G*eorgina Weldon was never quite the performer and entertainer nor the grand lady or talked-about social lioness she so fondly invented for her readers. Her story starts with parents and a childhood of such a cranky nature they must be examined with the care she gave to later episodes of her life. Her troubles started the day she was born, when she was presented with a mask fashioned for her by parents who were the kind that could not distinguish easily between the truth and a lie.

She came into the world on May 24, 1837. All day long the London streets were filled with people, running to see the Life Guards pass by or hanging on the Hyde Park railings to gawp or jeer at the rich. The greatest aristocratic houses in England were represented by the comings and goings of their lumbering and oversprung coaches, issuing from the squares about Mayfair and Belgravia. In the tens of thousands that milled about on foot there was that strange unvoiced sense of the exceptional that sometimes characterizes how mobs behave. Londoners normally turned out in such numbers only to riot or exhibit their feral curiosity—a fortnight earlier, for example, twenty thousand had gathered at Newgate to watch the murderer Greenacre hanged. Today the mood was different. The word "sightseer" was a brand-new coinage and exactly suited the occasion. Placid and orderly citizens of all classes wandered down the Mall to inspect the newly completed but untenanted Buckingham Palace, where it was said few of the thousand windows would open and many of the doors were jammed in their frames by green timber and shoddy workmanship. Directly in front of the palace squatted the enormous and foreign-looking Marble Arch, on top of which was to have stood an equestrian statue of George IV, a piece of triumphalism only averted by his death and the colossal overspend on the whole project.

There were many such examples of the new and the bold to gaze on. London, in its West End, was being almost entirely remodeled. Ancient lanes and houses had been pulled down and green fields obliterated. Behind Buckingham Palace the ingenious Mr. Cubitt was bringing soil from his excavation of St. Katherine's Dock at Tower Bridge along a canal that cut up from the Thames to the site of the present Victoria station. His purpose was to fill the marshy land round about and complete the building of Belgravia for his client, Lord Grosvenor. It was the showpiece of property development in the entire city. Filling marshes and leveling huge tracts were becoming a commonplace in that part of London. Thomas Cubitt's plans for neighboring Pimlico involved the wholesale tearing up of ancient market gardens: farms, even rivers, were not to stand in his way. Though it was true the speculation in property was running into something of a slump, the check was only temporary. The scale of new building in the capital was greater than anything seen before. For a brief moment this sunny Wednesday, London stood still and took stock of itself.

For the nobility it was an important working day, and most of those who peered from their coaches were in court dress. They were summoned in celebration of Princess Victoria's eighteenth birthday, which began with the formalities of an audience in the Drawing Room at Kensington Palace. It was an occasion of the greatest significance, for under the constitutional arrangements made for her the Princess at last burst free from the clutches of her mother, the regent. Those people of rank who attended the young Victoria that morning witnessed a telling little piece of theater. One of the many visitors she received was the Lord Chamberlain, who had ridden from Windsor with a letter from the King. The Duchess of Kent held out her hand to receive it on behalf of her daughter. Lord Conyngsby ignored the gesture and very pointedly gave the letter direct to the Princess. What was long promised had now become fact: the next monarch would be this almost unknown, unmarried young woman. As everyone understood, her accession was not far off. George IV had been fifty-eight when at last he became King, and his brother William IV succeeded him at age sixty-five. The taint of madness and scandal hung over both reigns. If God should spare Victoria, Britain could anticipate a profoundly different future.

As soon as she was old enough to understand, Georgina's father harped on the connection between these great events and her own birth. There was nothing particularly teasing about it either. Both parents made so much of the coincidence that she confessed later, "it filled my childish fancy with a vague idea of superiority and relationship with the Royal Family." Such ideas, which are normally no more than a harmless family joke, are supposed to wane with the passing of time; unfortunately, this one stuck. Georgina was to live her whole life with the unquantifiable feeling of superiority derived from that day. Encouraged by her manically snobbish parents, she was, she believed, blessed by greatness in some way: at the very least born to a rank in society that furnished its own recommendations and needed no apology or explanation. She was a full part of the old aristocratic supremacy, and the same gentle zephyrs that blew on Victoria's reign would also fill her sails. When things turned out rather differently—and it would be hard to imagine two less compatible Victorian histories than those of the monarch and her subject—then the fault lay not in her, but in other people.

It was certainly a wonderful day on which to be born. All England was *en fête*. The King lay at Windsor, unloved and unregarded, while at Kensington Palace his niece received twenty-two loyal addresses delivered by hand from every part of the country. In the evening hundreds of noble guests attended a state ball, where there was much quizzing of the short and excitable Victoria, who showed her gums rather a lot when she laughed. Once again, the King was conspicuous by his absence. Wellington had attended George IV in his last days and with his usual brutal candor let it be known around the room that the brother was in even worse plight. Lit by hundreds of candles, the noblest in the land gossiped on the white and gilt chairs set for their comfort. The sole topic of conversation was the future Queen.

Morgan Thomas and his heavily pregnant wife, Louisa, rode around London in their carriage that balmy May day, soaking up the atmosphere. Far from being at the center of things, they had no part to play and were not invited indoors to any great house: they were faces in the crowd. True, Morgan had a stare that could shatter glass and a coat in the old-fashioned color described as "King's blue." His wife wore a bonnet in which a plume danced as proudly as any other lady's, but their carriage would have given them away. There was a useful phrase in vogue to describe the aristocratic predominance: men and women of rank spoke of themselves as the Upper Ten Thousand. Morgan and his wife liked to believe they, too, were in that number—not angling to be admitted but already there and secure in their tenure. It was the deepest and most cherished of their fantasies. As evening approached, they crossed the river and rattled home to rural Clapham, where Georgina was born at a quarter to ten in the last of the summer light. For a few days and weeks there was anxiety in the nursery, for the Thomases already had a child, the sickly infant Cordelia. She died thirteen weeks later and was buried in Clapham Parish.

Georgina was destined to bear three surnames, but the first of these, Thomas, under which she was registered, is tied to a childhood that resolutely failed to budge from its anchorage in less progressive times. Her father was a William IV man, a Tory of the old stripe. At the time of her birth, Morgan Thomas was thirty-five years old and as reactionary as any man in England. His wife was a hapless woman who liked to protest she was not made for children and the family hearth. They were a strange couple, she by temperament as indecisive as her husband was truculent and hotheaded.

Morgan's position in society was a commonplace of the times: he was a lawyer never intending to practive law. His gentlemanly status had been expressed to his own satisfaction in a book published in 1834 by a writer named

Medwin. "Judges of the Exchequer were designated thus: one as a gentleman and a lawyer; another as a lawyer and no gentleman." Morgan was always ready to insist he was of the first kind. He had found and married his rather plain wife in Naples three years earlier, and if the venue was romantic, the circumstances were not. Both bride and groom were in their thirties, and whatever hand life had dealt them, it did not include friends and confidants. One unhappy and solitary human being was joined with another. Much later, at the time of his death, Morgan's younger brother, George, wrote an enigmatic letter to Louisa: "I ignore for the moment that I have treated you and yours with the greatest kindness, without mentioning the way I plugged the gap when you got married, without which it would not have taken place. I have always come to your aid when the means permitted and it was only after Morgan's gross and insulting letters that I broke off relations, necessarily."

The help that was given the newlyweds was almost certainly financial but may have included moral support for an unwelcome or overhasty union. These Thomases were turbulent and aggressive opportunists when it came to marriage, and Morgan may have been thought to have chosen his wife unwisely. It was a family fiction that he had courted her for ten long years—it seems more likely that he met her in Italy by chance. Louisa was once described by Count d'Orsay, the supreme arbiter of London taste and fashion, as "the offspring of Punch and Venus." The poor woman interpreted this as a compliment. To marry so late and in such a venue as the British Embassy, where otherwise only naval officers spliced the knot, might indicate to the sharp-witted or malicious observer a sudden inheritance on the part of a parentless bride. In this at least Morgan was his father's child. The marriage was much more favorable to him than to the luckless Louisa, and she was to pay a very heavy price.

The belief that he was a person of importance went very deep with this strutting, vexatious man. It was a matter of pride that his family had some mention in *Burke's Landed Gentry,* the second edition of which was brought out in that same year of 1837, for he was descended from those ancient Thomases who owned considerable land near Llanelli. The Lletymawr estates had been in the possession of his family since an honored forebear Sir

Hugh Trehearn followed the Black Prince to Poitiers. Morgan liked to emphasize this glorious ancestry. Perhaps, as the five hundredth anniversary of the Battle of Poitiers approached, he was inclined to make too much of it, yet it was easy to see why. For the first and last time in history, a French king had been taken in battle; more to the point, the entire chivalry of France had either been slain or surrendered. It was a huge payday for the Prince's army. The lowliest archer had three or four prisoners to ransom, and Sir Hugh and his little contingent went back to Wales far richer men than when they left. And there they languished.

Morgan's great-grandfather gave the family its English connection. In 1745 he married an heiress of the Goring family of Frodley in Staffordshire. Through the female line, the Gorings traced their ancestry back to Edward III, bringing Morgan to the point where he could assure his impressionable daughter that her family would "become entitled to the throne of England if anything should happen to the ruling family." She believed him.

The more recent past was much less romantic. At the turn of the century, Morgan's father, Rees Goring Thomas, married Sarah Hovel of Cambridge. This was almost certainly an undergraduate romance, spiked with a hardheaded opportunism, the like of which Georgina was one day to demonstrate herself. Hovel was a name well known in Cambridge, but not for its aristocratic connections. Thomas Hovel was a haberdasher and his brother John a saddler. These two had by diligence and hard work acquired property in the market area of town, as well as a parcel of fenland on the road to London on which the Leys School now stands. Rees Goring Thomas, of the illustrious Welsh ancestry, made himself comfortably secure by marrying the haberdasher's daughter—the last parcel of Cambridge land he acquired through marriage was sold out of the family in 1878. Rees took his bride out of Cambridge and into Surrey, where the family had bought the title to a small manor called Tooting Graveney, in the middle of which was erected a property called Tooting Lodge. It was in this house that Georgina was born.

There was just one small problem: the property did not belong to Morgan. He lived there as his elder brother's houseguest. To be a gentleman under these circumstances was a difficult part to carry off. There was already a nephew bounding about Tooting Lodge, a thirteen-year-old named Rees, who was destined one day to return the family to Wales. Worse yet: only a few months after the birth of Georgina, Morgan's brother, late in life, was given another boy. This finally slammed the door in the face of any hope he himself might have had of the Lletymawr properties and their rents. It was true he did not have to work, but neither was he rich in the way his heart desired. Riches were not quite the central issue—what he longed for was pre-eminence. He was a man who could not bear to be in another's shadow. This was a feeling he gifted in full to his daughter.

Georgina's mother had an equally illustrious family history. She was born Louisa Frances Dalrymple, of Mayfield in Sussex. The Dalrymples were an ancient family and claimed descent from the Earls of Stair. Her grandfather was General Sir Hew Whitefoord Dalrymple, the soldier who had signed the Convention of Cintra in 1808, which provided for his enemy the French to evacuate Portugal in British ships with all their impedimenta and a mountain of loot besides. The terms of the convention were considered so scandalous that Sir Hew never again commanded in the field. He was instead made a baronet and died in 1830. Of his two sons, the elder, who was also a soldier, sat in Parliament for Brighton. The younger was John Apsley Dalrymple, colonel of the 15th Hussars and lord of the manors of Cortesly and Hamerdon near Ticehurst in Sussex. He died in 1833. This man was Louisa's father. There were problems with this lofty background too.

Insecurity and disappointment made both Georgina's parents tremendous snobs. The careful and faintly comical allusions to an ancestry not half so grand as they pretended were second nature to these two, and were a form of vanity that ran—increasingly as the Early Victorian period developed—against the tide. Georgina grew up in a meritocratic age. This same Victoria, who seemed so light and biddable when she became Queen, came to preside over the greatest shift in social structure the country had ever experienced, calling for the wholesale redefinition of words like "art" and "culture," "industry" and "progress," and, most significantly of all, "family." This change in style and substance had no effect whatever on Georgina's parents. In 1837 Mr. Pickwick's friend Sam Weller had a characteristically sardonic way of expressing the essence of the old order: "Wotever is, is right, as the young nobleman sweetly remarked wen they put him down in the pension list 'cos his mother's uncle's wife's grandfather vunce lit the King's pipe with a portable tinderbox."

This was also Morgan's view of the world. He never mastered the new epoch. You had to look quite a long way down the descending orders of rank to arrive at his actual position in society—though of course his contemporaries could place him after only a few idle questions. This was a second son, educated at Cheam, entered under Mr. Wilding at Trinity College, Cambridge, with men who would far outshine him. He was hardly highborn: his great-uncle's saddlery overlooked the college gates. Later on, in supplying biographical details to yearbooks and the like, he lightly removed his mother from a haberdashery in Cambridge and described the Hovels and all his numerous cousins as "of Norfolk." In the same vein, he once claimed to have been presented at all the courts in Europe, which was—to put it mildly—stretching the point. This mania for improving the bare facts—and in him it became an actual mania—was passed on to Georgina. There was something very wrong with Morgan Thomas, and it seems to have been a willful attempt to make time stand still or even run backward. In this he was not alone, and there was in his generation a writer only too likely to understand him and his kind.

William Makepeace Thackeray went to Trinity at about the same time as Morgan; and like him read law at the Inner Temple. In 1837 he came back from a three-year sojourn in Paris, and in that year he, too, was presented with a daughter, born in London a fortnight after Georgina in much less auspicious circumstances. What distinguished Thackeray from Morgan Thomas and his kind were his energy and above all his talent. It was enough for Morgan to be a gentleman of independent means, however shaky those means were. But Thackeray had nothing on which he could fall back: what little he did inherit he lost at cards in a disastrous evening or two when a student at the Inner Temple. Necessity sharpened his wits. In satirizing the likes of Morgan and his foolish wife, he showed himself a man very much in the spirit of the times. The world was moving forward, and the gifted man looked outward and opened his mind and his senses to the new.

Part of the hackwork Thackeray did for *Frazer's Magazine* was to write the highly popular "Christmas Books," the last of which was published in 1850. He was by now famous through having written *Vanity Fair,* which some of his contemporaries placed higher than anything by Dickens. At the end of the book the plot is triumphantly resolved when the major surviving characters find themselves thrown together at a Rhineland spa. In the Christmas Book of 1850 Thackeray returns us to the Rhine in the company of a fatuous family called Kicklebury. His satirical portrait of them drew a reproof from the *Times.* The review, which was written to order by a friend of Thackeray's named Charles Lamb Kenney, greatly amused its target, enough for him to reprint it in the second edition of the work, with commentary. The one unanswerable point Thackeray had to make about the savaging of the Kickleburys was that the work had sold out. Kenney had written: "From the moment his eye lights on a luckless family group embarked on the same steamer with himself, the sight of his accustomed quarry—vulgarity, imbecility, and affectation—reanimates his relaxed sinews, and, playfully fastening his satiric fangs upon the familiar prey, he dallies with it in mimic ferocity like a satiated mouser." Yes, Thackeray rejoins: and the public loves it. Something is moving, something is in the air: there *is* no pity for vulgarity, imbecility, and affectation. The *Times,* he indicates with an unruffled assurance, has missed the joke.

Georgina's arrival did nothing to settle her parents' position. In the short term it greatly worsened it. The Thomas family had always found Morgan's violent temper hard to stomach. Clearly, he could not expect to go on living at Tooting Lodge forever, and the question had already been broached more than once as to when he would shift for himself. Georgina's birth made an issue of it. As soon as it was clear she would not follow her sister into an infant grave, Morgan and Louisa came under pressure to leave.

There may have been a second impetus. The family banked with their neighbor William Esdaile, who lay dying in Clapham. For two years Esdaile, who was a very old man but nevertheless the presiding genius of the bank he had built up, had done no business following malarial fever contracted in Italy. At the beginning of 1837 the bank failed. Whether or not the Thomas fortunes went down with it, it left Morgan with just enough unearned income to continue as a gentleman: the challenge was to find a house and a style that would reflect his high opinion of himself. Putting it another way, in the long gallery of snobs, what kind of a snob was he going to be?

Late in life, when the mood of retribution was upon her, Georgina published a letter from her brother Dalrymple. It read in part: "If you think to alarm me by threatening to unveil the fact that our grandfather Thomas was a drunken and dissolute lawyer and that Mother was a bastard you enormously mistake yourself."

Dal was by then a colonel of militia straight from the pages of a Thackeray novel. His exasperation was well merited. No one more than his sister had cultivated the legend of glorious Welsh and Scottish ancestry. But he also knew there was truth in at least the second allegation. John Apsley Dalrymple died unmarried. This clashes painfully with the entry in the cherished family copy of *Burke's Landed Gentry*, where Louisa is shown as wife to Morgan and "only child of John Apsley Dalrymple, Esq., of Gate House in the parish of Mayfield, Sussex." The discrepancy is only interesting to us because for Georgina to have learned about it must have been as a consequence of some bitter family accusations. We do not have to look very far for the major culprit. All the cruel candor in the family came from Morgan. As she grew up, it was a style very much to his daughter's taste. Both parents made her lofty, but she learned her recklessness from him. In her *Mémoires*, which were a settling of all the scores, Georgina went out of her way to explain to the world how her fearsome and aloof father ended his days in Dr. Blandford's asylum in Long Ditton, restrained night and day by four burly attendants. Without her testimony, this was a secret that might have followed the poor man into the grave. All in all, when the parents gazed down into the crib that first May evening, they were looking unknowingly at a wild child.

*I*magine her hand lax and pink against the linen of the crib. Who she is, what she will be, is written there in that moist palm as plainly as in any book. Many years later, one sultry afternoon in Paris, the palmist and psychic Desbarolles, who said so many interesting things to her, was the first to interpret a very pronounced line that ran from her Lifeline and ended in a fork or trident under the little finger. "Madame," the palmist explained, "you will write the most celebrated memoirs of the century, and at the same time, *useful*." He repeated this word to her several times, an instance, if any were needed, of his amazing powers. For had she not already begun these memoirs? The word "useful" rang like a gong in the stuffy room. It was exactly the adjective she herself would have chosen. The nineteenth century had done her wrong, not because she was a ninny, but because she was a woman of genius in a man's world. There was a vital subtext. The very people who ought to have championed her, her parents, the aristocracy to which she believed she belonged, had cast her aside. Her class had betrayed her. Another palmist, Madame de Thèbes, had also studied the curious branchings and forkings and came up with a different reading, but one that brought the story nearer to home. It was clear to her, she said, before giving Georgina back her mitten, that what the hand indicated was that she would most assuredly be divested of her £27,000 inheritance—if that had not already happened. The glorious thing about palmistry was that both statements were true, one not less than the other.

Until Georgina came along, Morgan was a man who cherished political ambitions. After leaving Cambridge he had gone on a journey through Persia with a friend, and this at least showed some enterprise (or was an example of his famous bloody-mindedness) since that country was then at war with Russia. In 1830, with this slight claim to fame and sponsored by his uncle, he stood as a Whig at the Cambridge parliamentary election, where he made an utter fool of himself and was soundly trounced at the hustings. Two years later he went up to Coventry with his mind a little clearer to stand as a Tory in elections to the first Reformed Parliament. His campaign throws great light on his character and helps explain the man he was to his children.

The task before him was a daunting one. Coventry was an uncommonly prosperous borough returning two members. One of these had enjoyed the confidence of the town for many years. Edward Ellice was a fifty-one-year-old politician of great distinction who had held office under the outgoing Grey administration and was a Whig whip. His son—also of Trinity—was a rising young star in the diplomatic service. Ellice's running mate was Henry Lytton Bulwer (briefly of Trinity), a man the same age as Morgan but already infinitely more experienced. Bulwer had that maddening aristocratic languor his opponent so much envied. As a twenty-three-year-old idler, he had been entrusted with £80,000 in gold by the Greek Committee, which he carried across Europe to the insurgents. As a special agent of the Foreign Office in Belgium in the revolution of 1830, he had an amusing story to tell of how the doorman of the hotel he was staying in was shot dead at his side by a stray bullet while he, Bulwer, was politely inquiring directions. He was hugely rich, apparently completely indolent, and already a very highly regarded diplomat.

Morgan arrived in Coventry on December 8 and made his way to the
King's Head. The Tory favors were light blue, and as he peered over the bal-
cony at the mob, he could see at a glance they were greatly outnumbered by
the dark blue and yellow ribbons of the Whigs. He and his fellow Tory had
hired some balladeers, who sang, hopefully:

> *Morgan Thomas and Fyler are two honest men*
> *They are not like Ellice and that East India grappler;*
> *I hope Ellice and Bulwer may ne'er sit again,*
> *But let's return Fyler and young Morgan Rattler.*

Unfortunately, the Rattler was no great speech maker, and his manifesto
made dull reading. It began, "I shall strenuously support the most rigid
Economy and Retrenchment, the Reformation of every Abuse in Church
and State, and all such Measures as may tend to promote the Happiness and
alleviate the Burdens of the People." His one piece of acumen was to declare
himself for the retention of tariffs on foreign imports. This was an important and popular point to make in Coventry, for the town was getting rich on
the manufacture of ribbons and watches, and free trade would flood the market with French goods. Overall, however, it was a lackluster candidature.
Then, quite suddenly, he was illuminated by the sort of forked lightning his
daughter was one day to draw down.

Making his way from the King's Head to the hustings, he was attacked
by the mob. This wasn't an unexpected turn of events; in fact, it was the
norm. A contemporary Coventry innkeeper with experience of these matters has left his unfailing recipe for election days: "To thirty six gallons of
ale and four gallons of gin, add two ounces of ginger and three grated nut-
megs. Boil the liquid warm in a copper; place in tubs or buckets and serve in
half pints; with a large cigar for each voter." The army pensioners recruited
by the magistrates to keep order were soon swept aside, or were maybe
themselves victims of this nutmeg surprise. However, Morgan was not quite
so green as he looked. On his way to Coventry he had noticed six hundred
Irish laborers digging the Oxford Canal near Brinklow, and these he now recruited to his cause. To give some generalship to his forces, he sent to Bir-

mingham for half a dozen prizefighters. The Whigs responded by alerting their own local pugilist, Bob Randall, who ran a pub in Well Street. Randall massed his forces. His orders were perfectly simple. He was not to murder anyone, but leave as many as possible hardly alive.

Inflamed by drink and religious bigotry, the riots Morgan Thomas managed to incite were remembered in Coventry for fifty years. His Irishmen suffered a terrible defeat. The local paper reported: "Many, thoroughly stripped, were knocked down like sheep, or escaped into the King's Head for their lives, in a wretchedly maimed condition, and the yard of the hotel presented the appearance of a great slaughter house, but the gates were closed and the place secured, whilst doctors were sent for to attend those injured."

When the dust settled and the vote was finally taken, in a booth festooned with his supporters' trousers, the Rattler found himself at the bottom of the poll, bested even by his running mate, Fyler.

Then as now, there was no disgrace in failing at your first attempts to enter Parliament. What marked out the Coventry election of 1832 was not just the scale of the rioting but its aftermath. To the disgust of the Whig Ministry and the outrage of the battered townsfolk, Morgan at once petitioned the House of Commons, contesting the result on the grounds that the electors had been intimidated. This was particularly rich coming from him. In the following year, after the case had been thrown out in committee, Halcomb, the member for Dover and a fellow lawyer of the Inner Temple, raised the issue on the floor of the House. When they found they could not silence him, the Ministry departed en masse to watch the boat race. As he left the Chamber, Ellice was heard to remark of Morgan with awful prescience: "That man will never represent Coventry as long as I draw breath."

The Rattler's humiliation was complete, but the victors had failed to identify something it would be his daughter's misfortune to emulate. No shame was too great for a man possessed of manic powers. Morgan Thomas contested Coventry another four times in his life, finally being elected in 1863. His stubbornness was comical, but it was also touching. The Tory interest in Coventry took early pity on him, and he made a second attempt at the seat in the year of Georgina's birth. Perhaps this time there was slightly more urgent reason to do well, and in one sense he was to be admired for going up there again to put his head in the lion's mouth. The Whigs were waiting for him. One of the broadsheets read: "And they went to the man Morgan, who is commonly called Tommy the Truckler, because he weareth two faces—one for Cambridge which looketh *blue,* and one for Coventry which is an *orange yellow . . .*"

Again he lost. His supporters softened the blow by presenting him with a Warwickshire watch. He wore it like a campaign medal. Just before the opening of the new Parliament in 1838, Sir Robert Peel invited more than three hundred jubilant new Tory members to his London house. Some of them had been Morgan's contemporaries at Trinity; some of them he had met through the Inner Temple. Counseled by Peel in small meetings, cajoled, flattered, cosseted, and inspired, the new members were in no doubt they were the breaking wave of an almighty sea change. Three hundred of them fresh from the hustings, shoulder-to-shoulder in Peel's house at Whitehall Gardens and surely soon to be the government of the country! Morgan was left on the outside looking in.

His participation in the age was to be more or less confined to such disastrous outings. When the entail on her father's estate was settled, Louisa's inheritance would give him that small portion of England—a few acres of East Sussex—sufficient to allow him to describe himself as a landed proprietor. Wanting to be the member for Coventry was a personal and not a political goal: he wanted it because it had been denied to him. His Toryism was of the old-fashioned and reactive kind. What he saw of what was happening around him he did not like and would not join. Yet behind the hauteur and exasperated bad temper was another more small-minded calculation—for all his disappointments, this was a world in which he did not absolutely have to compete. He was—but only just—a private gentleman. He could not fall; he need not rise. Even as early as 1837, there was a kind of redundancy about his position. He had no friends, the fashionable world outraged him, and in his own family he had been made to look a fool—not once, but several times.

The search for a place in England appropriate to his idea of himself was too much for him to contemplate. In 1840 he took himself and his wife off to Florence, along with Georgina and a new child, a solemn boy called

Morgan Dalrymple. The ostensible reason for their flight was the state of Louisa's health. In fact, they stayed off and on in Florence for twelve years, and the consequences to Georgina were to be enormous. Nothing blossomed in Florence: a dangerously narrow man took his bitterness with him and, as his children grew up, inflicted it upon them.

Florence

The Thomas family arrived in Florence in the type of commercial coach called a diligence on the last leg of a series of dusty and bone-shaking misadventures that dogged them all the way across Europe from Boulogne. They were set down outside the Hôtel du Nord in a state of complete exhaustion after a transit lasting nearly three weeks. Every flea-ridden inn, every insolent customs post, had provoked a quarrel. The diligence seated as many as fifteen passengers, inside and out, none of them worthy of Morgan's attention and on the contrary sweaty, vulgar, and for the most part disgustingly foreign. No concession was made to the sun—the Thomases arrived wearing much the same kind of clothing they had worn in England, Georgina in a crushed and dusty miniature of her mother's crinoline, the newly born infant, Morgan Dalrymple, swathed in flannel and half dead with heat.

They knew no one in the city. Those who watched them enter the lobby of the hotel saw they had little luggage and no servants. Though Florence was much more easygoing and welcoming than Rome, the Thomases made no great impression, either at first glance or on later acquaintance. It was not in their nature to be friendly—Morgan could hardly force himself to be civil—and they brought no news of any consequence. As for the little girl running about the lobby of the hotel, though she was plump as a pigeon, she evidently gave her parents no pleasure. The days passed, the family had still not visited the Uffizi, the father continued his supercilious silence over dinner: at last they were dismissed as dull. They were Kickleburys.

Morgan came to Florence for a very good reason. It was far from the scenes of his electoral nightmares, but much more to the point, the city was one of the cheapest places to live in Europe. A man with a high sense of his own importance but no money could hardly have chosen better. We can get some idea of the attractions from the affairs of another expatriate in much the same boat, Captain Fleetwood Wilson of the 8th Hussars. He happened to be there on a yearlong honeymoon when news reached him that he had been utterly ruined by his older brother, to whom he had lent all his money. The Wilsons were in a fix: they already had one child and another was on the way. Abused, betrayed, the gallant captain (considered by his generation one of the greatest horsemen in England) was at his wit's end. Then he found the Villa Strozzino. Built by a Strozzi three hundred years earlier, the villa sat on a hill with an elaborate arcaded front and two floors above. Fine trees decorated its lawns and gardens, and cypresses swayed ecstatically in the background. The internal arrangements were such that fifty years later Victoria herself occupied it on her visit to Florence. As Captain Wilson swiftly discovered, penury in Tuscany was a relative affair.

Morgan Thomas, the secretive and unclubbable newcomer, likewise chose his accommodation well. He rented the Villa Capponi, a short carriage drive from the city on its southern side. At one stroke, he entered into the kind of life so emphatically denied him in England. Like Strozzi, Capponi was a famous name in the history of the republic. Indeed, when Morgan rode into the city through the Porta S. Giorgio, he could see the proud boast set up by Niccolo Capponi above the portals of the Town Hall in 1528: JESVS CHRISTVS REX FLORENTINI POPULI S P DECRETO ELECTVS. Christ might have been the only king the Florentines could accept—the inscription had been a jibe at the departing Charles V—but things were somewhat different now. The Austrians were in occupation, and the greatest man in Florence was not a Medici, but the Russian millionaire Anatoly Demidov, who maintained his new bride, Bonaparte's niece, in the sumptuously appointed San Donato palace. The nominal ruler of the city and all the lands round about was the Grand Duke of Tuscany, cheerfully dismissed by his subjects as the Grand Ass. At the lower levels of society, the city was festering with every kind of adventurer and charlatan to be found in Europe. Morgan had been put in the unusual position—for him—of being monarch of all he surveyed, but what he saw he did not like very much.

The youthful Lady Dorothy Orford, a member of the Walpole family, which had deep roots in Florence, had recently made a much more dashing entrance to the expatriate community, having ridden the son of the 1835 Derby winner, a seventeen-hand horse called Testina, all the way from Antwerp. This was more to the taste of the locals. She later commented, "At that time, society in Florence was somewhat mixed: indeed, there were a great many people of shady character, in addition to others of none at all—so much so was this the case that the town had come to be designated 'le paradis des femmes galantes.' "

A paradise for whores was superimposed on, and undoubtedly drew some of its custom from, the well-established British colony. Many before Morgan had the same idea as he, some of them much more romantically motivated. Dante made the city a place of literary pilgrimage, and the Brownings were by no means alone in wishing to live and write there. There were many painters and sculptors in residence and a long tradition of amateur theatricals. All the same, the atmosphere inclined to the raffish. Thomas Trollope, brother to Anthony, settled in Florence in 1843 and has left a snapshot of how the Grand Duke's hospitality was abused at the Pitti Palace. At balls the English would "seize the plates of bonbons and empty the contents bodily into their coat pockets. The ladies would do the same with their pocket handkerchiefs." The Italian guests went further, wrapping up hams, chickens, and portions of fish in newspapers. Trollope saw an Italian countess smuggle a jelly into her purse.

Behind the walls of the Villa Capponi, where he could direct a household with more servants in it than he had ever dreamed possible, Morgan Thomas played out his fantasies of being a rich and indolent aristocrat. He was living in rooms with high ceilings. The trouble was elsewhere. When he looked farther abroad—when he looked outside his gates, in fact—it was Florence itself that he reprehended: not any bit of it, but all of it. Though the British colony was various, it contained more scribblers and painters than he was accustomed to meet and was headed by a man he quickly learned to fear and detest.

Her Majesty's minister plenipotentiary for Tuscany was Henry Edward Fox, soon to be fourth Baron Holland. Fox's wife was the attractive and flirtatious Augusta—"decidedly under three feet," the diarist Thomas Creevey once reported, "and the very nicest little doll or plaything I ever saw." It would be difficult to invent two people less likely to entrance the prickly and suspicious Morgan, who knew very well that Fox had learned of him and his political disasters through Ellice.

The author and socialite Lady Blessington drew a brief sketch of Fox as he was in those days: "Mr. Henry Fox possesses the talent for society in an eminent degree. He is intelligent, lively, and *très-spirituel;* seizes the point of ridicule in all whom he encounters at a glance and draws them out with a tact that is very amusing to the lookers on."

At any such meeting, Morgan was much more likely to be the butt of the conversation than an amused onlooker. Though he wore his hair in a dandified center parting and clung loyally to the blue and yellow favored by the Regency period, he was too short, too pugnacious, and far too provincial to be of any interest to such great men as Fox. Lady Blessington, who was really rather a good journalist, had noticed some years earlier the fascination the British had for the Florentine portrait sculptor Lorenzo Bartolini:

> Every Lord and Commoner who has passed through Florence
> during the last few years has left here a memorial of his visit; and
> every lady who has ever heard that she had a good profile (and
> Heaven knows how seldom the assertion was true) has left a model
> of it on the dusty shelves of Bartolini . . . Elderly gentlemen with

double chins resembling the breast of the pelican, requiring a double portion of marble in their representation . . . portly matrons too are ranged in rows with busts as exuberant as those that Rubens loved to lavish on his canvas . . . young ladies with compressed waists and drooping ringlets, looking all like sisters . . . and young gentlemen with formal faces and straight hair confront one at every step.

Bartolini stored these effigies on shelves in his studios, and they were inspected in much the same way as the work of Michelangelo. They were on the tourist list. Mr. Thomas and his wife belonged much more to that world of nameless and dusty nonentities than anything suggested by the glamour of the great palaces. Georgina later wrote of the Florence years:

My father disliked Society—he loved his home; my mother on the contrary liked Society. My father did not like women to wear low necked dresses; my mother on the contrary wished to be like other people. My father's opinion was that eleven o'clock at night was a respectable hour for leaving parties; this was the hour at which parties began. He obliged my mother to come home just at the time when she was beginning to amuse herself. My father would not call on this lady or that lady, or visit Madame A because she had a lover, or Madame B because she received Madame A. He would not even set foot at the English Embassy while Lord Holland was Ambassador, because gossip was afloat concerning Lady Holland. He seemed possessed with a passion for virtue, and he had been nicknamed at Florence "the policeman of Society."

This is as good a portrait of Morgan as can be found, but Georgina added another very telling sentence: "I had inherited to the full his mania to keep his reputation inviolate. I bristled with virtue."

When she was six years old, she had an early opportunity to support her father's reproach of local morals. In 1843 a penniless young artist named George Frederick Watts arrived in the city. Quite by chance on the boat from Marseilles, he had met Edward Ellice's brother, who at once effected an introduction to the Hollands. The policeman of society and his little sausage-curled lieutenant soon learned that Watts was the son of a man who had fallen so low as to be a piano tuner. To their complete amazement, Morgan and Georgina saw Watts being taken up by the Hollands, commissioned to paint portraits by the fabulously rich Demidovs, and the darling of all who met him.

While this may have secretly impressed Georgina as a striking example of how fame worked, Morgan had not come to Florence to have anything to do with art. The adoration of Watts, who was not only thin but unutterably gloomy and to many outsiders effete in the extreme, left him speechless. Augusta Holland commissioned a portrait by the artist in which she wore a *chapeau de paille*—"some lady having in a joke put one of the country hats on her head," as a smitten Edward Ellice reported to Lady Holland in London. On New Year's Day, 1844, Augusta presented the gangly Watts with a gold watch, specially commissioned from Geneva, murmuring, as she placed the chain around his neck, "We not only bind you to us, we chain you." It was immediately interpreted as the sign of a liaison. Morgan fingered his own Warwickshire timepiece from Messrs. Vale and Rotherham and reflected bitterly on the levels to which society had sunk.

The reason her father gave for fleeing London—his wife's ill health—was a common euphemism for poverty. If Georgina was ever worried about her mother, events were soon to calm her mind. At the Villa Capponi Louisa had another three children in quick succession: Emily, Florence, and the baby of the family, Apsley. Though the heat did not suit her and she never adapted successfully to having such a quiverful of children, she was as healthy as a horse. She lived to be eighty-three and was on this earth longer than her husband and her eldest daughter.

More sociable than Morgan in her timid, haphazard way, Louisa made the best she could of Florence. When Georgina was old enough, she took the child with her to the Cascine Gardens, where every day the *bon ton* gathered to gossip while the more gallant and amorous gentlemen threaded through the mass of carriages bearing messages and making their salutes. This morning concourse was, Georgina learned, to be compared favorably to Rotten Row or the Bois du Boulogne. When the weather was hospitable enough for walking, Louisa might descend from her carriage and stroll with her daughter under the trees by the banks of the Arno. There she would point out, not without envious longing, the roofs of the great houses on the opposite bank.

From May onward the town would be refreshed by new faces, birds of passage making the grand tour. They were eagerly welcomed by the expatriates. What was happening in London? Was it true that rain and a hundred thousand special constables had turned back the revolutionary Chartist mob—and was Mr. Gladstone truly one of those who was sworn in? Was it also true that railway speeds now regularly touched forty miles an hour, without hurt to the internal organs of the passengers? And plum—was that really a color a lady of fashion might adopt? Sometimes the tedium of the daily corso would be broken by the distant sighting of some scandalous liaison in its early stages, or whispered news of ruination in some other form, like gambling. These intrigues Georgina dutifully reported to her father. She showed an aptitude for similar detective work all her life—not much given to self-analysis, she was a master of the dossier method of investigating others. It was exciting and she was seldom short of material.

To a small girl groomed by her father to find outrage in everything, there was the additional frisson of the Austrian occupation. One afternoon an Italian lawyer absentmindedly spat on the ground while a patrol passed. The Austrian officer at once dismounted and, having the culprit pinned to the wall, ordered his troopers to line up and one by one spit in the unfortunate man's face. In 1851 there was an even more shocking case. Two young brothers named Mather were following an Austrian military band and darted across the road between it and the accompanying troop of horses. Two officers spurred their mounts and cut one of the brothers to the ground.

This was the sort of story to set Morgan bristling with indignation. Yet there was a diminishing return in feeding her father such tidbits. She gradually understood what it meant to be part of his police force. The fate of Charles Mather raised disgust and indignation all the way back to the floor of the House of Commons. However, Morgan's contempt for other people was quite unspecific—he was not minded to like the unfortunate Mather any more than the man who had struck him. In his eyes the whole world was out of step. When Georgina was very young, her father's vanity reinforced her own childish sense of superiority. To be a Thomas was to be a thing apart, not different from but better than all the rest. As she grew up, the unwelcoming house and the lack of invitations from others gradually began to cast doubt in her. The possibility existed that there was something seriously wrong with them all.

She was given tutors—a long roll call of them, not one of whom made any great impression or sowed the seeds of inspiration. Georgina learned to play the piano and completed a conventional and undemanding schooling in reading and writing. She once remarked, "I am sure if I had but studied Ruskin's *Elements of Drawing* I should have made a great artist." There is not the slightest nod here to the treasure house of art Florence was. She was intelligent but unlearned. The one gift she did possess she had been born with—a quite remarkably clear soprano voice.

It was said in later life that her mother took special interest in her singing. This may have indicated to some that Louisa herself was musical, but this was not the case. Every girl child of that time was taught to sing, in the same way she was taught to brush her hair, or show deference to her elders, or any of a hundred other little things. Singing was a way of moving from the schoolroom to the drawing room, and a young girl's voice was merely a further expression of the taste exhibited in the family's choice of furniture, its display of pictures and china. The role a good-mannered girl had in a family was almost too obvious to mention. A boy might, within reason, do as he liked and go where he would. No one expected much sense from a boy. For that he was sent away to school. His sister was domesticated as soon as was practicable. Singing was an outward demonstration of her complicity in the affairs of the family. She was in that sense her mother's child, an expression of her mother's taste and sensibility.

What is striking about Georgina's childhood is its extraordinary tedium. Pleasures a young girl of her class might take for granted in an English setting simply did not exist for her—like picnics, visits to relatives, parties, river excursions, or a trip to the seaside. She had some idiosyncrasies that stayed with her all her life. From her youngest days she exhibited a mild mania for collecting. She cut out armorial bearings from magazines and pasted them into books. She was among the earliest collectors of stamps. She made lists of Important Things. She kept a diary and recorded the uninspiring events of her day in scrupulous detail. This suggests a secretive and lonely child, but it is more likely that the Villa Capponi days were simply very long. We know from more famous Florence residents—from the Brownings, for example—that in the three summer months that began in June, the heat became enervating and a torpor settled over everything. Even a shaded garden became too hot to endure, and those families who could afford it moved up into the hills for air and the chance of a breeze. Once there, improving sight-seeing and visits to hilltop monasteries were scheduled for five in the morning. So, to be a child in the stiflingly hot summers, even with siblings, became a little like being the inmate of a prison.

Morgan had nothing to say to any of his children—they in turn were terrified to open their mouths in his presence. The rooms of the villa were extensive, there were servants in plenty, but there was nothing much to do. The only outdoor pleasure Georgina shared with her father was his passion for gardening, which he undertook in the winter months. She showed early on a very un-Latin enthusiasm for pets, especially dogs, treating them as little people, more loyal and certainly more loving than the two-legged inhabitants of the villa. Late in life she put this feeling into a letter: "I feel a horror for exaggerated love or friendship. It's just too well demonstrated to me that when the moment comes that one asks for something, or has need of something, the response is not worth a biscuit."

As she grew into womanhood, Georgina became nothing like the submissive little miss of the conventional fashion plate. Nor was she modeled on the enigmatic girls who decorated Leech cartoons in *Punch* with their smooth wings of hair and ultra-straight noses. The air of obedient calm required of young mid-Victorian women was quite foreign to her, and she had little chance to learn by emulation. Morgan saw to that. But if her upbringing had turned out rackety and unhappy, great changes were in the offing. Though he had lingered there a very long time, her father had always seen Florence as a makeshift arrangement, and its usefulness to him was as good as exhausted. The prime reason for moving on was right there under his nose. Georgina was no longer a child. In her adolescent form she was someone's future bride. There was much to be accomplished before this could come about, not least the family's reconciliation to society. Morgan would stir himself to exhibit his daughter to her best advantage, and then she herself could crown the family's fortunes by marrying well. The two things hung together.

This realization gave her power, perhaps more than she knew how to handle. The mystical writer Edward Maitland made a shrewd remark to Georgina when she was twenty. His opinion was colored a little by two things, both of them romantic. To begin with, he had fled the family home in Brighton, where his father was perpetual curate of St. James's Chapel. His rebellion took him to the California gold rush, and thence to Australia, where he had married and buried his wife within a twelvemonth. Maitland saw something in Georgina that her father had failed to notice: "I am but one of numbers who would be delighted to see your gifts and prowess winning success; and feel mystified at the waste of them, when we know that with better management it might have been otherwise. You yourself will see it some day, when your stormy youth is spent, and the *boy*—which you really are now—has developed into the *woman* which you are only in form."

This insight struck at the heart of the Florence years. All the other Thomas children grew up to be models of dullness. Georgina's brothers had upper lips as stiff as any in Victorian fiction. Her sisters were dutiful and long-suffering. That she was so different suggests a relationship to her father very far from the Victorian norm of duty and respect or, as was the case with her siblings, fear. It was as if she alone challenged Morgan, returning his systematic cruelties with some of her own. What was hoydenish in her as a child, running about the gardens of the Capponi in petticoats, changed as she grew only a little older into more dangerous forms of recklessness. If Morgan had hoped to crush her, things were turning out very differently. Not at all to his wishes in the matter, he had raised a rebel.

A few years later she explained her parents' expectations of her: "[They] never wearied of indoctrinating me with the belief that an eldest daughter should marry to the advantage of her younger sisters, from the point of view that if the oldest sister married a rich old man with a title, her siblings would find matches that were rich, young, and titled."

Many a diary hid the same thoughts. A beautiful young woman was, whether she liked it or not, a commodity; and a good marriage was one in which there was a significant amount of value added. Fifteen was not too young an age to start thinking of these things. Sooner or later she would have to come out in society—was that really to be at the edge of the crowd at the Casa Feroni, or mingling with the demimondaines at some sumptuously vulgar rout given by the Demidovs? Or was she instead to wait for a wandering Cambridge graduate or adventurous parson to turn up outside the Hôtel du Nord just as she had done, capture her in the street, and carry her off back to England? Her father's incorrigible vanity would never settle for that.

Morgan's thinking was way ahead of his daughter's. Sitting in state in his study, aloof and remote, he had begun to ponder a quite spectacular coup. It came upon him slowly like a gathering religious conviction, and once in place nothing would budge it. The details were perfectly simple and seemed to him to brook no abridgment. He would sell her to just that kind of man he most abhorred, and of a class from which he felt himself so bitterly excluded. It was his intention that Georgina should not marry for less than £10,000 a year.

The first time he ever spoke these thoughts out loud there must have been a peal of nervous hilarity at the breakfast table, followed by a plea from Louisa not to repeat them outside the house. The sum involved was ridiculous—to have that much income, a prospective suitor would need to be in possession of at least an earldom. (The letter Lord Conyngsby delivered to Victoria on the day Georgina was born was in fact an offer from the dying King of exactly that amount.) Louisa had grown used to her husband's erratic behavior. Should this new scheme ever get about among her friends at the Cascine Gardens, they would be ruined socially. Louisa was dutiful and submissive to a fault, but even with her limited knowledge of the world she knew they were regarded as Florence's nobodies. Ten years of Morgan's disdain had done its work. A £10,000-a-year man for the plump and argumentative Georgina was going to be as easy to find and trap as the Emperor of all the Russias or the Bey of Algiers.

It had, of course, occurred to both of them, ever since Georgina was a baby, that a shrewd marriage might greatly increase their own social position. That was the way the world was, and that was how what Bagehot called "the cousinhood of aristocracy" came into existence in the first place. Unfortunately, neither Morgan nor Louisa had gifts to bestow on the world. They had no friends of any significance, corresponded with no one, engaged in none of the controversies then in vigorous debate. When he wasn't gardening, Morgan kept up a desultory study of Dante, presumably for the pleasure of seeing sinners punished. Of the Victorian England he had deserted at its birth, he knew next to nothing. Yet the campaign to marry off Georgina to such advantage to them all had to be fought in London, at balls and levees or wherever beautiful young women were set out in display.

In Morgan's day Almack's Assembly Rooms had been the ground on which the greatest battles were fought. Controlled by the seven super-rich patronesses who managed the guest lists, it was said by the diarist Captain Gronow that in his time only five of the three hundred officers of the Foot Guards were admitted. (He happened to be one of them, which was the point of the story.) Though Morgan believed persons of lesser rank were acceptable nowadays, the truth was he had no clear idea how to set about promoting his daughter. Twelve fatal years in Florence among the Waterloo veterans and hapless exiles had done nothing to educate him otherwise. A local example of the old school was a man named St. John ("a scion of a noble house") who wagered an Austrian cavalry officer to follow him wherever he went through the city. After a hectic chase, St. John put his pony at a parapet of a bridge and leaped forty feet into the dried-up riverbed, killing the pony outright. The Austrian declined the invitation to follow. St. John was the kind of man Morgan was looking for, only with money and in England.

When Georgina was told of her father's great scheme, it probably left her in two minds. On the one hand, the plan was so outrageous, so impossible, that it filled her with the same almighty ambition as his and nourished in her that old sense of being born to greatness. For her the Florence years had hardly been distinguished, but now that did not matter, or not as much as it might to a lesser soul. Her destiny beckoned: life in a country seat, with a fine town house, a rich man who loved her, and a circle of jealous and admiring friends. This was the fulfillment of all her wildest daydreams; novels were based on plots like this. The other possibility was that her father had set the bar so high exactly to deny her any kind of a marriage at all. In some somber fashion it was his method of possessing her. In this way of looking at it she was his and would never be another's.

In 1852 Morgan and his family left Florence. In the informal history of the expatriate community, as recorded in memoirs and reminiscences, it is as though he had never been there. You did not have to be a poet or a peer to get something from Florence; nor did you have to be a roué. But the policeman of society left no record. One of the sidelights cast on the city in those days was the vigorous efforts made by the more pious English to import Protestant Bibles to Tuscany, a campaign that might seem close to Morgan's heart. In 1851 Captain Wilson, who was hardly in the mold of an evangelical bigot, went to visit an Italian friend imprisoned by the Austrians for the possession of a smuggled Bible. "In the afternoon I paid a visit to Guicciardini in the Bargello. It really makes one's blood boil to think that even the

abuse of justice should enable any Government, however despotic, to incar-
cerate a man merely for reading a bible and making free use of his conscience."

This is a recognizably Early Victorian tone. Wilson was a gentleman,
who believed like many of his kind—like Morgan Thomas himself—that an
English gentleman was the greatest masterpiece ever created by man. But
beneath the languid airs and graces, which the Hussar officer certainly had
in full, there had to be some fire, some subterranean force. A man must have
his demons. Morgan makes a poor comparison with the gallant and penniless
Wilson. He had his demons, but there was something empty at the heart of
him. A weaker man, or perhaps a poorer one, might have used the Tuscan
years to seek preferment at home in England. A more intellectually curious
one might have embraced the city for its own sake, or at any rate looked
about him. From all that rich stew of society, the only thing Morgan Thomas
took away with him from Florence was his butler, the secretive and sardonic
Antonio.

Going Home

1

The road is dusty, the coach unbearably stuffy. The landscape has very soon palled. One valley is much like another, one ridge reveals the next. She is sweating in her stays, her waist nipped in painful imitation of adult fashion, her legs in stockings, her feet crammed into dirty white silk shoes. Not a button is to be loosened from her bodice, not a hem raised of her skirts. Clothes, like the empty conversation, the conventional diet, are to be endured. She belongs to the kind of family in which all the children are considered as miniature and largely ungrateful adults for whom the future has already been mapped out. Her brothers will never work, in the sense that engineers or doctors work. They will probably become soldiers. Though it might be privately comical to imagine these lumpy and unimaginative boys as standing in the breach at some future clash of arms, it is not so funny at all to consider her own position. Though she is hardly more than a child, her future has been even more ruthlessly dictated.

What she sees in the mirror is what she is. She is a commodity. What she wants can have nothing in it that doesn't correspond to what her parents want. Even before she has truly entered the world—as expressed by the mystery of other people—she is preparing to leave it.

Time moves as slowly and maddeningly as the coach in which she sits, but even so, in five or six years' time, what little freedom of action she possesses now will have disappeared. Part of her commodity value is obedience to a man. It was her father, and all too soon it will be her husband. The sweat thickens in her hair and gathers behind her knees. The road unravels. At the end of it (the child's fantasy) might be a prince, a castle, and rolling acres. The person not likely to be waiting is a poet or a dreamer, or anyone who lives in a garret. Though there is much in the world—as, for example, the young Austrian officer who leans in through the carriage window to inspect the passports, or the distinguished-looking German scholar on his way to Rome, or any of a hundred interesting examples met along the way—most of the observable world is nothing more than idle scenery. About England, where she is going, she knows next to nothing: she knows the names of shops but not the names of cities. Victoria, whose star she felt she was to follow, has turned out to be distressingly family-minded and moralistic, besotted with her prim little husband. As for her own talents, her father speaks at least as good Italian as she, her voice is untrained, her reading patchy and inconsequential. She is already a little on the dumpy side. And she is sweating.

*I*t happened that Wilkie Collins and Charles Dickens were traveling to Florence at exactly the same time the Thomases set off in the opposite direction, and a letter by Collins to a friend has left us a snapshot picture of travel by diligence along those dangerous roads of northern Italy. He explains how strings were tied to the trunks and luggage riding on the roof and each passenger sat with the loose end in his hand. The intention—no matter that the coach was in motion—was to prevent theft. "It was like sitting in a shower bath and waiting to pull the string—or rather, like fishing in the sea, when one waits to feel a bite by the tug of the line round one's finger."

The tedium of the journey, the bad inns and low cunning of the peasants met along the way, the occasional interrogations by unpleasantly brusque Austrian patrols, all conspired to produce in Morgan the conviction that he was at last leaving the shadows and coming back into the light. Let others take what they could from Italy: he was free of it. He was not as rich as he would like, and he was no longer young. However, Louisa's inheritance was clear of entail at last: he could throw out the agricultural laborers who were now in disgraceful occupation of Gate House and set about making himself a landed proprietor. That had a ring to it. He had enough money to send both his sons to Eton; and sprawling next to Louisa as the coach rattled along, its canvas window coverings clattering, sat the petulant girl on which the last and he hoped best phase of his life depended. Somewhere, perhaps even on this road, returning home to some noble house in a carriage emblazoned with arms, was the man to marry Georgina and, by so doing, elevate the whole family.

The diarist Charles Cavendish Greville had summed it up in 1843: "This year is distinguished by many marriages in the great world, the last, and the

one exciting the greatest sensation being that of March to my niece. A wonderful elevation for a girl without beauty, talents, accomplishments or charm
of any kind, an enormous prize to draw in the lottery of life. All the mothers in London consider it a robbery as each loses her chance of such a prize."

Morgan understood well enough that his stake in this market was slender. But he also knew, or thought he knew, that nobody got what he wanted
by chance. There was a campaign to be fought. That was how it had been in
his own day, and that was how he imagined it to be now. His firsthand
knowledge of English society was nearly fifteen years out of date, yet he
supposed that what went in the days of his youth, went on still. It had better, for he knew of nothing else.

He was to be proved wrong. Even leaving aside his wife's eccentric taste
in clothes—her high color and preference for red shawls led Georgina once
to describe her mother as looking like a macaw—there was something fusty
and old-fashioned about the whole family. Though they were English to the
people they met along the way, there was an ignorance in them that surprised
their fellow countrymen. A significant example of this was found whenever
Louisa mentioned her daughter's wonderfully clear soprano voice. Anyone
who asked out of courtesy to whom they had sent her in Florence for lessons—to Signor Giulio Uberti perhaps?—was met with a studied silence.
She had received no lessons. The same was true of the art and literature of
the day. Morgan knew that his bête noire Watts was back in England but not
that he was recently engaged on enormous historical and allegorical paintings in which his social conscience wrestled with the ills of society. (They
were sometimes called muffin paintings, after Thackeray's satirization of a
"George Rumbold" painting in which Rumbold—his name for Watts—had
painted such a huge canvas that a mere muffin had a diameter of two feet
three inches.) Meanwhile, what was this absurd thing called the March of In-
tellect—whence to where? The Great Exhibition had been and gone—what
had been the attraction of looking at a lot of farm machinery and the like,
displayed in a building made of glass by a man who was gardener to the
Duke of Devonshire?

For Georgina, going home was the adventure of her young life. She was about to rejoin what was the greatest nation on earth at its most prosperous. Everyone knew that Britain was best. Even her father believed that. Surreptitious study of fashion plates showed her that a ball gown was now worn off both shoulders and that hair was curled only at the back to fall lightly on the neck. In calling on others, it was de rigueur to wear a long fringed shawl over a demure dress, the whole set off by a beaded reticule, dangled, it would seem, by the middle fingers of the left hand. There was much to ponder here, but the imaginative leap was to picture the man who would capture her.

The year that Morgan left England, Thackeray wrote the potboiling *FitzBoodle Papers*. Its story begins farcically with the remark by his hero "I have always been considered the third-best whist player in Europe . . ." FitzBoodle, we discover, is the second son to a title stretching back to Henry II; his absurd opinions and brief adventures first entertained the readers of *Frazer's Magazine*. To the modern taste the empty vanities of FitzBoodle and his redoubtable stepmother, Lady Flintskinner, are too easy a target. In the early Thackeray there is cleverness, but also a faintly studied quality. *FitzBoodle* and the other works like it were slight, not because they were too cruel, but because they were too cautious. There were plenty of readers ready to discover in Thackeray a kind of social anxiety, an insecurity. They saw, or thought they saw, in his own phrase, the flunky that hid behind the gentleman. But, unlike Morgan Thomas, Thackeray grew up with the new age and learned from it. His vision deepened and darkened. In a letter written when his eldest daughter was in the same situation as Georgina, young and beautiful and eligible, he strikes a much more somber note. Speaking of a society to which he was now himself an adornment, he wrote:

> They never feel love, but directly it's born they throttle it and fling it under the sewer as poor girls do their unlawful children— they make up money marriages and are content—then the father goes to the House of Commons or the Counting House, the mother to her balls and visits—the children lurk upstairs with their governess, and when their turn comes are bought and sold, as respectable and heartless as their parents before them.

This was new and beyond the comprehension of a man like Morgan. Even more to the point, it was not a thing Georgina herself could understand. At the time she left Florence, an American girl her own age had come to Europe with the sole intention of being heard by Rossini. Genevieve Ward, young though she was, knew what she wanted and headed straight to Florence to get it. She had been told she had a good voice and was determined to make herself famous. Rossini was encouraging. He found her distinguished local teachers (one of whom was Uberti), and two years later she opened at La Scala. That kind of dedication was way beyond anything Georgina possessed, then or ever. She had the voice, but not the vision.

Morgan was in no great hurry to face up to London. He wished the journey home to be a way of applying a little finish to his daughter. They broke their return first by the shores of Lake Constance, where his younger brother, George, was living in style with an invalid wife, the Baronne de Hildprant. For a sixteen-year-old girl with hardly any understanding of the wider world, this was interesting enough. At Schloss Hard Georgina found the kind of company she had been warned against at the Villa Capponi: indolent, not in the slightest way intellectual, gossipy—and amorous. True to his character, Morgan did not like his brother any more than he did his Florence enemies. On the other hand, his daughter could not be sheltered from the importunities of other people forever. The days at Schloss Hard turned into weeks, the weeks into months, while he watched Georgina try out her new freedoms.

Her looks and personality were of great interest. In appearance she was judged to be perhaps a little too much on the short side, a little too full of figure, to be the ideal of beauty. Her conversation was startlingly direct, and in one respect her aunt and uncle must have studied her with special doubt in their minds. She was already—and particularly among men of mature years—an accomplished sexual tease. Many of the scrapes she got into later in life came from this inability to treat men in a realistic way. She was arch in their company and sometimes irritatingly so. Weak men, or vain ones, might find her little-girl act provocative, but wiser heads found something missing in her, perhaps a commonsensical understanding of the limited choices life could afford, not just to her but to anybody. She was not, in the way the French apply the word, a serious person. Even this early in her life it was easy to see that she had great energies, but many fewer talents than she supposed. She talked far too freely, scoffed and wheedled. She wrote on June 21, at the end of a day of sunshine and persiflage: "I first experienced what Mama told me some time ago about young men making themselves agreeable to me."

Young though she was, she had discovered the power sex could wield. This amorousness needed some explaining later on in life, and she had a ready answer. She was scientifically amative: "I loved everyone who loved me and there were endless outcomes—lamentations, reproaches, tears on all sides. But there we are! I am a loving person. Phrenologists tell me that my bumps of love and friendship cover my entire head! One is not mistress of one's temperament and of one's skull, not at all."

Even this early, her bumps dictated events in an unfortunate way. Among the party lounging and sketching, going out onto the lake in boats and exclaiming about the wonders of nature, was a familiar family legend, the source of many an outrageous story. He was the fiery and voluble vicar of Llanelli, a man named Ebenezer Morris, whose living had been presented to him by Georgina's grandfather. The Reverend Mr. Morris was sixty-three and decidedly eccentric. His preaching was considered so entertaining that on one occasion the gallery of the church threatened to collapse from the press of people gathered to hear him. He was also a man of colossal and unforgiving temper, perfectly able to knock down a parishioner for some imagined insult. In his battles with neighboring clergy, he composed scathingly brutal and quite scandalous letters and pamphlets. In Llanelli he was a notorious and much-discussed figure.

As well as flirting with the young men who ran after her and deriding the enthusiasm her uncle held for romantic scenery, Georgina romanced the Reverend Mr. Morris, whom she dubbed Cannonicus. She was successful enough to have him embrace her a little too freely and kiss her without the innocence usually employed toward a child. Emboldened, he wrote her a love letter. One can think of half a dozen reasons why he might instantly regret what he had done. This was the first test of her capacity to behave more like a young lady than a hoyden. Could the situation be defused by tact and common sense? Was this the kind of letter that anyone else would have torn in a hundred pieces or hidden in the trunk of a tree? Was it an occasion for the young to moralize the old and bring the reckless philanderer to the error of his ways, as happened in fiction?

She chose differently. She gave the letter to her mother. Louisa gave it to her husband. For all Morris's long friendship with the family (which included being a lifelong drinking crony of his patron, Rees Goring Thomas) Morgan did not hesitate. The poor man was confronted with the evidence, humiliated, and shown the door. Georgina had done the right thing and learned a useful lesson: she might not be the cleverest girl in the world, but she was certainly able to stir up passion in the opposite sex. Moreover, she had found a new way to make her father angry. Shortly after the incident, the Thomas family left Schloss Hard, still postponing London and heading toward Brussels.

*I*n the winter of 1853 the Thomases took a house in the rue de Luxembourg. Morgan bought a carriage with a form of armorial bearing painted on the doors. "We went about in our carriage, and all our ancient admirers, on foot, stared at us as if we were risen from the grave," Georgina commented. Her father had managed to secure a letter of introduction to the ambassador: he was positioning himself for the campaign that lay ahead. If he had gone abroad like a loser, he intended to come back with a different story to tell.

Brussels, like Florence, sustained a large British colony, and for the same reason. It was cheap to live there, and titled European families were ten a penny. A man might fill his mantelpiece with crested invitations and *cartes de visite*. Perhaps the very best people were in Paris, but there was enough going on in Brussels to replicate that older, frowstier form of society that was to Morgan's taste. So, interspersed with the names of son Dal's fellow Etonians who came to stare and wonder, we find the Baron de Pfuel, Limmander de Nieuvehoven, and—Louisa's finest social acquisition—the Baronne de Goethals. There was war in the air and everyone was talking about Constantinople. Some of the insouciant young Englishmen Georgina saw lounging about at balls and parties she would never see again. One of her beaux was William Scarlett, whose uncle was to command the Heavy Brigade at Sebastopol.

Brussels was intended by her parents to be a kind of finishing school. They stayed a season, and Georgina sang before an audience for the first time at the British Embassy. The recital—which may not have been more than one song—was well received. For the first time in her life it was exciting to be a Thomas. Though she was by her own description "wild," she was also "irresistible." Her triumphs came entirely as a consequence of her own

efforts—to her surprise people liked this turbulent and impulsive girl from
Florence. Now that the family was out in the world a little more, her father's
peculiarities became more obvious. It was the first chance she had to com-
pare him with other fathers, and she began to form the opinion expressed so
forcibly in the years ahead:

> My father, who as a consequence of his proud and violent char-
> acter had always been more or less mad at last became so, despite
> being gifted with rare and valuable qualities. His mother's
> favourite, he had been spoiled as a child, and he reaped what all
> spoiled children reap. He inspired hate and terror in everybody. As
> for me, I never addressed a word to him in my life, and he only
> spoke to us to call us to table and to tell us we were damn fools. If
> my mother had only a little common sense or principle, she would
> not have endured such a hell, neither for herself nor for her chil-
> dren, and I blame her much more than my father for all that has
> happened.

There is a characteristic element of exaggeration in this. At the time,
darting about Brussels, discovering clothes, learning to waltz, and reaping
compliments wherever she went, life had taken an unexpected twist. It was
fun. Evidently, some young women made their effect by hiding shyly behind
their mothers' skirts. That was not Georgina's way. She was bold, careless
even. A lifelong habit of bathing in cold water had been set in Florence.
Now, much farther north and in the depths of winter, she bounced from the
bath pink and eager, hungry for breakfast and the chance to meet new people and shine in their company. Wherever she went she demonstrated a similar animal exuberance. She was happy.

While retaining the lease on the house in the rue de Luxembourg, Morgan finally took his family back to England in 1854. Dal was at Eton, but the
other children had never seen England and only Georgina had been born
there. It was exciting to be home, but it was also daunting. The country was
more interested in cholera and the imminence of war than the arrival of the
Thomas family. Georgina's flirtatious experiments followed her across the

Channel: no sooner had they set foot in England than Morgan intercepted a love letter to his daughter from a mysterious G.V.—presumably by stealing it or reading it surreptitiously. His reaction was illuminating. He summoned the butler, Antonio, and had him take it to the bemused local police. Meanwhile, Gate House in Mayfield was prepared for the family as its permanent seat, and Georgina's first scattered impressions of her native country were gathered while driving about Brighton and East Sussex to be introduced to the local gentry. She was not impressed. That vague sense of superiority so lavishly rekindled in Brussels was not to be squandered on mutton-eating squires and their sullen children.

At first, England disappointed Georgina. Life at the Villa Capponi had been dull, but wonderful things had happened to her since. Though her father watched her like a hawk, she had already received two declarations of love and turned any number of heads. Neither of her sisters was of an age to be seen in a romantic light: she was the center of attention in whatever drawing room she found herself. She confirmed the earlier suspicion that she was far more forward and direct than her English contemporaries. In an age that placed so much importance on the niceties of address, how to behave with self-effacing quiet was something it was already too late for her to learn. Her father had been right about one thing: once you described yourself as of good family, the number of friends and acquaintances you might make in life was small indeed, at any rate in the Sussex hinterland. However, farming had never been so prosperous in living memory, and Morgan and his family had come back to a golden decade for corn prices. The best of the country gentlemen had "no enemies but time and gout," as one admiring foreign observer put it. That did not necessarily make them entrancing company.

If Sussex was dull, London was a different matter. Though Morgan might find as much to deprecate there as anything he had found in Florence, his opinion counted for nothing. The London he came home to had almost doubled in size from the one he had left. Its sophistication and complexity were quite beyond him. There was more "dash" to affairs than he remembered and a great deal more irreverence. Whole new classes had sprung up and with them manners that were beneath Morgan's dignity to interest himself in. He was safe for as long as he stayed in the West End and kept himself away from anything approaching talent. The truth was that Morgan could not and never would find a niche in society. His time had passed.

For Georgina London was a city bathed in dangerous adventure. Rotten Row, of which she had heard much as a child, had been recently widened to accommodate the Sunday carriage rides of the rich and titled. She duly made her baptismal appearance there, stared at in what she considered an insolent way by any number of young men on horseback. She found them all distressingly tall. It was no use attempting a conversational finesse by comparing the scene disfavorably to the Cascine Gardens—this was the real thing. The carriage row in Hyde Park was a showcase of the aristocracy. The Prince Consort rode out there. As the elegant carriages ambled their way back and forth along the mile-and-a-half route around the edge of Hyde Park, on fine days—just out of sight but not out of earshot—as many as twelve thousand bathers swam in the Serpentine. The scale of London and the juxtaposition of its classes were beyond anything she had ever seen. Like her father, she discovered much that she must learn. The greatest part of it was where and how to fit in. To be fashionable was to know far more—perhaps to discount far more—than the elementary education she had received in Florence.

In 1855 Georgina went back to Brussels with her mother for Carnival, and on February 17 attended a ball at the Baronne de Goethals'. It was the scene of one of the great moments in her life. Among the company was a Portuguese baron named Pedro de Moncorvo. He was twenty-seven years old, the son of a former ambassador to the Court of St. James. Georgina was dressed in the costume of a Parisian grisette, and the evening passed in a delirium of romantic enchantment. Here, with all the force of a novel, was the perfect situation—a beautiful girl heated by the dance, pursued by a dark and handsome stranger. Writing fifty years later, Georgina claimed to have loved him with all her heart, and when she was sixty-six, she went all the way to Bemfica to visit his grave. Moncorvo was probably the first man to see her for what she was and not attempt to change her. They met no more than ten times, during which he alternately scolded and cajoled her. For the first but not the last time in her life she was, so to speak, living to the tune and lyrics of the best kind of song. Four days after her eighteenth birthday, her father intervened, and she was banished from Brussels and sent into exile at Boulogne.

On June 18, wracked by love, playing the piano with tragic abandon, she opened the door of her lodgings to find Moncorvo on the doorstep. Unchaperoned, they walked on the cliffs overlooking the town.

> He asked me if I had deceived myself in allowing that perhaps I loved him. I answered "If I loved you, what would be the use?" "Forgive me," he said. "If you loved me we could be married in that church" and he pointed to the church of Boulogne. I made no reply, his lips almost touched my cheek. I drew back gently. He did not kiss me. He departed that same afternoon—and I have never seen him since.

It is a perfect vignette. As she grew older, she realized he may have loved her with a seriousness her youth and ignorance did not allow for on the day. For the rest of her life she wondered what might have happened if she had done as he asked and married him against the wishes of her parents. And though a year later he married a Portuguese comtessa, he continued to write her affectionate letters, enough for her to make that long sea journey when he died. What makes the story so poignant, in light of what was to come, is that the girl on the cliffs was still the girl from Florence, the wayward boy in the body of a woman, the original and untempered Georgina Thomas. She lost him out of inexperience.

It is sad to see her later embroider the story, explaining that she could not marry him because of a devotion to a higher thing, her art. She was an eighteen-year-old girl who had for the first time in her life been faced with a real decision, touching real feelings. Moncorvo was asking a lot of her—he was very much older, he was poor, and he was Catholic. But the truth was that—too early in her life for her to understand and profit from the experience—a man was prepared to take her exactly as she was. In this brief and shimmering image of them on the cliffs, we are watching a man who has seen something of the world and a girl who has not. Moncorvo was not saying "take me back to England so that I can sponge off your father." He was inviting her to come with him to Portugal.

When he pointed with a sweep of his arm to "the church of Boulogne," the gesture also took in the villa where Dickens and Wilkie Collins stayed with their families, and the place where Thackeray and his daughters had rested in the past. Perfectly visible was the massive embarkation camp from which the French Imperial Army had set sail to the Crimea. Even while they spoke, many of those who had marched down to the quays garlanded with flowers were being blown to pieces at the Malakhov Redoubt.

Georgina knew nothing of such things. Moncorvo was the first to lay bare her ignorance of the real world. She may have had practical misgivings, and certainly the peculiar urgency and danger of his visit must have weighed with her. Watching the hazy sea, trying not to look into his eyes, she learned from Moncorvo that afternoon what love was, rather than what a well-arranged English marriage could confer. She chose the wrong option.

Treherne

*I*n the autumn of 1857 Morgan and his brothers changed their name to Treherne. The battle of Poitiers was now five hundred years old, and the family was able to show that the two surnames had been interchangeable down the years that followed Sir Hugh's adventures in France. They were merely reclaiming what was theirs by right and reverting to a more profoundly ancestral form of address. From Morgan's point of view, there was an element of the *ruse de guerre* in the alteration. Like his forebear, he had gone away one person and (he hoped) come home another. A change of name was a partial cancellation of all his earlier mistakes. While it might please his eldest brother to stand contemplating his Lletymawr estates as a Treherne, it did Morgan no harm, either, to lord it over his Sussex neighbors under the new title. In a way, it was as good as an elevation.

There was more of a problem with how to identify the new Trehernes when they came up from the country to London. They were not rich, nor were they well connected. Families—brothers and sisters, uncles and aunts—usually made a simple enough matrix for the giving and receiving of hospitality, as did work or political allegiance. None of these helped describe the Sussex Trehernes. To go about at all in society meant they had to have some circle of acquaintance, and it is probable that the greater part of it was provided by Georgina. When carriages were summoned and Georgina parted regretfully from her hosts after what she hoped was an irresistible contribution to the evening, the question arose: who was she? Parsed, this meant, who were her parents? Mr. Treherne himself had no cronies, political or otherwise, and belonged to no clubs. He was estranged from his own family. His wife was a dumpy and unfashionable lady happier when she was in the country. If it was asked what this family wanted, what advantage it was trying to seek (a perfectly understandable inquiry), no easy answer was forthcoming. The change of name might indicate that Morgan wished to be considered Welsh, but he would have been bitterly disappointed to have given this impression.

When Thackeray's *The Snobs of England* was published ten years earlier, it made the whole country anxious. Some of those who read the work in serial form wrote in to ask whether *they* could be accounted snobs, and Thackeray cheerfully included the details of their lives in his next installment. How far did a man like the new Mr. Treherne come under the title? The word derives from Cambridge undergraduate slang in use during Morgan's time at Trinity. In the narrow sense, the Welshman was indeed a "snob" as much as he was a "tassel"—his parentage bridged town and gown. Thackeray's extension of the meaning to include anyone wishing to be something he was not was useful in principle but applied so indiscriminately by him that Morgan and many others might have wondered whether anyone at all in society could escape the term.

One of the small miracles of literature is how Thackeray escaped the crude and gluey morass that was *The Snobs of England* to begin in the very next year his literary masterpiece, *Vanity Fair*. There he devoted a famous chapter to how to live well on nothing a year. The new tone is more realistic and generous: "The truth is, when we say of a gentleman that he lives elegantly on nothing a year, we use the word 'nothing' to signify something unknown—meaning, simply, that we don't know how the gentleman in question defrays the expenses of his establishment." This describes Morgan's situation when seen about town in London or Brighton. His innate anxiety led him to claim more than he possessed, in wealth as well as rank, but he was not as fatuous as some of Thackeray's more helpless victims. Nor was he in the slightest way ingratiating. He paid no man his loyalty. If the question turned on whether he was a gentleman at all, most Victorians would have concluded that he was. They might have gone on to say that he was not a very pleasant one, nor a very distinguished example of the breed. That was beside the point. Morgan's desire was not so much to remake himself in a different image, but to consolidate what little rank he had. In that respect, he *had* gone away one person and come back as another.

His daughter was the immediate beneficiary of the new surname and the first to give it luster. In October 1857 Miss Georgina Treherne was included in the cast list of a private musical extravaganza devised in honor of the Duchess of Cambridge, called endearingly *Hearts and Tarts*. The performance took place at Ashridge in Hertfordshire, the home of Lady Marion Alford, a widow in her forties who kept up a lively artistic and political salon. The Queen of Hearts was played by Princess Mary of Cambridge, whom Queen Victoria always found so wanting for her terrible size, her dirty ball gowns, and the racy company she kept. The Princess had been childhood friends with Constance Villiers, which explained her presence in the cast, as well as that of Lady Villiers's father, Lord Clarendon, who acted as stage manager. His fellow minister, Lord Granville, played the Knave of Hearts and had as his father in the play the newly succeeded Duke of Manchester. In fact, only Georgina was without noble connection. Princess Mary, perhaps confused by the surname and the obscurity of her background, remembered her afterward as a handsome young lady from Cornwall.

How had Georgina come to be in such august company? It pleased her in later years to describe herself as wracked by shyness, but of all her fantasies this rings least true. She was certainly very pretty—the Pre-

Raphaelite Frederick Sandys considered her one of the most beautiful women in England (though in this and practically every other area, his was a very unreliable opinion)—but it was her voice that gave her the entrée.

There was a very long established tradition of musical entertainment in great houses. If you were well bred and could sing, you could do something very useful for your hostess and add to the charm of the occasion. It did not much matter if people talked through your rendition of some touching ballad—you were there to see and be seen. And it *was* a wonderful means of social introduction. At some of the grander functions, duchesses filled the first chairs, and the audience was ranged back in strict order of precedence. Invitations to these evenings—when they took place in the London high season—might exceed a hundred. The better houses had music rooms, but in other places the company crammed into drawing rooms and sat in bundles on the stairs. If there was not much glamour in it for the old, for the young it was exciting. For their mothers it was a battleground.

Constance Villiers liked and remembered Georgina for her performance on this particular evening at Ashridge. Hidden in the playbill is the clue to how she may have come to take part. The prompt for Georgina's performance in *Hearts and Tarts* was a wonderful old piece of Regency flotsam, Freddy Byng. It may have been his sponsorship that got Georgina into such august company. Poodle Byng (who was given his nickname by the Prince Regent because of the tight blond curls he wore as a young man) flits in and out of Victorian memoirs like an elderly and homeless bat. It was the Poodle who so scandalized the court in the first months of Victoria's reign when she was still considered a green girl by playing cards and making eyes at her, until he was gently shown the door. The fifth son of Viscount Torrington, he was fond of very young women and is said to have married his mother's chambermaid. He seems to have traveled light in Victorian society and been tolerated in the houses of the rich for his manners and gentle heart—because he knew everybody and was so very old. His only official duty anyone could remember had come in 1824 when he was given the job of escorting the King and Queen of the Sandwich Islands about London as a representative of the Crown. He did the best he could to amuse these two monarchs but could not stop them from dying of influenza two months after they arrived. Acting with unusual decisiveness, he had them embalmed in brandy and shipped back to the South Pacific.

Byng seems to have been genuinely besotted by Georgina. Three years on, Thackeray, who knew the Poodle rather better than he knew Georgina, surprised her by buying a wedding ring in Cockspur Street. Later in the afternoon he ran across the decrepit old man and broke his heart by saying, "Poodle, you have lost your singing bird. Miss Treherne has married some other fellow." Poodle Byng found her when she first came out and introduced her to those of his many friends who spent part of their time and wealth on private concerts and recitals. If he was amorous, he was also kindly: after irresistible blandishments from Georgina, he helped get her parents presented at court in 1858. Even Morgan could see the use of a sponsor like that, however old and decrepit he might be.

Georgina at twenty possessed an enchanting and very idiosyncratic soprano voice (her diction was considered exceptionally clear and distinct), and what she lacked in manners and sophistication she made up for by being seen everywhere. If she was coquettish—and this could certainly be leveled against her—then it was all very artless and inconsequential. Suspicious mothers and society hostesses alike were quickly reassured that this was no Becky Sharp, no girl on the make. She was if anything naive to a fault. Her dearest friends were the people she met last night. They were replaced without embarrassment by those to whom she was presently talking. So, for example, early on she spoke of Lord Lansdowne as a dear friend and ally. The fourth Marquis was an undersecretary of state for foreign affairs and a political scalp worth having. Whether he could separate Georgina from any of half a hundred young women he might have met under similarly brief circumstances was quite another matter.

Georgina was beginning to exhibit her father's ability to improve the facts. She had only to be in a noble house once to affect a lifelong intimacy with its owners. The most casual kind word addressed to her was an affirmation of undying love. She was odd like this and had a number of other social faults, including a garrulity that sometimes led her into indiscretion. She was not a girl to keep a secret.

Poodle Byng soon found her an appropriate milieu in which to shine. This was at Little Holland House, the former dower house of Lady Holland. After her death it had been purchased by Mr. and Mrs. Thoby Prinsep. Prinsep was an amiable and elderly retired official of the India Office and his wife, Sara, one of the famously beautiful, famously eccentric Pattle sisters. Georgina was especially delighted to discover there someone she could claim to know from the Florence years. The last time she had seen him was in the Casa Feroni, when she was six. The principal adornment of Little Holland House was her father's most reviled artist, George Frederick Watts.

Watts was now forty-one years old. He was the centerpiece of all Mrs. Prinsep's bustling social energies, a position he had more or less proposed for himself. "He came for three days; he stayed thirty years," his patroness observed dryly. The salon he helped her create included many of the Pre-Raphaelites, and figures such as Tennyson and Thackeray, Dickens and Carlyle, but it was really given over to Watts's enigmatic genius. George Du Maurier left a description of Sara and her sisters—"Elgin marbles with dark eyes," as Ruskin once called them—handing out tea to their guests with almost Eastern obeisance:

> Watts, who is a grand fellow, is their painter in ordinary: the best part of the house has been turned into his studio and he lives there and is worshipped till his manliness hath almost departed, I should fancy . . . After the departure of the visitors we dined; without dress coats—anyhow, and it was jolly enough—Watts in red coat and slippers. After dinner, up in the music room Watts stretched himself at full length on the sofa, which none of the women take when he is

there. People formed [a] circle, and I being in good voice sang to
them the whole evening, the cream of Schubert and Gordigiani—
c'était très drôle, the worship I got . . .

This was a different kind of ambience altogether from Ashridge, and
Du Maurier's breezy insouciance captures it exactly. The house itself was as
good as in the country, removed by trees and meadows from the harsher,
more unforgiving light that shone on soirees in Grosvenor Square or Belgravia. It was a low and sprawling building, the interiors decorated by
Watts's frescoes. Some rooms boasted wonderful blue ceilings, and others
were hung with Indian rugs and cloths. Behind a door covered in red baize
lay the hallowed center of the house, the source of its energies, Watts's studio. For Georgina it was a perfect stage, nonpolitical, gossipy, and faintly
loose. There was enough oddity already existing at Little Holland House for
her to feel at home. Sara Prinsep swept about the rooms in her own version
of Indian dress, coaxing and wheedling Watts and permitting in her other
guests what seemed to stricter hostesses a dangerous bohemianism. Her husband's library was kept out of the way, and there were no books on display
in the main rooms, forcing visitors and habitués into torrents of conversation and persiflage.

As to Watts, nobody could quite make him out. He had an almost perfect mixture of worldly vanity and ethereal otherness. Tall and thin, very
good-looking in youth, now with a hint of pain and suffering peeping out
from behind biblically long and straggling whiskers, the time he spent in
Florence—and in particular the gift for portraiture he discovered there—
had set him on the road to fame. If there was a question mark against his sexual appetites or lack of them and if men found him ridiculous, he was all the
same a society portraitist of the highest rank. This was a label he hated, for
Watts had it in mind to paint the large allegorical works with which he had
started out, and which the fame of the Florence portraits had eclipsed. As
soon as Georgina met him she made up to him unmercifully and had the reward—the accolade—of a sitting.

Watts had the reputation of making his subjects look younger and more
beautiful than they were in life. In his Florence portrait of Augusta, Lady

Holland, she looks out directly at the viewer under a slightly tilted head, her huge eyes shaded by the Italian straw hat she wears. Her lips are smiling and there are dimples in her cheeks: she wears the expression of someone sharing a pleasant secret with the artist, and so with us. It is the portrait of a clever, sensuous woman, well aware of the effect she is making. Watts finished this painting in 1843. Fourteen years on, the portrait of Georgina makes a striking contrast. Shown in three-quarter profile, she wears a similarly wide-brimmed hat, and her hand lightly supports her chin and cheek. She has highly arched and plucked eyebrows and looks out a little past the painter with unsmiling eyes. Although she is only twenty, her face is full and the neck plump. Augusta smiles out at the world with sardonic humor; Georgina's expression is faintly suspicious. It is an unfinished woman that Watts has represented and not an entirely likable one. He wrote at the time of the portrait:

> I must tell you, Bambina mia, that I miss you very much and the studio is very silent. The Bambina's vivacity was pleasant enough to the dull Signor, who was affected by the exhilarating contagion; now, coming from Lincoln's Inn weary and listless, I miss the vivacious little Bambina, and though Little H.H. is always charming and I am always made much of and spoiled, especially when I am tired, I miss the effervescent stimulant that was sparkling and overflowing all about the house, yet I was always in a fidget about the wild little girl, and very often not a little unhappy.

There is the accent of a spinster aunt about this. What put him in a fidget and made him unhappy? Was it anything more than having his peace and routine disturbed? Something deeper? In the next sentence he adds, enigmatically, "I depend upon her to be prudent and wise, not less merry I hope, God forbid she ever should be."

The portrait, of which Georgina was enormously proud, has nothing in it at all merry or skittish. At first blush Watts might have been writing about someone else altogether. He liked very young girls, as he was to prove in a disastrous marriage to the seventeen-year-old Ellen Terry, and he was also fond of moralizing. But the artist in him was painfully honest. He had seen a gaucheness in Georgina that he put into words in another, later letter: "I want you to be very wise in the choice of a husband, for everything will depend on the person or persons with whom you may live. If you are fortunate in this respect, you will be as you ought to be, an ornament and a delight to society; if the contrary, I dread more than I can say for the poor little bambina. I do not think you could be happy as the wife of a poor man . . ."

In one way it is pretty obvious conventional advice. But Watts was writing to the girl who thought of herself as destined for a £10,000-a-year man, a story she must have told him. Fey though he was, however foolish he might act with the young, he was all the same still the piano tuner's son. His remarks seem to distinguish between a life spent in society and not. That was something he knew all about, but a thing too unpleasant for her to contemplate.

And was there anyone truly rich, eligible, and well connected among the people who flocked to Little Holland House, drank its tea, and admired its painter in ordinary? Not Watts himself, nor any of the Pre-Raphaelite Brotherhood. Of the writers Mrs. Prinsep cultivated all were rich men, but their property was intellectual. Thackeray might gaze in amazement at a cheque for £2,000 from his American tour, and Dickens was by no means a poor man, yet theirs was a different kind of wealth. Thomas Carlyle had once explained this in a letter to Jane Welsh, the intelligent and ambitious girl he was trying to persuade to marry him—and it was a sentiment likely to have found favor at Little Holland House: "Kings and Potentates are a gaudy folk that flaunt about with plumes & ribbons to decorate them, and catch the coarse admiration of the many headed monster for a brief season—and then sink into forgetfulness . . . but the Miltons, the de Staels— these are the very salt of the earth; they derive their 'patents of Nobility' direct from Almighty God; and live in the bosoms of all true men to all ages."

One of the occasional members of the coterie Georgina had now joined and who did belong to that rather less exalted nobility of plumes and ribbons was Lady Charlotte Schreiber. Charlotte Schreiber had strong Welsh connections. Her first husband was Josiah John Guest of the Dowlais Ironworks, the M.P. for Merthyr Tydfil for twenty years until his death. Guest practically owned the town and employed most people in it. His wife was a daughter of the ninth Earl of Lindsay and a Welsh scholar—she translated the *Mabinogion* into English when she was still in her twenties. After her husband's death in 1852, she ran the iron and coal companies he left her under her own name. She had recently—and in some eyes shockingly—married Charles Schreiber of Trinity College, Cambridge, tutor to her eldest son. In Dorset the family kept up Canford Manor in all its magnificence, though (as the ever-vigilant Morgan discovered) under the terms of a trust the house and Lady Charlotte's personal share in the fortune was forfeited by reason of this second marriage.

It was at about this time, when the eldest son, Ivor, came into his majority and Canford became his, that Georgina first met the Schreibers. In the winter of 1856 Lady Charlotte and nine of her ten children crowded into a house at Marine Parade, Brighton, while a search was made for suitable and more permanent accommodation in London. Not until April of the following year did they find Exeter House in Roehampton, standing in sixteen acres. During their stay in Brighton they became acquainted with the Trehernes, in the general sense of being present at the same ball or party and included on the same subscription lists for concerts. The fourth son of the family was Merthyr Guest. He was a year younger than Georgina, a restless and underachieving student at Trinity College, Cambridge (where his brother had taken a first). Very comfortingly and after only a few meetings he declared himself infatuated with her. When the family moved to Exeter House, Georgina was soon invited there by Lady Charlotte. She also saw her from time to time at Little Holland House, where Merthyr's mother was wont to engage Tennyson in conversations about the Arthurian legends. She had no knowledge of the depths of her son's feeling for the pretty and amiable Miss Treherne. For the time being, Georgina said nothing to enlighten her.

*I*f coming out in society and making a mark in it were part of Morgan's plan for his daughter, Georgina had already done a great deal to satisfy his ambition. Her voice had carried her into drawing rooms that he would have difficulty in entering on his own merits. He had taken a house in Stratford Place, a small gated cul-de-sac off Oxford Street from which to direct both her affairs and his own. In the country he was a magistrate and a ruthless persecutor of trespassers and poachers. On his own land he set spring guns without the slightest qualm. He had by no means given up hope of a seat in the House of Commons. He was friendless and his relations with his brothers were as strained as ever, but by his own lights the new Mr. Treherne was making progress in the world. He was very deliberately old-fashioned, and there were as a consequence huge gaps in what he knew about the age in which he lived. Style and the surface of things had always meant nothing to him. He was a reactionary and proud of it. In certain circles—say among military men—there was no harm in that. On brief acquaintance and with the addition of only a little humor his position could even seem endearing. He polished a way of expressing himself that he was to use to the electors of Coventry in a famous speech: "I have a thorough and heart detestation of the Whigs . . . I have a parrot at home that cries Damn the Whigs! and although I should be very sorry to use such language myself—even if I do express myself strongly sometimes—I cannot say that my feelings towards the Whigs are more friendly than those of my parrot."

Georgina was troublesome to him but no more than she had ever been. Although by now she was of an age where he might have expected her to be settled and not emptying his purse running about London as a young lady of fashion, there were some encouraging developments. It was never Morgan's practice to give a compliment, yet Georgina's impetuous charm had at least secured the interest of an eminently worthy family like the Schreibers and she had the friendship (or so she claimed) of Lady Constance Villiers, daughter of the Foreign Secretary. From such connections who knew what might follow?

And then the roof fell in.

In January 1858 Lady Sudeley gave a ball in Brighton to which Louisa and her daughters were invited. The occasion was a happy one. Lord Sudeley, whose family owned large estates in the town, had just succeeded to the title. It was the first entertainment of the new year, and the 250 guests who assembled in the Pavilion Rooms had another lively topic of conversation, in addition to Lord Sudeley's good fortune. A few days earlier, amid scenes of incredible pomp and attended by thirteen crowned heads of Europe, the Queen's eldest daughter had married Frederick, Crown Prince of Prussia. She was seventeen years old. That very Saturday, there had been an immense press of people at a congratulatory Drawing Room, at which the young Princess stood by her mother to receive her guests. Victoria was amazed and delighted at the cordiality shown to the Royal Family in what was for her a watershed experience. (The Princess Royal left England the following Tuesday in a blizzard of snow, attended by immense crowds. At Buckingham Palace the Queen had parted from her daughter in floods of tears, and this mood was communicated to the entire household, who sobbed and wailed as at a funeral. Lady Desart, a lady-in-waiting, said later it was the first time in her memory that Victoria completely lost control of herself.)

There was much to discuss, then. Louisa might borrow a little from the glamour of the royal wedding by having boys at Eton, for the school had telegraphed the happy couple on the day of the wedding and asked permission to drag the honeymooners' carriage through the streets of Windsor, which they accomplished most gallantly and inexpertly. And of course, since the subject of marriage in general was more than usually on everyone's lips, did the company know that Georgina, etc., etc.? Nothing had been fixed, no formal announcements had been made, but Merthyr Guest was *such* a prepossessing young man and seemed so enamored of Miss Treherne, etc., etc. Of course he was very young and had first his career at Trinity to contemplate, but he was a dear kind boy. People who knew the Schreibers rather better than Louisa did might have been startled at this piece of wishful thinking. A really shrewd observer might have looked behind the understandable note of triumph and discovered an ancient doubt: the development of the plot was only so good as the steadiness of the principal character in it, which was to say Georgina. Was she going to do something stupid at this critical moment?

She was. The officers of the 18th Hussars, who were in barracks at Preston Park, had been invited to the Sudeley Ball. The 18th was hardly a very fashionable regiment: it had only recently been reconstituted, and of the officers there was not a title among them. It was true that General Scarlett, the hero of Balaclava, had himself served as a cornet with the old 18th; one of the present cornets had the honor to have been born under a gun at Waterloo. But the regiment was originally raised in Yorkshire and re-formed there; and though it had taken part in the festivities surrounding the royal wedding, it was too new to have fought in the Crimea or to have had any part in the putting down of the infamous Mutiny in India.

Among those of the regiment who accepted for Lady Sudeley was a young lieutenant named Harry Weldon. While he cut a fine figure in patrol uniform and was reputed to ride well, his experience of soldiering was practically nil. Like many of his troopers, he came from Yorkshire. He had the languid manners appropriate to a junior officer and was good-looking in a stock sort of way, but he was shockingly provincial, for whom the past glittering month or so—of Brighton and London—had been bewitching. His expression was frank and open, and he was altogether the sort of boy you might entrust at a ball to fetch an ice or search for a shawl, but one whose name you asked only to forget. He was twenty years old and in the present company, a spear-carrier, an extra. If Morgan Treherne, M.P., had searched the *Army List* for a week, he could not have come up with a less appealing candidate for Georgina's attentions.

To his stupefaction, therefore, a day or so after the ball this young man, this whippersnapper, this uniformed nothing, rode out from Preston Barracks to Mayfield on his horse, Multum. Flakes of snow fell romantically about his head: when the butler asked him his business, he explained he was there to see Georgina. Antonio (who may have been impressed at a wearisome journey undertaken in vile weather, but knew his master's temper only too well) went off to see Morgan. Morgan sent back word that the gentleman was not to be admitted. The suitor—for that was the purpose of his visit—turned his horse's head and set off on the long ride back to barracks. Georgina was summoned and closely questioned. A slow thrill of horror began to run through both parents.

Lieutenant William Henry Weldon was the son of a coal merchant from the Sheffield area. According to Georgina, writing in later years, old Mr. Weldon actually delivered coal in sacks on a horse and cart, a piece of spite that may or may not have been true. Harry's father died when he was a child, and his mother now lived in a two-bedroom cottage in Beaumaris. There was a grandmother still alive from whom he would inherit, and he claimed to be coming into a trust fund two months hence when he reached his majority. In letters that he had the extreme impertinence to send Morgan, he diminished the value of this fund's income from the £2,000 that he may have boasted of to others. In fact, he halved it, perhaps out of prudence or maybe as a demonstration of his good faith.

If he hoped to impress his prospective father-in-law by such honesty, the plan backfired badly. When he offered to have his solicitor write to clarify matters further, Morgan ordered the long-suffering Antonio to reply to the letter, not deigning to take up his own pen. Unfortunately, Harry Weldon either was having trouble reading these signals or had badly misjudged the fanatically snobbish Trehernes.

Ten days after he had first been shown the door, Louisa burst in on her daughter while she was still in bed. "Here's a letter from that blackguard Weldon. And look what he's written! Oh the vile swindler! A thousand a year when he's twenty one on the 8th of April. Another £2000 when his 84 year old grandmother dies and another two thousand when his mother dies. And she's still young—what is it, hardly forty! Oh, I'm very happy he doesn't have two thousand a year now—you'd be mad enough to want to marry him! Two thousand a year is beggary, but a thousand a year is starvation, it's to die of hunger!"

If Louisa really spoke these words, she stands accused of the same mania that afflicted her husband. Georgina may have recalled the conversation precisely because it threw a bad light on a snobbish and not very worldly woman. What alarmed and infuriated her mother, however, were the circumstances that had led to the letter. They took some explanation. It is unlikely (a crowded ballroom being what it is) the two had passed more than twenty minutes in each other's company unchaperoned. What, then, had been said? The question was not one of Harry's income, but of Georgina's common sense. He had met and been smitten by a pretty girl. Of all the things she may have told him about herself, it would seem the one thing she had not mentioned was the situation with regard to Merthyr Guest. Nor the volcanic temperament of her father.

Or maybe she did—maybe riding over to Mayfield was for him the romantic equivalent of the forlorn hope, beloved of gallant (and suicidal) officers in every army of every epoch. Maybe she did tell him that her father would have him for breakfast, and the sheer thrill of that was enough for him to volunteer himself. He knew next to nothing of society, had no connections of any kind, and in every sense had nothing to lose: why not make his play for her in as gallant a way as he knew how? Proposing to pretty young women was not a crime, and Georgina's father was hardly likely to shoot him from an upstairs window. (Luckily for a great many people in the nineteenth century, Morgan and firearms seem to have been strangers. That is, among his own kind. Poachers in Mayfield spoke darkly of his use of spring guns, aiming to blow the head off anyone daring to take a pheasant on Treherne land.) There was one further possibility. Maybe Harry saw her, was bowled over by her, and what Mr. Treherne interpreted as confounded impudence was an advanced form of lovesickness. He must have that girl or destroy himself in the attempt.

Morgan came up with a sobriquet for the unfortunate Hussar. He was swiftly known over the Gate House breakfast table as Ananias, the foolish man who lied to God and paid the penalty. The story comes from the Bible, Acts 5:1–6:

> But a certain man named Ananias, with Sapphira his wife, sold
> a possession, and kept back part of the price . . . and brought a cer-

tain part, and laid it at the apostles' feet. But Peter said, "Ananias, why hath Satan filled thine heart to lie to the Holy Ghost, and to keep back part of the price of the land? Whiles it remained, was it not thine own? and after it was sold, was it not in thine own power? why hast thou conceived this thing in thine heart? thou hast not lied unto men, but unto God." And Ananias hearing these words fell down, and gave up the ghost: and great fear came on all them that heard these things. And the young men arose, wound him up, and carried him out, and buried him.

In later life and in the full knowledge that Harry would read her words, Georgina declared the nickname well merited. If she thought so at the time, it throws a lurid light on the whole Treherne family. Was Morgan really to be compared to the apostle Peter or to God? And had it escaped all of them that a little while after, Sapphira followed her husband into the same grave?

In the short term the problem resolved itself. The 18th Hussars were ordered away back to Yorkshire. If it had been a case of lovesickness, the traditional cure seems to have worked. Harry Weldon reflected without bitterness that though he had lost this particular skirmish, he had hardly lost the war. In April he came into his trust money, which had appreciated to £7,500. He was young and good-looking, and the world was filled with more or less beautiful women. Were he to stay in the 18th, he might become at the very least a major. If he exchanged into an Indian regiment, he might one day have his own command. Instead, according to Georgina, he went through the whole of his inheritance in eighteen months, which hardly bespeaks a broken heart. He was easygoing and venal in just the right proportions; a model of a certain kind of junior officer who might continue exactly as Georgina had discovered him: a supernumerary at balls and banquets, a cheerful card player, and a modest rake. But if he thought it was all over, he was wrong. Thackeray at his most cynical could not have dreamed up a better twist to the plot.

In May, Merthyr Guest came to his mother and wished her permission to propose to Miss Treherne. Lady Charlotte was startled, for it seemed to her that Georgina was no more than a friend to him and a cruelly joshing one at that. Merthyr explained otherwise. He confessed that he had been seeing

Georgina and corresponding with her for much longer than his mother suspected: in fact, since the winter of 1856. He could not now contemplate life
without her. Charlotte Schreiber did everything she could to dissuade him.
The first favorable impressions Georgina had made had begun to wear off,
and while Lady Charlotte enjoyed her chats with Tennyson, the rest of the
coterie at Little Holland House filled her with the deepest suspicions. However, her own second marriage placed her in a weak position. She grudg-
ingly gave her consent to an engagement, on condition that it remain secret
for a while and that Merthyr not attempt to marry without her permission.

Overjoyed, Merthyr went down to Mayfield to ask Morgan for his
daughter's hand. He was hardly greeted with open arms. As soon as he left,
Morgan began bombarding the Schreibers with letters that did not waste
time on felicitating the young couple. He wished to know the exact extent of
the fortune involved. So far as Morgan was concerned, this was the best offer
he was going to get for his daughter, and it merely remained to settle terms.

The tone of these letters was deeply offensive to Lady Charlotte. It
seemed her son had been trapped by an adventuress. At Exeter House there
were tears and recriminations, Georgina first saying she must obey her father's wishes and in the next breath saying she must marry Merthyr or per-
ish. A good-hearted compromise was worked out, without Morgan's
knowledge. No decision of any kind would be made until Merthyr came of
age in January 1859. Then, if the two young people were still of the same
mind, matters could be straightened out with the ogre of Mayfield. Meanwhile, they might continue under the tacit understanding of an engagement.
This seemed to please Georgina and it delighted Merthyr. It was the summer
vacation, and Ivor Guest invited his brother to accompany him to Scotland.
Georgina was annoyed at this and tried to prevent Merthyr from going.
They parted acrimoniously.

Only a month after Merthyr's interview at Mayfield and while he was
still in Scotland with his brother, Lady Charlotte paid an afternoon visit to
Little Holland House, probably to check up on one of her daughters, a
young woman who had also been taken by the free and easy atmosphere of
the house. Instead of her daughter, she discovered Georgina "closeted alone
with Lord Ward in Watts' studio, Watts being absent at Bowood." The loca-

tion was shocking in itself—nobody but the painter crossed the threshold of the red baize door, unless by invitation. The two might as well have been discovered in Mrs. Prinsep's bedroom, so great was the impropriety. The identity of the man found with Georgina was the second awful surprise. William Ward was twenty years older than she and an enormously rich widower. Whatever Lady Charlotte saw when she burst in on them—and it cannot have been innocent—it was enough to persuade her son to disengage himself at once from any undertaking to marry.

Lady Charlotte dropped Georgina and all the Trehernes forthwith. Nothing was said, nothing needed to be said: Georgina made no attempt to defend herself. It was disaster. She had recklessly thrown away connections she and her parents had striven for over four years. Word of Georgina's betrayal of her hospitality got back to Mrs. Prinsep, and she was dropped there too. Watts's prophecy had come true: the Bambina had made the wrong choice, and her wildness had gone beyond what was permissible even in the easygoing ambience of Little Holland House. Maybe it would have been seen differently if Georgina had had some offsetting talent, some serious application to an art or to a cause: that might have mended fences with Mrs. Prinsep. But, stung, Georgina now began to make blustering and unpleasant remarks about her hostess. Watts knew what side his bread was buttered on. She lost his friendship too. The end came on June 28, as recounted in Lady Charlotte's diary:

> I had thought it my duty last week to write and tell Merthyr how Miss Treherne was going on with Lord Ward, and how she went about telling everybody that her engagement to Merthyr was at an end. I, this morning, heard from Merthyr in reply, greatly grieved, poor fellow. He mentioned having written to her and to Mrs. Prinsep for an explanation and I was anxious to hear from the latter what sort of reply she intended to make to him. I did not now find her at home . . . and so the next morning I went again to Little Holland House and had a long interview with Mrs. Prinsep. Her opinion was that Miss Treherne cares nothing for Merthyr, but would gladly marry Lord Ward if she could accomplish it.

Morgan must take some of the blame. His dealings with the Schreibers and with Mrs. Prinsep had been peremptory in the extreme. In other circumstances, Charlotte Schreiber would perhaps have felt it her Christian duty to rescue Georgina from the clutches of such a monstrous father. Toward her own children she showed an almost supernatural solicitude. (When her fourth son, Montague, embarked with his regiment at Gravesend, en route for India, she left Wales, where she had been staying with the ironmaster Talbot, and traveled for eight hours by train, only to find the troop convoy had left. Distraught, she tried to persuade the Custom House to let her follow the fleet downstream, where she was convinced they would remain at anchor until dawn the following day. She was at last dissuaded and got home to Roehampton at one in the morning utterly exhausted.) Though she did not much like Georgina, she would have exerted herself on her behalf in the same way, if it were not for one thing: Georgina herself had flung away the prize. Ward was almost old enough to be her father, and though he was amazingly wealthy, he was never a serious lover—and she knew it. She had indulged herself with a man for the sake of momentary pleasure. She was brought back to Mayfield in disgrace and more or less made a prisoner of her father's. He forbade her hardly to leave the house.

*T*he awful consequence of being Morgan's daughter was at last plain to her. Taken together, the actions of father and daughter put the kind of marriage she had been promised and the future she envisaged for herself out of the question forever. She had behaved badly and he hardly any better. Socially they were doomed. Nor had Morgan's political star shone as much as he would have liked since changing his name to Treherne. In 1857 he went up to Coventry to make his third assault on the constituency.

> *To the Freeman of Coventry 'twas Treherne who spoke—*
> *Ere the Tories are beat there are crowns to be broke!*
> *So here's to the man who freedom would earn,*
> *Let him follow the colours of Morgan Treherne.*

Neither the candidacy nor the ballads had improved with age. Morgan came fourth out of five on the ballot and, when given the courtesy of a speech, held up his famous presentation watch, declaring bitterly: "It is a good watch; I value it highly, though it has cost me dear, for it has kept better time than its presenters of 1837 have kept faith with me."

In April 1859 he tried again and was once again defeated. This time he was stung into reminding the electors of Ellice's boast that Morgan would not serve Coventry for as long as he had breath. Ellice (who had not even come to Coventry to oversee his reelection, pleading gout as his excuse) at once denied he had ever said this and forced a humiliating public retraction. Victorian England was not so large that Morgan's antics at Coventry and Georgina's at Little Holland House could not be connected. Insofar as they were known at all outside Sussex, father and daughter had contrived to make too many enemies. The campaign to find the £10,000-a-year man lay in tatters.

Harry Weldon, meanwhile, was smoking cigars and playing billiards in barracks in his native Yorkshire. He had completely forgotten Georgina, and there had been no correspondence between them since January 1858. To his consternation, he was summoned back from the wilderness. The plump and enchanting girl he had bid for and lost now amazed him by writing to him. Unlike Ananias faced with the wrath of God, he was explicitly commanded not to give up the ghost. On the contrary, under conditions of the greatest secrecy, he found himself egged on to indiscretions he must often have pondered in the quiet of his quarters. He took leave to travel to Brighton.

> The day is fixed, my beloved! On Thursday! I think, darling,
> the best way for us to meet is for you to be waiting for me in a fly at

the bottom of the colonnade, your horse's head turned towards the left and the vehicle itself not quite at the edge of the street: almost—but not quite—opposite Ayler the hat woman. I am sure to be there by half past ten. Keep the blinds of your carriage down and have patience, my Harry, not to look out. Then, darling, when I see you are there, I will open the carriage door, jump in, and you tell the coachman beforehand to drive out of town.

On this particular occasion, he had enough gallantry to obey her instructions up to a point. But there was prudence in Harry, or maybe it was callousness. That Thursday, which must have cost her dear in deception, ended in farce. At half past ten she burst out of the hat shop, saw the carriage, and ran toward it. She flung open the door. Inside, in the dark, his soldier servant greeted her with the gloomy words "Mr. Weldon is not here."

Though setbacks like this did not deter her, if she was looking for gallantry in Harry she was soon disappointed. He wanted her physically with a passion that delighted her but was in most other ways the least gallant officer in the British Army. Just how much she told him about Merthyr and Lord Ward is unknown, but it would hardly have made a difference—Harry knew nothing about society and cared less. All he saw was that a plum had fallen into his lap. She was used to the indolence of titled young men; her brother Dal, newly commissioned in the West Kent Militia, was busy learning the same laconic, drawling manners. Harry's lazy good humor came from a different and more homely source. Money burned a hole in his pocket, the army bored him, and he had no plans. She had all the plans. His letters to the prison that Mayfield had become were ordered to be wrapped in sheet music from Chappells. She even told him what scores to buy—Verdi. There were a handful of clandestine meetings.

Writing many years after, her nephew remarked, "No doubt existed that this was anything other than a love match." He was quoting family history, for he himself had yet to be born. The evidence is all the other way. Harry was being driven along by forces out of his control. The only other explanation is that he was cynically abusing her. Of this time, when all her greater plans had been dashed to the ground, she writes of Morgan:

As we never dared open our lips in his presence, scarcely daring to breathe without his snubbing us unmercifully, and as he allowed us no amusement whatever, not even that of teaching the choir in the church at Mayfield, I left the paternal roof, where otherwise I should have been so happy, without much regret. I had no taste or need of marriage; in a convent I should have been the happiest of women, without a desire, without an aspiration: I was endowed with the most placid temperament in the world.

She was fooling herself. There is something quite manic in her pursuit of a little provincial Hussar she hardly knew. This is a woman in her twenties lighting matches in a gunpowder factory. At last, at the beginning of 1860, Harry came to her and explained that he had squandered his entire inheritance and all that was left for him to do was to go to India and there blow out his brains.

Instead, they married secretly at Aldershot on Saturday, April 21, 1860.

5

t was snowing in London that day. There was war in the air, as well as snow. All the docks and installations had been fortified, and the previous month the Queen had received 2,500 Volunteer officers in review. Millais, Rossetti, and even Watts joined the Artists' Rifles, riding about Wimbledon Common on horses they could hardly manage. Most amazing of all, the decrepit and tottering Poodle Byng enlisted in the Queen's Westminsters and was present on parade, just as he had been for George III in the levy of volunteers fifty-seven years earlier. It was a strange time for the happy couple to be rattling toward Dover and the Continent, but a letter from Lord Clarendon to the Duchess of Manchester may hint at the suddenness of the marriage: "Don't you remember Miss Treherne, who sang so well at Ashridge & the Poodle was so in love with? She has just eloped with Mr. Welldon a respectable man of 3000 a year but who her father did not think fine enough for her. My sister knows her very well & had a letter from her to say how impossible it wd: have been for her to have acted otherwise."

The £3,000 a year did not exist, of course. What was the reason for her being unable to act otherwise? Whether she was pregnant going across to Dieppe we do not know (though she was very soon after). Although Harry was married in uniform and attended by his fellow officers, he sold his commission the same day. At Paris Georgina wrote to her brother Dal, asking him to intercede with her father. But it was no use. Morgan cut her off without a penny, and she never saw him again.

Harry had won his prize after all. The circumstances were less than ideal. He had met her parents only once, at the Sudeley Ball. He knew her only through the days and nights they had stolen together. She knew nothing at all of his family and astounded him by supposing Manchester to be a town in Yorkshire. As the coach headed south and Georgina practiced her French and Italian on the natives, their destination was—where else?— Florence. Less than two years after being presented at court, a week after shaming her parents, she was talking with a wildness and lack of realism he must already have grown used to, of going on the stage. No matter that the Mediterranean sun began to shine on them and leaving aside the question of whether or not she was already pregnant, they were effectively ruined. The only way back from a fiasco like this was through love. Or genius.

Weldon

1

The new Mrs. Weldon returned to Florence with an adult's view of what had been her childhood landscape. Harry was dismayed to find recent history being vigorously rewritten by his bride. The little girl who once bristled with virtue had become a confident gossip and name-dropper. She could assure people that Watts, who as a young man had painted Napoleon's niece when *she* was newly married, had also painted her, to the acclaim of all London. She had met Thackeray, amused herself with Millais. Lord Clarendon and all the Villierses were special friends and Princess Mary such a lump. Tennyson was a rather earnest man with a complexion much ruined by tobacco. On the threat of war and revolution, of the political mood in England—on any matter whatsoever to do with politics—she was on less sure ground. Human society was for her always a matter of style and not content. It was hats and gardens, wallpapers, sheet music. She seemed not to understand that the world was being run by someone, or that there were wheels within wheels.

Georgina was, or would like to have been thought, "a fashionable." A fashionable woman was described by the width of her crinoline, the depth of her neckline, the exact amount of false hair added to her coiffure. Only a fashionable would know what jewelry to select for a given occasion or how well or badly to play at cards. But the term extended beyond clothes and appearance and crossed the line between the sexes. Books, plays, towns, streets within those towns, drawing rooms, furniture, the naming of children and dogs, the livery of servants—the list continued. It was easy to see what would not do. For example, until the Crimea veterans started to come home, beards were thought very de trop among men, and only certain kinds of mustache would pass. But after the investiture Victoria gave her Crimean soldier heroes in Green Park, beards might be allowed. In the same way, Wellington had detested his officers wearing uniforms in public, but now (for a while at least) it was thought rather a good thing.

Fashionables might be treated satirically by their lessers, but the codes they established were very powerful. Georgina understood this world and all its nuances, without quite realizing that it interlocked with the world of real events. Though she came back to Florence a fashionable, it caused her no reflection that Italian unification was just about to knock a nail into the coffin of the English colony she wished to impress. In Florence itself the Grand Duke had abdicated, and the British Embassy, scene of so much revelry and intrigue in her childhood, had been withdrawn. Florence's revolution had been peaceful, yet for the old Waterloo veterans still tottering the streets there was the unmistakable scent of gunpowder in the air. Garibaldi was in Naples. An era was ending.

Harry's enjoyment of the honeymoon was tempered by some unpleasant surprises. For such a careless name-dropper, his wife was extremely exact in matters of household budgeting. The cost of a night in a coaching inn, the loose change left over from a wise—or careless—choice of wines: in such things she showed a decided taste for petty detail. He had married a list maker. It was a foreshadowing of what was to come. She made lists, she argued indignantly over bills, handled servants with superb contempt. It was a side of her he had not reckoned with. It was true she had a hundred ideas and inspirations and an absolute passion for improving the bones of a story. But the grand lady she liked to be in the daily concourse of carriages at the Cascine Gardens and the musical genius she felt to be her true destiny came down in bed to a rather erratic woman who tried to amuse him by imitating the sound of birds and animals. In the mornings, staying at this or that hotel, she would sing for him, at alarming volume, breaking off only to scold a maid or question the reckoning of last night's supper. The Florence of galleries and palaces left them both unmoved. They were at their best in cafés and restaurants or as the guests of some gullible family, hoping for news of England.

Harry could play the part of a languid consort: it was the sort of thing he did well, and he was a clubbable, even on occasion a twinkly, personality. But he was much more realistic in temperament. Walking in the city and its gardens, listening to her chatter, it was better not to think too deeply of the comparison between Florence and whatever a little town in Anglesey had to offer. When they came home again to England—or as he had constantly to remind her, Wales—they would pay the full price for their folly.

For a few weeks, all was well. They went to Capri, where they met the minor Pre-Raphaelite John Brett, who sketched her portrait. Such flattering attentions were no more than the embers of the romantic fires she had lit so briefly among the Little Holland House set. Her flirting days, the gamble she made of her youth and beauty for such high stakes, all this was at an end. Marriage did not extinguish her beauty, but to marry meant to settle down. In the case of the new Weldons, without money and influence, it meant to disappear. Their host Brett was an instance of how obscurely the obscure might live. To be praised by Ruskin for a particular painting was a fine thing, but it was not the passport to wealth and riches. In a year or so, with the whole Pre-Raphaelite Brotherhood shipwrecked (to some extent on the rock of marriage), Brett left Capri and took himself off to Putney, where he built himself a most amazing house and took up astronomical observation and was largely forgotten. Here on Capri, talking and lounging, life seemed so wonderful, so fabulous. Whether or not she had married Harry for love, she was clearly mad about him now. He was her Proomps, her Darling Boy, her Dear Old Man.

Brett was a few years older than them both and unmarried. He had been born into a soldier family and could recognize in Harry a lazy lustfulness, a sort of garrison town gift for making himself attractive to women. The husband, he observed, had little intelligent conversation and was perfectly ignorant of art and culture. His wife was beautiful but also distressingly empty-headed. The pencil sketch Brett did of Georgina shows her sleeping, a plump arm extended above her head, her chin full. Around her neck is a choker of coral. There is not a line on her face. The whole drawing suggests ripeness and indolence, a Mediterranean abandon. This is Georgina at the magic hour, the shutters open to a blissful silence as the sea begins to take up the tint of the sky. But the idyll could not last. Harry finally dinned it into her that they could not stay where they were. The sun, the sea, all the romance of Italy, had been no more than a cruel backdrop to what seemed like a hopeless future. For the second and last time in her life she climbed into a diligence and quit the Mediterranean.

Back in England, and on the road to her mother-in-law's cottage in Beaumaris, she miscarried of a boy.

The miscarriage was a shattering blow. In her memoirs almost the only good word she has to say about Harry in any of his guises is that he sat by her bed for weeks nursing her through illness and despair. The location was unpromising. On the road into Beaumaris there lay a short row of cottages, one of which was occupied by Harry's mother, a redoubtable and, according to Georgina, coarse-grained widow who came originally from Eccleshall in Lancashire. The newly marrieds moved in as neighbors. They, who had so recently sat where Nero sat, now found themselves in four rooms and an outside privy, with no money, no prospects, and no friends. Watts's portrait, which hung on the wall alongside Harry's boyhood collection of stuffed birds, was a ghastly reminder of what had been.

Georgina lost the baby to what turned out to be an incurable gynecological defect. The enormity of this news—taken with the desolation of all her other prospects—might have brought a lesser woman to her knees. (It is the one subject on which she stayed silent in later life.) There were investigations done by doctors in London, cures attempted in the Rhine spas. The physicians she consulted saw a plump and comely young woman of twenty-three with a very ready presence, not at all the textbook wraith or hollow-eyed neurasthenic. Georgina was an otherwise healthy patient with unbounded energy and apparently unending reserves of courage and fortitude. They could not help her. It is quite clear that she desired children. Whatever had gone wrong with her own childhood she wanted to redress with children of her own. She persisted with the doctors long past the stage of a second or even a fourth opinion. In this, at least, the willfulness she had shown before her marriage came suddenly into focus. Being barren was something she simply could not allow to happen; and when it was proved beyond a doubt that she was, what was most valuable to her—her power over events—was taken away. Love in a cottage was all very well, but without the long perspective offered by children, where would her life with Harry lead?

Some of her new neighbors took pity on her. The kindly Lady Bulkely called, which she had never done for the elder Mrs. Weldon. All the same, the scale of her Beaumaris life was more like shipwreck than anything else. She responded with a new and unfamiliar determination to make the very best of things. She gardened furiously in a handkerchief plot overlooking the sea, kept a dog, made light of her circumstances, and absolutely insisted on her rank. She engaged two Welsh girls as maids at £8 a year and started the long climb back.

Without children, without the possibility of reconciliation to her own family, her single resource was not so much her talent, of which she had little that had been properly educated, but her energy. In the Beaumaris years it was this that made her famous. She astonished everyone who met her.

Harry's indolence, which had looked so well in uniform, soon enough seemed to her a mysterious force, a sort of disease even. She loved him dearly but found him completely without ambition. After a while he had himself elected to the Beaumaris Artillery Volunteers, where he found undemanding duties and congenial drinking companions among his fellow officers. Georgina organized a choir drawn from the ranks, augmented by child altos and with herself as principal soprano, and gave charity concerts. Harry thought her mad. His own plans were rudimentary in the extreme. He was waiting for his grandmother to die.

*G*eorgina had been told several times just before her marriage that she should put her singing voice to advantage and turn professional. The advice came originally from Frederick Clay, an amateur composer who held a clerk's post in the Treasury. Clay was a year or so younger than she and not much better trained as a musician, but he was a considerable melodist and an ambitious young man. He had been charmed by her and remained her friend through thick and thin. "The Sands of Dee," a Clay ballad which for forty years every young woman in England offered when music was called for, was dedicated to her. It may have been that he knew enough about her to make this idea of singing professionally a subtly practical suggestion, as a way out of the disgrace she had brought down on herself at Little Holland House. It was a delicate matter to broach, for young ladies of good family did not take this route very often. Lords might marry opera singers, but their daughters hardly clamored to go on the stage. Fredling, as she called him, may have been trying to help, but it was not completely welcome advice. His own hold on the musical scene came from two little operettas he had written. He was much better known as James Clay's son and the man who first introduced Gilbert to Sullivan.

The composer and conductor Julius Benedict gave Georgina the same encouragement to turn professional. This was a much more weighty endorsement of her talents. Benedict had the unmistakable air of the maestro about him (he had been a pupil of Weber's and was surely the only man Georgina ever met who had shaken hands with Beethoven). It was Benedict who brought Jenny Lind to England to sing in oratorio and he who shepherded the singer on her triumphant tour of America. His admiration for Georgina's voice seems to have been unqualified. Benedict understood very well that the Upper Ten Thousand knew little about music they did not make for themselves. They went to the Italian Opera as a form of social snobbery. Otherwise, they were taught by poor devils who came to the house as servants or by their mothers. Their accomplishments were consequently very modest.

Benedict—and there were increasing numbers of others like him—saw that musical patronage was passing from the aristocracy to the middle classes. The Royal Academy of Music was a striking example. It was founded in 1822 and given its charter in 1830, but its fortunes had until recently been mixed. The original patron was Lord Westmorland, a soldier and diplomat, and an amateur composer and fiddle player. The committee that formed around him was entirely aristocratic. It took as its principal duty the management of a modest fund and a property off Hanover Square. The question of music education hardly came into it. The institution lurched from one disaster to another. When Westmorland died in 1859, the Board of Professors tried for ten years to increase their role from being merely advisory to the directors, to a share in the running of affairs. The committee's response was simple and direct. If the profession of music led to unseemly wrangles of this kind with titled gentlemen, they would rather have nothing to do with it. They voted to resign the Royal Charter. The professors took legal opinion, and it was only by their energies that the Royal Academy of Music was saved.

Georgina's own interest in music was purely amateur. As her experience of Little Holland House had shown, it was much easier to meet a poet or a painter on more or less equal terms than it was to discover a composer, especially an English composer. The division that existed in the Royal Academy of Music ran right through society. The gifted amateur from her own rank in society and the professional music maker hardly ever mixed. There is a telling anecdote in Fenimore Cooper's account of his visit to England, as early as 1828: "Respectable artists such as would be gladly received in our orchestras walk the streets and play the music of Rossini, Mozart, Beethoven, Meyerbeer, Weber, &tc., beneath your windows," he reported. The poverty they dwelled in astonished him quite as much as the quality of their playing. He even found a man who pushed a grand piano about on a cart and gave recitals "quite equal to what one finds in society." In forty years much had changed, but the underlying point of the story remained the same. Music professionals were doubtless very worthy, but they were not exactly cherishable.

Benedict was one of the men who changed all this. At the time he first met Georgina he was conductor of the Italian Opera. If *he* thought she could turn professional, it was advice not to be dismissed lightly. In the long winter of 1860 she must have thought about this many times. If she had truly compromised her social position by a runaway marriage—as it must have seemed with the wind whistling through the cottage door and snow blanking out the view of Baron Hill, behind whose walls Lady Bulkely gave court to the even more illustrious Pagets—maybe a professional career as a singer was the only way out. Harry had no opinion one way or the other. He knew none of the people she knew and had no particular wish to make their acquaintance. Georgina could, if she wished, ride bareback in a circus. It was all the same to him.

She did not in the end respond to Benedict. Every life has opportunities that are not taken up—in this case fatefully. Benedict was a pleasant old man, but he was after all merely a German. To do what he proposed was to admit defeat, not only to people who had known her in London but, more important, to her parents and brothers and sisters. The composer could not know how important it was for her to be counted among the elite. Fame of the kind given to Malibran or Jenny Lind was not what she was after. She had already touched the hem of what she wanted—to be in the same company as the

Duchess of Cambridge or Lord Clarendon and his adorable daughter. To be irresistible in a room filled with duchesses, simply because she was beautiful and in some small way dangerous to know—that was her real stage.

Perhaps it was through Benedict's good offices that she received an offer to join an amateur choir giving concerts to the British volunteers who had gone to support the North in the American Civil War. This was more appropriate to her idea of herself. She went very willingly and after her duties in Canada (where she was, she says, feted as "the Napoleon of Song") made a visit to Washington, flirted her way into the British Legation, and did what she did best, which was to entrance older men.

The head of legation was Lord Lyons, a bachelor diplomat in his forties who had been in Florence at the end of Georgina's stay there. William Russell, the *Times* correspondent made famous by his reporting of the Crimea, was also a guest. The whole of the North was baying for his blood after dispatches he sent from the Battle of Bull Run, seeming to suggest Yankee cowardice. At the same time, his reports were so vehemently antislavery they upset the South and contradicted the generally favorable line his own editor took with the Confederates. As a consequence Russell was more or less in hiding, both from his public and from his employer. Georgina's visit occurred at an electric moment. There was talk of war between America and Britain for insults received and slights offered. Lyons was to say later that had there existed an Atlantic telegraph cable at that time, war would have been inevitable. Though Georgina knew nothing of it, there were contingency plans already laid to evacuate him and his staff to Canada.

The Washington episode throws light on her incurable naïveté. To have wangled her way to the center of an international crisis as well as a civil war took some doing. It was soon clear that most of what was being talked about in the Federal capital went straight over her head. She was not there to learn, but to be seen and swooned over. Russell met the challenge. He got up a parlor game in which those in the legation formed a secret society, the members of which were named Bully—Bully Warre, Bully Anderson, and so on—with himself as the Bold Buccaneer. Georgina was inducted as Sister Sal. The young men of the legation staff took a shine to Harry and his rather brash but flirtatious wife. One of the Bullys—Frederick Warre—became a lifelong friend of Harry's. As for Georgina, she was loud and reckless. Her opinions of Anglesey society were quite scandalous, and though she pressed on Lord Lyons her claims to know Florence well, he was not impressed. Nor did William Russell entirely recognize her descriptions of literary London. What could not be denied was her colossal and childlike enthusiasm. Like life lived as a child, every day was a completely new beginning, and what had gone wrong the day before was sunk without trace. She could be spiteful and vindictive, but these were moments that passed as quickly as clouds.

*O*nce back in Anglesey, things came to a head with Harry's mother, who could be forgiven a certain bewilderment at the way things had turned out for her boy. In 1863 old Mrs. Weldon had taken enough and announced her intention of removing to Chester. War immediately broke out between the two women on the most trivial of issues. They were glad to be rid of one another, but the problem was that of forward delivery of the mail. Harry's mother instructed the post office to send on all mail addressed to Mrs. Weldon. Georgina at once struck back. She let it be known that in Anglesey society, *she* was that person. The other Mrs. Weldon, who had lived in the neighboring cottage a great many years, quite understandably objected. She might not be Lady Muck, but she did have rights over her own surname.

The Beaumaris postmaster failed to arbitrate, and Georgina revealed the first signs of a litigious nature. Letters were exchanged between the two Mrs. Weldons, who lived only a few yards apart. Solicitors were threatened on both sides, and Georgina composed a magisterial letter to the Postmaster General. That was a characteristic Georgina flourish—go to the top, brook no contradiction. (There had in fact been an earlier example of her passion for litigation. At Holyhead a woman passenger on her way to Ireland stumbled down the steps of a railway carriage and injured her foot. Georgina, a bystander, darted forward and impressed upon the poor woman the need to sue the company. The lady was uncertain; Georgina insisted. Her husband was drawn into the discussion. Unfortunately for him, he thought he was talking to someone with a close knowledge of the law. The passengers accordingly sued, lost the case, and were ruined.)

Harry's mother was a fearsome enemy while she lived, but death seemed to mellow her. In 1876 a medium by the name of Towns raised the shade of Hannah Weldon at a séance. He described for the company "a very fat woman, not at all pretty. She squints. She has a large hooked nose and wears her hair combed flat with two large buns at either side. I can't see much of her mouth or neck, for one side of her face is completely swathed in cotton wool and she wears a red flannel cloth around her head."

"It is my mother-in-law!!! The description is exact!" Georgina exclaimed.

Once on the Other Side, Hannah proved to be an unexpectedly loyal voice. (Georgina received a spirit letter from her eight years after her death, which read baldly, "Continue to do harm to Harry Weldon.") In the immediate here and now she was not quite so accommodating. Until Georgina arrived to plague her life she had lived in comfortable retirement with Mrs. Rawson, her sister. These two knew their place, and living in a little cottage was no bar to their comfort. They were respectable people, the sort to be invited to a ball or party only when the guest list was very long indeed, but perfectly happy to be nonentities. It did the elder Mrs. Weldon's nerves no good at all to hear the younger Mrs. Weldon dismiss the Pagets as "very humbuggy" while the rest of Anglesey society was impressed beyond measure at the condescension shown them by such great people. There is a London journal entry for 1862 that gives the tone of Georgina's reckless appraisals:

Harry went to lunch with Mother and I went off to Effie Hopetoun. It was so nice and they were all so kind and gave me quantities of monograms. I saw all Effie's diamonds and things. Miss C the old reptile came. We went off to Lady Theresa Lewis at 4. I amused myself very much as I did not stick in the concert room, so I talked to Alice Gurney and her husband who seems a darling little pretty man. Lady Ailesbury, Lady Alwyne Compton, Mr. Vivian and Clay and all the musical celebrities there. Lady Agneta Yorke sang all out of tune and the *Inflammatus* was not suited to Miss Browne's voice. Sir John Harington most haffable and admiring. I sang well, I am thankful to say. So it was jolly and Benedict was fulsome.

The company might seem exalted, but she was soon able to join it on more equal terms. In 1864 Grandmother Weldon died, the old lady who six years earlier Harry had blithely asserted had only weeks to live. Grandma Weldon left him £4,000 and some scraps of land around Chesterfield. In 1867, quite incredibly, this land—which Harry seldom visited and Georgina had never even seen—proved to have coal under it. It was wonderful, almost unbelievable news. Harry Weldon was now the £10,000-a-year man of Morgan Treherne's dreams. He had got there by a strange route and was hardly the titled proprietor Morgan had set his heart on. (A £10,000-a-year man living in a four-room cottage with an outside washhouse was a difficult idea for anyone to encompass.) But the plain fact was that Georgina was now best placed of all the children.

Unfortunately, there was no longer any communication between her and her family. None of her brothers and sisters offered to heal the breach between her and Morgan, nor did her mother dare to write. In Morgan's household there was only one side to any question. Though he had lost his daughter, there was a turn to his fortunes that offset that. In 1863 Ellice, who had for so long barred Morgan's way to a parliamentary seat, died in his sleep in Scotland. For the last time the Rattler put himself forward to the Coventry voters. As the result of the by-election was announced, a sweep stood on top of the highest chimney of the City Hotel and yelled ironically to the crowds below, "All's up! Morgan's in!"

He had achieved his goal in life almost too late to savor it. He was assiduous in his duties and enormously pleased to add to his parliamentary seat the deputy lieutenancy of Surrey, but his mind was faltering. In 1866 Georgina wrote to him:

> My dear Papa,
>
> I hear that Apsley is going to be married, and now that I myself have been married more than six years, I trust you will feel with me that this would be a very delightful opportunity for us all to be re-united and to let bygones be bygones. My unhappy girlhood is by me now quite forgotten and forgiven and I am quite prepared to be a kind and affectionate daughter to you—if you will but forgive my one act of subordination we could all be so happy together.

Morgan made no reply, merely remarking to his eldest son that "a person had written" to him. It wasn't perhaps the best of letters in its phrasing (he was to be "forgiven" for her unhappy childhood), but it took a man of very great rectitude—or cruelty—not to respond. A year later, just after making a will that specifically excluded Georgina ("I wish to mark my strong disapprobation of her conduct in marrying her present husband William Henry Weldon without my knowledge and against my consent"), he succumbed to the insanity that had been circling him all his adult life. He died in the asylum at Carshalton and was buried in a tomb he had provided for himself in the parish church of St. Dunstan's, Mayfield. It is not clear that Georgina was invited to attend the funeral.

*A*ll family deaths herald a new beginning. However, the hoped-for reconciliation between Georgina and her mother never took place. Sussex was as forbidden to her as ever, and the frost between the members of the family never melted. Losing the baby and finding herself barren had been a cruel blow to Georgina which she dealt with entirely on her own. Now that Morgan was gone, she hoped she might be accepted back into the fold. Louisa in her old-fashioned and artless way simply crowned Dal the new head of the family, and he kept his sister firmly at arm's length. While Flo and Apsley might feel sorry for her, she had the bitter and lifelong enmity of Emily to contend with. Flo married first. Her husband was an officer of the Life Guards who scandalized a garden party by remarking to a young woman serving at a tea stall, "My wife is ill. When she is dead and buried I shall marry you." Flo died a few months later. Emily married a man named Bill Williams who was land agent to the Duke of Newcastle. He was painfully dull. Apsley married a hapless girl named Mamie.

Though she sang for her supper in many of the great houses and lived among people her mother could only ever dream of meeting, Georgina was growing increasingly disillusioned. After a charity concert organized by Mrs. Gladstone she wrote: "I was furious and so was dear Harry to see that horrid old crow and humbug Jenny Lind put herself down for five solos and me for one." She adds, "Jenny Lind the image of a shrunken crab apple! She sings through a veil and it might be in any language but her style is good and altogether if she was nice her singing would be nice. Deacon accompanied lovelily and I sang *The Keeper* so as to draw tears from most eyes. J.L. looked as though a toad had croaked and took not the slightest notice."

This is overreaching. The Swedish Nightingale was then in her early forties and one of the richest artists of any kind in the world. Julius Benedict had secured her £20,000 for a single tour of America, and from her stupendous life earnings the singer had endowed an entire hospital in Liverpool and the wing of another in London. She was in fact the consummate professional. Georgina was just one of any number of pretty young society sopranos that fell in her way—and not so young any longer either. Jenny Lind lived in state and was the friend of kings and princes. Georgina, when she was not in London, famously received visitors to her cottage in Beaumaris in her apron, her pug Dan Tucker yapping at her feet. Over the teacups she would confide her most cherished and almost her only artistic opinion. She had taken to explaining that superiority was its own form of exile:

> I have already given some idea of the select society in which I ruled and reigned and of which I was the "Peri," the "Queen of Song," the "Semiramis," the "Corinna," the "Nightingale," the "Muse" etc, and all those other pretty flattering names which are accorded to the worst amateur, as well as to the greatest artist. I was acquainted with all the richest and noblest among those who were in the habit of throwing their money out of the window, and as my runaway marriage, beneath me and *sans façons,* had not been the signal for a shower of wedding presents, I thought that my friends would have seized this opportunity of repairing their want of generosity, in order to give me proofs of their appreciation, their admiration and their gratitude. How often, with eyes suffused with tears, with smothered sighs had I not been accosted with—"Ah, Mrs. Weldon, what ought we not to do for you who lavish so bountifully your divine gifts on your fellow creatures? What have you not a right to demand of us?"

The labored facetiousness of this is quite awful. Was it the job of the richest and noblest to repair a bad marriage? And did it really help her case to describe the hospitality they offered as being akin to throwing money out of the window? It was ridiculous bravado of her to write, "Mrs. Gladstone sent me an impudent invite. So I sent word that I should come if I had nothing better to do." The fact was she had run after such opportunities ever since losing the baby in 1860, and if it was all now beginning to pall, that was hardly the fault of her hosts. When she was only thirty-two, she wrote, "The sun has quite gone down on my beautiful past." It was probably the most poignant sentence she ever wrote. She had tried to make the whole world love her without being able to see how impossible an ambition that was.

Some of her despair was with Harry. Though he continued escorting her wherever she went in high society with his customary and impertubable good humor, he was not the man she had married. There was a reason. Harry was unfaithful and had been since 1863. The details were woundingly prosaic. Shortly after his mother moved to Chester, he went to see her on a filial visit. There he met Mrs. Annie Lowe, a dressmaker and widow of a Fusiliers' officer. They commenced a relationship, and in time she gave him a son, Frank. Had they known of it in the Beaumaris Artillery Volunteers, his friends might have shrugged and smiled. This was very much the scrape he might get himself into, even so soon after the tumult of marriage to Georgina. It was worth a drunken cheer to learn that Harry had a clandestine child by this other woman, after all the fuss and bother with Georgina's doctors. There was clearly nothing wrong with his shot and shell. However, if they reasoned that their support was needed to help get him out of a tight corner, they were wrong. Harry had found the woman in his life.

Georgina remained in complete ignorance of the liaison for fourteen years. Though Harry kept Annie Lowe a secret, there was no doubt left in his wife that the love she so craved was not in any case going to come from him: not in the form she most desired it. Harry tolerated her and even indulged her. But he could not be changed into Moncorvo—he could not be altered a whit from the easy-natured spendthrift he was. Georgina's whole existence depended upon being thought irresistible. That had been the story of how she and Harry met, after all, and giving up all for love was one way of glossing their hasty and imprudent marriage. The strangest thing of all was that he did better than she in most social situations, partly because it mattered so little to him. Freddie Warre was back in London, and the two men renewed their Washington friendship. It did not include Georgina—

Warre did not like her and once described her to her face as "Georgina Graspall." It was a candid as well as a brutal assessment. She was importunate. Women of rank did not put themselves about in quite the brash way Georgina did. If they wanted to be in the world, they cultivated politics or the arts. They triumphed over men in the world of men. For all her running after social fame, this was a skill of which Georgina knew nothing. Meanwhile, Harry was elected to the Garrick Club, where he amused himself with Freddie Warre and other cronies in that pleasant and undemanding manner that made him such a popular figure.

Georgina was beginning to disappoint people. She began to realize that she made enemies much faster than Harry made friends. Even her most loyal supporters—and they were very few—saw in her a woman who was somehow detached from the realities of life. The thing she lacked most was a clear view of what was possible. All her energies flew off with centripetal force, bringing her back nothing but harm. There were scandals—none of them very great and some of them farcical. An example was when Harry asked her to make herself "agreeable" to Sir William Thompson, a distinguished surgeon and devoted amateur of the arts, in particular music. The elderly and susceptible Sir William was soon besotted, only to find that he was not being loved for himself but instead being asked to invest in a granite quarry in some part of Wales of which he had never heard. In general, society began to tire of her foolishness, her grand opinions of herself. It is at this time of her life that she began to end her account to friends of how she rejected the fabled Moncorvo with the remark "and this is why and how I became a great musician." It was a desperate piece of wishful thinking.

Her bachelor friend Clay liked her, but even he must have winced when she claimed to know all the singing teachers in London, all of whom worshiped her genius. She had gone to Canada as a member of a choir, yet by her account of the tour a listener might be forgiven for thinking it was to give solo performances. Certainly, she had sung for the Gladstones, for Palmerston, Lord Lansdowne, and many others. But being asked a service of them—to provide part of an evening's musical entertainment to a company that might exceed a hundred—was confused by her as an invitation to deep and lasting friendship, even intimacy. She seemed not to realize how others saw her talent, or the frame in which it existed. In the *Mémoires* she writes of another social acquaintance, this time with a quite reckless abandon:

> In 1868 the composer Arthur Sullivan (who died quite recently and was buried in St. Paul's, his tomb covered in palms and laurels) pestered me as he pestered all women with his disgusting familiarities. I was even obliged, laughingly, to get my husband to tell him to leave me alone. He was a tiny little fellow, quite dark, with enormous hands on very long arms and nigger feet. In our circle one called him Jackie—he was a comical little thing who made everyone laugh. As a musician he was a very facile plagiarist, a real parrot: when he imitated Handel, Fred Clay, Mendelsohn *[sic]* or Gounod, he was very good, but when he tried to be original his music was nothing. For myself, I never patronised his efforts and although he tried to cling to me like a monkey, I told him squarely what I've just now written. My husband eventually told him "Jackie, don't bother my wife or I shall be forced to horsewhip you."

These are the words of someone who has long lost touch with reality. The truth was otherwise. In those late sixties she cultivated Sullivan just as she did Clay and Julius Benedict because she was contemplating a dramatic change of direction. It began to form in her mind that she should cross the chasm that separated the amateur from the professional. She would open an Academy of Singing.

6

There was in Victorian England an enormous and apparently unquenchable interest in choral music of all kinds. A pious and churchgoing public was still in the full grip of oratorio-mania, which had begun with Handel in the previous century and showed no sign of abating. The year she met Harry there was a representative newspaper account of a concert organized in Bristol: "The Harmonic Union performed the greater part of *Judas Maccabeus* . . . under the able direction of Mr. Philip J. Smith. The whole of the music was sung by members of the Society, both the solos and choruses, which speaks well for the continued prosperity of the Society. The body of the hall was nearly filled by the vocal and instrumental members, leaving but a limited space for visitors."

This happy scene, in which members of the public were mere visitors or spectators, was often repeated in London and throughout the provinces. Choirs were huge. On even average occasions at Crystal Palace or provincial festivals the audience could count on an orchestra and chorus of more than a thousand. The music critic Ernest Walker, who was born the year Georgina conceived her idea of opening her own school of music, described this hunger for the English form of oratorio and how it skewed the works of composers:

> They set, with apparently absolute indiscrimination, well nigh every word of the Bible; and when they were not writing oratorios of their own, they were still making them out of the mangled remains of other men's music. Operas of Handel, masses of Haydn, instrumental music of Mozart and Beethoven—all were fish to the net of this insatiable oratorio-demanding public; and most English composers devoted the greater part of their energies to satisfying it

in one form or another. From the middle of the 18th century down to the renascence which is the work of men still in their prime, English music is a darkness relieved by the wandering lights of talents that in happier circumstances might have been geniuses.

It was into this darkness that Georgina wished to plunge. Two things came together to push her plans forward. The first may have been a startling act of chance, or it may have been sublime opportunism. She met Sir William Alexander, who was Attorney General to the Prince of Wales. There was a very slight family connection, for as a young man Alexander had been of great assistance to the Thomas family when Morgan's sister and her young husband had been drowned in the Pyrenees on a honeymoon boating trip. The lawyer, who happened to be on vacation in the same region, had handled all the legal problems arising out of the accident. This was enough for Georgina to describe him as "a dear friend," though this tragedy took place when she was nine. In fact, in another part of her *Mémoires*, she had to be prompted by the medium Desbarolles even to remember the death of her aunt. As Georgina discovered, Alexander, now laden with honors, was charged by the Earl Marshal with some reorganization of the College of Arms. With the artless energy for which she was famous, she asked him to make a place for Harry when one should become available. Her own interest in heraldry stood as guarantee for what must have seemed to Alexander a long shot. Captain Weldon, as he had taken to calling himself at the Garrick Club in London, was not armigerous, had little formal education, was a man who had sold his commission after only two years in the 18th Hussars, and lived more than two hundred miles from London in a terrace cottage. He had never before evinced the slightest interest in genealogy.

The Duke of Norfolk was sounded out and proved unsympathetic to Harry's candidature. This was hardly surprising (she told her French readers the reason for this was that Harry was not a Catholic, but it is not difficult to think of other objections). Then a strange thing happened. Alexander completed the work for which he had been commissioned and, when offered a £500 fee for his services, waived it in return for the favor she had asked. After some hasty coaching from Georgina, William Henry Weldon was appointed Rouge Dragon Pursuivant, with rooms in the exquisite seventeenth-century College building below St. Paul's. He succeeded the immensely scholarly Cockayne. The new Garter king of arms was Albert Woods, who was knighted in November 1869 and continued as Garter until his death in 1904.

This was a privileged and select club to which Harry had found himself admitted, for in addition to the grant of arms that was the bread and butter of the job, the Pursuivants and Heralds represented the sovereign at foreign investitures. During the last three years of his tenure, Cockayne had been to Portugal, Russia, and Italy, and Woods (as Lancaster Herald) to Denmark, Belgium, and Austria. The post carried a small honorarium but immense kudos: Harry was nominally a member of the court. Of the society that Morgan had so desperately wished to join, Harry was now an honored record keeper and custodian. The man whose correspondence had been answered by Morgan's butler ten years earlier was now besought by families ten times higher in the land than a mere Treherne. Georgina's pleasure in the appointment was focused on one point, which may have been her purpose all along. Henceforth the Weldons must live in London in accommodation suitable to their position.

The second impetus for an academy of singing originated in Beaumaris. Harry's godmother had a friend, Mrs. Jones, a rector's wife in the remote parish of Llangwyfan in Denbighshire. The Reverend John Owen Jones and his wife had ten children, of whom one, seventeen-year-old Gwendolyn, was in their opinion possessed of a wonderful voice. Mrs. Jones went begging for advice to Beaumaris and found to her astonishment that the answer to her prayers was right there in the town—none other than the highly connected and prestigious "musical oracle," Mrs. Weldon. Introductions were effected and Georgina reviewed the problem with characteristic aplomb. "I knew all the singing teachers in vogue—Benedict, Deacon, Campana, Pinsutti, Vera, Randegger. They were all my devoted admirers. My word was their command, and they would have gone to any trouble to have the honour of accompanying me."

This was astounding news for Mrs. Jones and the nervy Gwendolyn. What they brought to Beaumaris was a dream, the faintest of hopes, a cry from the very depths of obscurity. Nowhere could be more hidden away from society than Llangwyfan, and yet now, suddenly, they found their lives bathed in light. One did not have to know too much about London music circles not to know that between them the men Georgina mentioned so casually were at the heart of public music education and had as their private clients some of the greatest names in opera. And could they really help Gwendolyn? Georgina left them in no doubt. Something could be easily arranged if the trembling ingenue could be brought up to scratch. She set the young singer a regime, of practicing only a few notes over and over, while she herself set off for a spa trip to the Rhine. When they met again, Georgina remarked loftily, "I had gained a great deal. She had become aware of her own defects." The rectory at Llangwyfan was further convulsed when Mrs. Weldon began to muse that she herself might be persuaded to take up one or two more of the Jones girls, if suitable premises could be found in London.

The illustrious Alberto Randegger and his colleagues were soon enough dropped from the discussions: what was envisaged was an academy of which Mrs. Weldon would be the principal. The methods of voice production and training were to be of a revolutionary character, and the object was to produce concert artists of international caliber. The pupils would live within the academy and pay board. Drawn from the very best families (which should have sent a warning shot across Mrs. Jones's bows), they would sing at the best of amateur concerts; but the intention was to send them out into the world as recitalists and opera stars. This was a process that might take five years. There was a final dramatic flourish to the plans: did the Joneses know that Captain and Mrs. Weldon had taken up a lease on Dickens's old house in Tavistock Square?

avistock Square was developed in 1824 by Thomas Cubitt, who had a happy relationship with Bloomsbury's principal landowner, the Duke of Bedford. As can be seen today, the uniform high quality of the Cubitt designs gave a character to this part of London which, though it was never fashionable in the same sense as the Grosvenor Estate in Belgravia, was considered highly respectable. On the east side of Tavistock Square (which was gated until the Act of 1893) was Tavistock House, one of three large houses set in generous grounds. Tavistock House boasted particularly fine mulberry trees. When Dickens and Wilkie Collins passed the returning Thomases on the road to Florence, the greatest of all Victorians had been in occupation of this house for three years. Dickens bought the run-down property leasehold from the Bedford Estate and set about extensive renovations with his usual energetic pernicketiness. In November 1851, pacing up and down for inspiration in his new home, with the builders still at work, he began *Bleak House*. (An early working title was *The Bleak House Academy*.) But in 1855 he learned that Gadshill Place in Rochester was on the market, a house he had dreamed of owning as a child. He sold Tavistock House in 1860 at a dark time of his life. An old lady took up the leasehold, followed by the Weldons.

In many ways the house was perfect for Georgina's purposes, for one of the many alterations Dickens had made, and which still stood, was the creation of what he used to call "the smallest theatre in London," where he indulged his taste for amateur dramatics. Bloomsbury was famous even then for its society of artists and writers, taken together with a strong leavening of lawyers. In many ways it was an inspired purchase for the Weldons. As an address it suited Harry, and as a site for the projected academy of singing it could hardly have been bettered. Dickens himself died at Gadshill in June 1870, four weeks after the Weldons moved into Tavistock House.

The new owners came to London with Gwendolyn Jones and two of her sisters. Georgina was in a frenzy of excitement. There must be an inaugural fund-raising concert for her academy, and it must take place immediately. Nothing else would do. She wrote Clay an excruciatingly facetious note enlisting his help. He himself would perform, along with a comic singer named Arthur Blunt, but the centerpiece was to be her own debut as a professional.

Tavistock House had grown frowsty since the Dickens days, and the Weldons were strapped for furniture on the scale the house required. Georgina at last admitted that the concert could not be held there. But something must be done! After some setbacks the new Lady Dudley offered Dudley House as a location. (She was the second wife to that same Lord Ward who had been caught with Georgina in Watts's studio twelve years earlier.) The date was set for July 5. Another society acquaintance, Sim Egerton, was given the task of publicizing the event. In the end he rounded up 250 people, including a bemused Ferdinand de Lesseps, engineer of the Suez Canal. Twelve years later Georgina confessed that she expected £3,000 in donations and subscriptions from this one concert: this was the chance for her society friends, as she perceived them, to pay their dues. She could not command their respect, but she believed she had earned it. They would do the right thing.

She drove away that night with the distraught Jones girls and total receipts of £199. The concert had been a complete fiasco. She had been betrayed by overexcitement and a lack of planning. But much more than an artistic and financial fiasco, it was a social rebuff. The Welsh girls might wail that they had been made to look fools, had sung badly, worn the wrong dresses, but Georgina knew that something even more disastrous had taken place. She had suffered the kind of snub from which there was no way back. Nothing had been said, but what she considered her own class had spoken. It was Little Holland House all over again. The favor she had asked of Lord Ward, now the Earl of Dudley, had not helped her, but ruined her. The 250 invitees had not even contributed a guinea a head. Many had given nothing at all. Worse than that, in the way that these things worked, within the week theirs would be the only opinion that mattered in London. The all-powerful engine of society gossip had doomed her. She wrote:

> Entering the profession is the most disagreeable and humiliating thing you can possibly imagine, but it is no more humiliating in my opinion than the way people fight to get to one party or another in Society and the way Dukes and Duchesses are run after for no reason or object in life that I can see. I always hated Society and its mean ways and never have I asked to go to a party in my life. Whatever I go through now is for a purpose, and in my opinion as well as many other good persons, a good one . . .

Not given to reflection and often unable to distinguish between what she would like to happen and what was going to happen, Georgina crossed over on that one disastrous evening from fantasy into brutal fact. Turning herself into a professional musician required far more planning and much greater talent than she possessed. She had the support of Benedict and Clay—though not for much longer. She did not have Sullivan, whom she suspected of having set people against her. But even if he were innocent of any malice, she knew in her heart that something had happened for which there was no remedy. It was not that people did not know her: they knew her all too well. All the gaffes and little pieces of spite she had so liberally strewn in conversation, all the reckless flirtations, had been remembered. The truth was that society, which she pretended to reprehend, had already made a judgment, long before she stepped before her audience at Dudley House. The world, which she so freely judged, had now judged her. By the weekend, when she had a chance to find out by cautious inquiry what the full reaction had been, she realized she was not even a notoriety. She was a nothing.

Georgina had no business sense and no desire to learn it either. She had rushed into a promotional concert with a poor program and little groundwork. What had let her down more than all this was basic human weakness. Her dreams were bigger than her abilities. It is cruel to add to her anguish, but it happens there was another more glorious story of singers and singing entrancing London at exactly the same time and indeed in the same place. Comparison with Georgina's professional debut is painful but serves to show up the enormous gap she was trying to bridge.

As a young girl, the rich Bostonian Lillie Greenough had persuaded her mother to bring her to London to learn singing. She auditioned for Manuel García, who heard with a sinking feeling her party piece "Three little kittens took off their mittens to eat their Christmas pie." García asked her how long she had been singing, and Mrs. Greenough answered for her daughter. "Since she was a little girl, monsieur." "I thought so," García commented. But within the year, Lillie had married the American banker Charles Moulton and gone to Paris, where she was considered one of the finest sopranos of the Second Empire. It was true that Moulton made her rich beyond the dreams of most people, but she was also dedicated. She befriended Liszt and Auber, sang for the Emperor and Eugénie, and in June 1870, on a whim, came back to London. She and her husband took rooms in Park Street and left cards. Within days they were inundated with invitations, one of which was to a *matinée musicale* at Dudley House. Lillie sang for her hosts only a few days before Georgina's ill-fated concert. "The piano was in the beautiful picture gallery," she wrote, "all full of Greuze's pictures bought from the Vatican: it has the most wonderful acoustics and the voice sounded splendidly in it. Lady Dudley is a celebrated beauty . . ."

The engagements continued: dinner with the Duke and Duchess of Sutherland, then with the Rothschilds, who pressed her to stay for Ascot week; an at-home with Lady Anglesey, an audience with the Prince and Princess of Wales. The Covent Garden diva Adelina Patti was fetched to meet her, and Sullivan followed her around like a dog, entreating her to sing in his operetta, *The Prodigal Son*, which he was getting up for Lady Harington. At the Ascot races she joined Delane of the *Times* at the open table he kept for a hundred guests, come who may. On her birthday Lady Sherbourne took off a diamond ring and gave it to her. At Twickenham she dined with the Comte de Paris and the entire Orléans family. It was not just that Mrs. Moulton was rich, nor were her hosts exhibiting a group hysteria in vying with each other to hear her sing. They were responding, as best they knew, to excellence. Georgina had never sung as an amateur to audiences such as this, nor could she begin to hope for support from them in her professional career. The two sopranos were worlds apart, not just in connections but in talent.

Lillie Moulton's trip ended with a garden party at Chiswick, as guest of the Prince and Princess of Wales once again. The three little princesses rolled around the lawns "like three fluffy pink pincushions, covered in white muslin." Huge Japanese sunshades had been set up to shelter the company from the sun as they strolled and chatted, or drank their sherbets at little tables set on the terrace. Lillie found herself talking to the Prince of Wales, who asked her where she had dined last. She mentioned the Comte de Paris.

"What day did you dine there?"

"On the 17th, Your Highness."

"Are you sure it was the 17th?"

She explained that she remembered the date well, because it was the day before her birthday. The Prince of Wales asked whether it was a large dinner and nodded when told that all the Orléans family had been present.

"Did you know that they had a *conseil de famille* that day?"

"No. I heard nothing of it."

"The whole family signed a petition to the Emperor Napoleon to be allowed to return to France and serve in the army." The Prince studied her. "Can you imagine why they want to go back to France when they can live quietly here and be out of politics?"

The remark was intended to be genial, but it had its shaded side. Edward was no stranger to the lighter, dizzier character of the Second Empire, but it was as if in that one remark he consigned it and all its vanities to oblivion.

Lillie returned home to Paris and on July 17 drove to St. Cloud for dinner with the Empress. When the Moultons arrived, instead of a flurry of servants in the vestibule, there was only one distracted official. The dinner had been canceled. Then, at the last moment, Eugénie sent word they were to be admitted. Other than members of the imperial household, they were the only guests. The meal was taken in terrible silence, interrupted by a stream of telegrams. At the end of the meal, the Emperor, wracked with kidney stones and ashen white, hauled himself to his feet and almost absentmindedly bade the company good night. He had already sworn to take the field at the head of his troops but could barely mount the stairs in his own palace.

Two days later France declared war upon Prussia.

Gounod

1

An almost insensate war fever convulsed France. In Paris hapless German tourists were knocked to the pavements and beaten senseless. People ran about the streets all day long, looking for something to cheer. The curtain was rising on one of the most catastrophic events in French history, a conflict in which England for once had no interest or treaty commitments. The Foreign Office and the British ambassador had been taken completely by surprise. Clarendon, who had smiled so kindly on Georgina at Ashridge all those years ago, died suddenly at his home in Grosvenor Crescent on June 27 and was replaced as Foreign Secretary by Granville, who had been Knave of Hearts on that same glorious evening. On appointment, he unwisely announced that not a cloud obscured the pleasant prospect of peace in Europe. A fortnight later Napoleon declared war.

In Paris Lord Lyons found himself once again vexed by a flood of cables and dispatches. His afternoon carriage rides with the ever-faithful Bully Sheffield and Bully Malet, who had followed him from the Washington posting, were now sorely disturbed. In normal times the curious might set their watches by his grave progress in the Bois de Boulogne. Now, yet again, Lyons was forced to make contingency plans for the evacuation of the embassy. That was, he hoped, a thing of last resort; but it did not help that in Washington Prévost-Paradol, the French ambassador, predicted a Prussian victory and then drove home the point by committing suicide. His was almost the first shot fired.

In London sympathies were divided between the two belligerents. Patriots bore in mind that the Crown Prince of Prussia was married to Victoria's eldest daughter. The Queen was much gratified to hear from her son-in-law words indicating a complete reprobation of sinful Paris. (The Prince, meanwhile, was curtly dismissed by Bismarck in a conversation with William Russell of the *Times* as "that dunderhead," and an enraged Russell asked permission to quote him.) Many found the Germans—as represented by those who flocked to the spas and watering places favored by the British—sociable and well behaved, with a reputation for exquisite manners. They were, as they constantly assured their Anglo-Saxon friends, much more in tune with them than with the French. And this struck some as no more than the truth. Those who had tasted the pleasures of Paris in the Second Empire—its wit and irreverence as well as its monumental hedonism—suddenly remembered tendencies to bombast and ungentlemanly arrogance among the French. There was a strong feeling in England that the war had been foolishly provoked not by Bismarck, who was its actual author, but by the Empress Eugénie. Certainly the grounds for it, understood to be an insult offered to the French by the Kaiser, subtly reworked as an insult to the Kaiser by the French ambassador at Ems, was the stuff of opéra bouffe. As in Offenbach, war had descended out of a clear blue sky.

One of the multitudes of Parisians caught up in the patriotic hysteria was the composer Charles Gounod. The day Lillie Moulton dined with the Comte de Paris in London, without quite realizing she had walked into the conclusion of a historic *conseil de famille*, happened to be Gounod's fifty-second birthday. He celebrated it in Paris with some aplomb. On the face of it, the empire could not have boasted a more solid and conscientious citizen. Member of the Institut de France, Academician, officer of the Légion d'Honneur, the composer had got from the epoch his full share of rewards. There was little frivolous and nothing bohemian about him. His *Faust* had been triumphantly revived in March of the previous year, and plans were in train to start rehearsals at the Opéra of a sellout revival of his most successful opera, *Roméo et Juliette*.

He was the very model of bourgeois success—heavy, mannered, sometimes even somber in character, with an oracular way of expressing himself suitable to his artistic eminence. His name appeared on prestigious committees. His opinion was sought at the best salons. He lived in a fine house at St.-Cloud with his wife, two children, and his mother-in-law, the redoubtable Mme Zimmermann. Photographed in about 1870, his image shows an imposing figure with slightly dandified clothes, arms folded, a full beard already turning white. The way he holds his head and the expression on his face are challenging, magisterial.

He had another side. Paris in the nineteenth century was a city particularly rich in caricaturists, and what they brought out was the size of his head and a peculiar quizzical intensity in his expression. The photograph taken of him in 1870 is how he saw himself. In caricature he always looks disheveled. His eyes are huge and dark, and his brow slopes back an immense way such as to indicate deep and passionate thoughts. He seems on the point of tears or as if caught in some guilty act to which he must now confess. Even if one knew nothing at all of his personal life, these sketches would seem to show a weak and vacillating personality.

The caricaturists were responding to well-known failings in him. In particular he was a colossal flirt. At soirees, or to enliven the slumbrous afternoon calm of a French at-home, he was given to singing at the piano, sometimes complete operatic scores. On these occasions he invariably rendered the female part of his audience brimful of tears. Not every composer can sing, and there was an element of party trick in Gounod's ability to caress his audience. A woman once asked him how he came to write such beautiful music. "God, madame, sends me down some of His angels and they whisper sweet melodies in my ear," he murmured. He meant it.

In 1852 he married Anna Zimmermann, whose father was a professor at the Paris Conservatoire. In fact he almost balked at the last fence. Going to the Zimmermanns with a letter explaining how impossible it was for him to marry, he was greeted on the doorstep by his future mother-in-law, who swept him into the drawing room to make his proposal. He put the letter back in his pocket and proposed. This suggests the plasticity of the caricature and not the jaw-jutting determination of the photograph.

There was a price to pay for being Gounod. Intimates knew he was prone to massive attacks of melancholy and self-loathing. When he was in the mood, nobody could be more tragically afflicted than he. In the early months of 1870 he had just such an attack:

> My work costs me the most painful efforts and racks my brain. I fight against the void, I think I've written something acceptable, and then when I look at it again, I find it execrable. My mind wanders and grieves, *I don't know where I am*. It would be a help if only I knew how to deal with such a horrible condition. I can't see clearly any more: I don't know where I'm going . . . twenty times melancholy overwhelms me, I weep, I despair and I want to get away . . . I open my notebook and shut it again. Nothing! My mind is empty! Oh Lord, what better can be done than to accept this desolation and nothingness! I thought I was worth something! I didn't want to be a nobody.

For some these thoughts expressed the very essence of Romantic agony. This was how great creative minds were supposed to speak to their demons. But insiders, while they might admit he had a difficult and also vexatious job, knew that Gounod's mental resilience was suspect and would have been so whether or not he composed music for a living. Never far from the Gounod entourage was Dr. Antoine Émile Blanche, who had a clinic at Passy. Blanche had treated Gérard de Nerval for madness and was to attend the last days of Guy de Maupassant. Dr. Blanche was what was described in those days as an alienist and his clinic effectively a private asylum. Gounod's

overwhelming despair had already sent him to the clinic in Passy more
than once.

At first the war galvanized him. He took the man in the street's view of
the coming conflict and composed a fiery patriotic song called "À la Fron-
tière!" (His fellow composer Richard Wagner was meanwhile telling French
friends passing through Munich that the only way out was to bomb Paris and
burn it to the ground. This was ungrateful, because it happened that
Gounod as an unctuous young man had met Wagner on the beach at Trou-
ville and persuaded the German to adopt Catholicism. Gounod was, very
improbably, Wagner's godfather.) But after a little while his native prudence
reasserted itself, and as the crisis deepened, he evacuated his wife and children to Varangeville, near Dieppe. He wrote them twice-daily bulletins.
"Prayer is your *only* weapon! You must load it! The *soul of the French* must
be the gunpowder that fires French bullets!" he explained to his wife.

Prayer proved less effectual than Prussian efficiency. As the summer
months passed, so did some of the hysteria. Things were looking black. The
Louvre was emptied of its treasures which were taken to the coast at Brest.
Most theaters closed and the Opéra became a military depot. The Emperor
had gone at the head of his armies to the eastern frontiers, but the news from
there was not good. One morning a spectacular victory was announced, and
Paris was delirious with joy. In the afternoon the report from the front was
contradicted: the Imperial Army had suffered heavy losses. Despair rushed
in like seawater. On September 1 the unimaginable took place. Paris was utterly staggered to learn that Napoleon had capitulated at Sedan. The surrender was unconditional and the Emperor himself captured.

The fine detail was dramatic enough to satisfy any composer. The defeated Emperor met Bismarck in the upstairs room of a squalid cottage near
Donchery, hastily requisitioned for the purpose. The last time they had met
was at the Paris Exhibition three years earlier, when the first performance of
Gounod's *Roméo et Juliette* had been part of the glittering celebrations.
Then, Bismarck in his white uniform and helmet with eagle mounted had
been a raree-show all of his own. Things were very different now. While
waiting to learn what his fate was to be, Napoleon walked up and down the

cottage garden between rows of potatoes. The escort that came later in the day made all clear. On a command from an indifferent young subaltern, the party drew swords, as it would for the capture of the merest private. The empire was at an end.

Gounod at once fled Paris to Varangeville and on September 13 embarked at Dieppe with his family for England. London presented a stark contrast to the panic and uncertainty of Paris. On his earlier visits, when the City of Lights had been the undisputed style capital of Europe, Gounod found his English admirers wooden and the streets of London dirty and unkempt. Exile changed his point of view. Now everything seemed wonderful. He lived first at Blackheath with some English friends named Brown before finding accommodation in Park Street, near Regent's Park.

A letter he wrote to Crown Prince Frederick—whom he had never met—throws some further light on his personality. As the Siege tightened around Paris, Gounod read with alarm how leafy and prosperous St. Cloud had become a battleground. In his letter he asked the Prince to use his influence to spare the house, or at least ensure the German gunners were made aware of its illustrious owner, a man always friendly to German art and the suitably reverent composer of *Faust*, no less. Surely there could be some special consideration given in what were trying circumstances. (In fact, the house *was* in the middle of the battle zone, and both French and German patrols occupied it during the fighting.) Frederick seems to have made Gounod's letter public, which did nothing for his reputation in Paris. There, famously, as the Siege took hold, even people of the highest rank were starving. Georges Bizet joined the National Guard and was given a rifle he did not know how to fire; he spent much of his time scavenging for food. In October Gounod wrote to his brother-in-law:

> We ought all to be standing face to face with the Prussians at this moment. Every one of us, or not a soul. And it astounds me that three million Frenchmen and 30,000 cannon were not summoned, over a month ago, under one and the same flag (not that of France alone but of humanity in general) to repulse this invasion of

machines rather than of men. Here comes Mrs. Brown. Goodbye for a while.

On an even more unfortunate note he tried to explain that while blood was being spilled in France, those who had fled also experienced their own agonies. But Gounod's exile was personally exhilarating. His presence in London that winter had not gone unnoticed by the music world, and by comparison with his Parisian relatives he spent a pleasant and calming time. On February 26, 1871, he was invited to meet Julius Benedict at his house in Manchester Square, off Wigmore Street. It was a happy occasion: Benedict, who had recently naturalized, had even more recently been knighted for his services to music. What was more congenial than for the Stuttgart-born Englishman to extend the hand of friendship to the distinguished French exile? This was the kind of social engagement Gounod understood very readily and something he had done a hundred times before. It was a meeting of music makers attended by their acolytes and admirers. After a while, Gounod was pressed to play the piano and noticing a woman in the room with a lively eye and a forward expression, elected to accompany himself in the song "À une Jeune Fille," directing his performance almost exclusively at her. It was a wonderful piece of theater: typically Gallic, probably ironic, for the lady was no longer young, and thus tender and witty in just the way Parisians could carry such things off.

The woman, who was with her husband, was of course Georgina. Bursting into uncontrollable tears at the beauty of the moment and the compliment she had been paid, she retreated behind the window curtains to drink a glass of water. She made sure she stayed there until all but the principal guest had left. Only then did one supremely talented flirt come face-to-face with another.

ounod was nineteen years older than Georgina and may have worried that the slim good looks of his youthful self had fled forever. But if he had anxiety on that score, it was unfounded. He was exactly the kind of man Georgina had been looking for in one guise or another since childhood—an older, more mature figure with a knowledge of the world, a practicality and assurance she need not try to match. Gounod would provide the worldliness and she the romantic idealism. She soon discovered things about him that surprised her by the way they chimed deliciously with her own personality. Gounod was an artist, but he was also a troubled man. He was more like his caricature than he cared to admit. He had, she saw, his mystical, incoherent side, his sense of the unutterable. He had a haplessness and childlike innocence when it came to subjects other than Wagner, whose music he admired—for example, such mundane matters as contracts and royalties, or more tellingly marriage and children. He had secrets, emotional luggage he carried with him that he hinted would make her hair stand on end, and was sentimental to a fault. Of course it mattered to Georgina that he was famous, and he did not blanch when she applied the term "genius" to his musical talent. His calm acceptance of her adulation was proof in itself of genius. But maybe his greatest attraction to Georgina was that, like her, he longed to be loved. It did not matter that he *was* loved, that his loyal wife loved him. The love he wanted was unspecific and not even particularly sexual. She recognized that in him straightaway. This great man was made just like her. His heart was bleeding and his mind misunderstood. As to the rest of him, his gifts and personality, there was an obvious way of describing his allure. Charles Gounod was everything that Harry Weldon was not.

The starting point for their relationship was very flattering. A few days after their first meeting, he called at St. James's Hall, where she was re-hearsing, and overheard her singing Mendelssohn's "Hear My Prayer." His admiration for her voice was immediate and unfeigned. His good opinion was worth having. Gounod had known Pauline Viardot when he was Georgina's age, and Viardot was still counted as one of the greatest operatic sopranos of the century. For her he had written *Sapho* and, the gossip ran, shared her favors with her weak and complaisant husband and the unlikely third party Ivan Turgenev. That was one of his murky secrets. Like Gounod, Viardot had fled the war and was living at Devonshire Place, off the Maryle-bone Road. Turgenev, who had secretly helped to fund her, had rooms a few streets away. (He had brought back from the war a characteristic Turgenev-ian story. The distant shelling of Strasbourg had brought down the chimney stack of the villa in which he was staying. He had noticed this chimney when he first took up the let of the property and mentioned it to the architect, who happened to be French. "That stack, m'sieu, is as strong as France itself," the man replied.)

In more recent years Gounod had worked with the equally illustrious Marie Carvalho, who had created the part of Marguerite in *Faust*. Gounod might be two-faced about many things, but a professional tribute from him was not likely to be dishonest. Having heard Georgina sing, he said at once, "I was struck by the purity of her voice, by the sureness of her technique and the noble simplicity of her voice, and I was able to prove to myself that Benedict had not been exaggerating when he spoke to me about her remark-able talent as a singer." It was, he added in a memorable phrase, "*un voix des deux sexes.*"

This is a very startling commendation, and we suddenly see her exactly as she saw herself, but through the eyes and ears of another. Gounod was without question a colossal flirt, but he was also a complete professional, be-side whom Fred Clay was merely a Treasury clerk with an imperial beard and modest musical accomplishments. Gounod was the real article. Many people—Liszt was one of them—believed him to be the supreme composer of his generation. There is dispassion in his estimate of Georgina's voice: about things like this, we would like to believe, artists do not lie. They may lie about money or love, but not this, not art. At the time he first heard her sing, he had no way of knowing who she was and to what use she had put these talents.

She met him, in fact, at a disastrous moment. After the humiliation of the Dudley House concert, she had undertaken a debut tour of Wales and Anglesey with Gwendolyn Jones—"Beauty and the Beast," as she put it, casting herself in the role of Beauty. It had not been a success. The halls they booked were drafty and unwelcoming, audiences were sparse, and local agents were nowhere near as scrupulous in accounting for the box office as she would have liked. Not everybody in North Wales wanted to go out on a cold and blowy night to hear two unknowns sing. Contrariwise, at the end of the tour where there was at last a decent audience, Arthur Deacon, the accompanist, was so annoyed at the incessant chatter during the recital that he closed the piano lid and left the stage. He did much better than that even. Before the concert ended, he had left the hall and the town in which it was located.

Back in Denbighshire, Mrs. Jones had begun to revise her estimate of Mrs. Weldon's plans. The tour had been an artistic and financial failure, and Tavistock House, the seat of the National Academy (for that was how it was being puffed now), was still no more than Georgina's private residence and a rackety one at that. Gwen was ill. In fact, she was dying. Disgusted, Mrs. Jones withdrew her remaining daughters a year later.

The day after meeting Gounod for the second time, Georgina called on him and asked him for an engagement to sing at a charity concert being got up for the victims of the Siege. He asked her to stay for tea. Together they sat down and sang the entire score of *Faust*. According to Georgina, Anna Gounod and old Mrs. Zimmermann were entranced—"it was a perfect shower of tears and compliments"—and both ladies told her she was "born for Gounod." He himself declared that she was the Pauline for which he had been searching in his efforts to complete his opera *Polyeucte*. The meeting was a small triumph. Nobody of comparable musical rank had endorsed her talent with such enthusiasm. A real musical oracle had spoken, and she had jumped from nothing to everything in the space of a single afternoon.

That night in Tavistock House there was an opportunity for a clearer, calmer appraisal. In purely personal terms his praise had been intoxicating, but if she was thinking as a businesswoman, a fellow professional—which is what she had after all chosen to be—it was not the most helpful outcome of the encounter. There was more to come. What she needed from Gounod was some endorsement of her plans in the here and now—her academy in the making. The slightest assistance in this area would be worth a ton of publicity in any other form. Perhaps anyone other than Georgina would have seized on this aspect of their meeting and tried to think up ways of exploiting it. There was not the slightest doubt that he found her physically desirable and that some of his warmer exclamations were founded on that. But he *was* a great composer, and a golden opportunity was staring her in the face. For the time that he was in London, Gounod could make a huge material difference to her plans. It was for her to make of it what she would.

George Moore remarked of Gounod that he was "a base soul who went about pouring a kind of bath water melody down the back of every woman he met." This was exactly the attention Georgina wanted, and it replaced common sense. The academy was completely neglected as they began a flirtation which, while it still had a musical content, soon extended to looks and sighs, letters, and on his side prayers. The experience was not unlike living inside a Gounod song. In the beginning she may not have been able to control the course of events as well as she would have liked. He was hardworking, he was impetuous and temperamental as many artistically gifted men are, but he was also venal in a quite astonishing way. Georgina wanted a hero. As Mme Gounod could have told her from long experience, she was getting a little boy. The solution that occurred to Georgina was simple. She must reinvent him.

Gounod had already made settings to some well-known English poems and was mulling over a much larger work. It was to be an imposing allegorical commentary on the fate of his country, for which he himself would supply the text. His London publisher, Novello's, arranged for the first performance to be heard in the newly completed Albert Hall on the occasion of the International Music Festival. It was an inspired piece of publicity. Immediately after the fall of Sedan, the Queen had heard with satisfaction a sermon preached to her, of which the text was from Isaiah: "Woe to the crown of pride, to the drunkards of Ephraim, whose glorious beauty is a fading flower." But the Siege and the agony of the Commune swung the

public mood toward pity for the French. When Georgina saw that what
Gounod had written was on the theme of a martyred France, it was another
cause for grateful tears. She soon described him, with typical exaggeration,
as "the Messiah of the Gospel of New Music." This sounds foolish in hind-
sight, but when on May 1 Gounod made his contribution to the international
festival with an oratorio he entitled *Gallia*, the composer, who also conducted the performance, was cheered to the roof. The reception accorded
him quite overshadowed Sullivan, whose *On Shore and Sea* premiered on the
same night.

Gounod had been in England only eight months. As he walked off the
podium, he must have calculated that there were new triumphs he might accomplish here to enhance his somewhat faltering muse. No one outside
France had ever completely come to grips with *Faust,* and his fame with
English audiences rested more on *Roméo et Juliette.* But now he had the royal
plaudit for a very different kind of work. Away from the concert platform
he had an outlet for his more personal musings. Putting it bluntly, he had
someone who had never heard his stories before and so did not wince when
he told them. Sitting in the audience, Georgina saw through tearstained eyes
a man she had begun to consider "a god," though one whose human attri-
butes she more than anyone else in London had secret knowledge of.

Gounod was a tentative and uncertain dramatist in some of his operas,
but he knew how to make an effect. A fortnight after the triumph of *Gallia*
he burst into Tavistock House in a distraught state. In an impassioned speech
to both Weldons he bared his soul. They struggled to understand him as he
marched up and down their drawing room, talking a torrent. But it was all
quite predictable and when at last it came out, quite banal. He could not
stand to live with his wife any longer. After twenty years of marriage he had
no alternative but to separate from her. His artistic life was being ruined. Ex-
clamation marks spattered the carpet.

Anna Gounod was one of four daughters born to Pierre Zimmermann.
In appearance she was thin, with a small head on a high neck. Not many of
Gounod's intimates liked her. Bizet detested her. Georgina (once she got the
new lie of the land) thought her ugly—"a Japanese crockery dog . . . a little old brown woman"—and commented blithely, "She was odious, I

confess; but I pitied her. Why had God made me so amiable and her so disagreeable?"

Part of the reason for Anna's disposition was Gounod's habitual philandering. He tended to fall in love with his younger admirers (it was said the younger the better), and there was a history of such brief liaisons, for the moment unknown to Georgina. In character these interludes were all more sentimental tosh than anything else: Gounod liked to exact devotion, not desire, and repaid it with long, liquid looks, whispered secrets, sighs. The lover in Gounod was a perpetual adolescent, and Anna could not help but notice an old pattern reestablishing itself. Her husband and Mrs. Weldon were becoming a mild scandal in both London and Paris, and it was time to go home.

The house in St.-Cloud had not survived, and though the last shot was not fired in Paris until May 25, the provisional government was in control, and a terrible vengeance was being wrought on the Communards. In the midst of all this, their old friend Auber, director of the Conservatoire, had died and the post was vacant. These were practical reasons not to dally in London, but there were also patriotic considerations. Were the Gounods to be counted cowards in the new Republic; or, worse still, traitors?

Gounod had opened his heart to the Weldons on May 16. Five days later Anna went back to France, taking her children with her. It says much for her courage and patriotism. A week or so later Mme Zimmermann followed. On June 19, on the first anniversary of Georgina's arrival at Tavistock House, Gounod moved in, bringing with him all his possessions, several valises of music he had already written while in London, and the unfinished score to the opera *Polyeucte*.

*V*ery quickly, Gounod discovered something brought home to Harry a long time before: he was involved with a skillful manipulator of men more than with a wanton sexual being. While Georgina flattered him relentlessly and fed his ego, she was not all that interested in sex. Possession might mean one thing to him, but to her it meant quite another. She had, so to speak, collected him: he was added to her list of worthwhile things in the world. It was pleasant—up to a point—to be addressed as "Divine Being," but Gounod may have been looking for more earthly pleasures. These she could not give him—not out of any delicacy or consideration for Harry's position, but because it was not in her to give herself, to make good the promise that her titillations excited, with Gounod or anyone else. She was a tease, and an accomplished one; but that was that. Georgina was not the seductive and compliant mistress of a Frenchman's dreams. Her admiration for him had a disconcerting Anglo-Saxon pragmatism.

He began to realize he was a long way from Paris as far as other matters went, too. One of his complaints about Anna was that she had ruined his digestion, a very grave thing for a Frenchman to suffer. Georgina responded with energy. She ordered an immediate regime of cold baths. Nor did it help that when he wished instead for a doctor, she insisted he consult her own. There were two further shocks to Gounod's system on meeting this man: Dr. McKern was a devout Plymouth Brethren and an even more ardent devotee of hydropathy than Georgina herself. When a man says his wife does not understand him and hurls himself onto the bosom of a younger woman, he does not always expect to be plunged into a cold bath for the wound in his heart.

Harry watched. His role is enigmatic. He had brought Annie Lowe to

London and was secretly enjoying the sort of sex that Gounod may have had in mind for himself. He had the Garrick Club to amuse him, and much to his surprise he found the work of Rouge Dragon Pursuivant to his taste. The house in Tavistock Square was sufficiently chaotic to accommodate a neurasthenic French composer, and all the evidence is that Harry tolerated Gounod's presence in his home with cheerful equanimity. Events were bringing out the frantic side of Georgina, but "the old man," as Harry called him, posed no threat at all. It was true that people were starting to talk. But Harry seems never to have minded talk. What such scrubs as Sullivan thought about Gounod's ambush was beneath his consideration. He may even have seen the funny side of things. Georgina had exasperated him for years with her fantasies of high society. Now she had exchanged these for the care and solacing of a faintly preposterous figure when he was in his slippers, a corpulent French genius driven mad by the barking of Georgina's four dogs and given to taking snuff, smoking cigars in bed, and, like a good Parisian, an expert at spitting.

He was there by invitation, of course, but he also chose to be there. Many people in London would have been happy to have taken him in after his wife left for Paris. Maybe Blackheath was a little out of the way, but he knew Ernest Gye, for example, who owned the lease on Covent Garden and was general manager of the Royal Italian Opera, as it was then called. Most of those connected to the music world would have been happy to settle him. He could as easily have stayed where he was in Park Street. He entered Tavistock House too willingly, and the decision did not go unnoticed. To his surprise, Georgina was assuming a sort of proprietorial right over him more important than any sexual hold she may have had. A vivid example of this happened only a week or so after Anna left. The composer was canvassed by intermediaries of the Paris Conservatoire to be its new director. Gounod himself had entered the Conservatoire in 1836 when Cherubini was its director, and to be sounded out in this way now—at the beginning of a whole new epoch, the Third Republic—was a signal honor. A year or so earlier under Napoleon III he would have accepted the post without hesitation.

He discussed the offer with Georgina. To his dismay, she advised him to refuse. He pointed out the advantages to her of accepting. She could come to Paris and study under him. The professional career she was trying to make for herself would be so much more easily accomplished. She would soon have engagements everywhere in Europe. There were difficulties, of course—his wife, her husband—but they were surely outweighed by the benefits. This was the opportunism necessary in a famously fickle way of earning a living. The point is an important one. Picking a quarrel with his wife so that he could surrender himself to the suffocated mother in Georgina was certainly infantile. But about the music business and its politics, Gounod was vastly more experienced than she. He knew everyone in Paris. It was a city she had hardly ever visited. Her given objection to the offer from the Conservatoire was that once there he would write no more great music. About this and so many things to do with how other people's minds worked she was wholly ignorant. It really came down to this: she did not want to lose control of him. Incredibly, Gounod gave way. He wrote to the Conservatoire and refused the offer.

In July he went to Paris to get the Opéra revival of *Roméo et Juliette* back on track and to talk to his publisher, Antoine de Choudens. It had been pointed out to him by Georgina, who was good at this kind of thing, that his English royalties far exceeded his French. For her Choudens was just a name: he must be brought to heel. Gounod thought so too. But arguing with his publisher did nothing to improve his standing among the music community in Paris: people were asking searching questions about what Gounod was up to in London. However—and it is an indication of his eminence among his contemporaries—his oratorio *Gallia* was chosen to reopen the Conservatoire and so signal the resumption of musical life in the capital. The piece had a particular significance, over and above any other candidate, because it was entirely free of association with the old regime. In many ways it was heaven sent as a work of semiofficial art—solemn and patriotic, written in a form not generally part of the French repertoire yet certainly earnest enough to satisfy the most carping of critics. As to Gounod himself, now that he was on French soil again, the composer was understood to be partially reconciled to his wife, enough to avoid an outright scandal.

There was just one small problem. Gounod stipulated that Georgina must sing the solo soprano part. This took away some of the patriotic value of the piece and renewed gossip that Gounod was being led by the nose. Was there no French soprano in the fledgling Third Republic adequate to sing this role? Nobody had ever heard of Georgina Weldon. Gounod insisted.

Georgina traveled alone to Paris, which she had last seen eleven years earlier, in the days following her elopement with Harry. On October 29, 1871, she gave the first French performance of the work at the Conservatoire, followed a week later by two evenings at the Opéra-Comique and a final rendering at the church of St.-Eustache, attended by seven thousand people. Gounod conducted all the performances himself.

He had given her a stage beyond her dreams. Her reception was polite rather than enthusiastic, and she was understandably wracked by nerves, but somehow or other she carried it off. Nobody and no occasion had ever asked more of her. On the face of it, conditions favored her. *Gallia* was scored for solo soprano, orchestra, chorus, and organ and was in a form she knew very well, the dominant English musical form of the period. It was true she found the Conservatoire "a pokey hole," and she was highly conscious of the scrutiny she received from the master's contemporaries. There were some nerve-wracking details to the piece she had not properly taken in at the Albert Hall, chief of which was that the soprano part carried the melody on its own for a full seventeen minutes. In the two performances of the work given at the Opéra-Comique, the management added some backdrops and stage furniture and required Georgina to wear a costume with an enormous train. She only just survived tripping on it, to the sniggers of the supernumeraries. At times the chorus drowned out her voice. In the finale of the piece she had to walk backward across her train and seat herself on a suitably scriptural rock. "The chorus behind me (which were lamentably out of tune) were supposed to be my *brothers* and did not support me at all. At the moment when at last, seated safe and sound on my stone, I had to look around and gaze sadly at the Gallic-Israelites as they passed at the back of the stage, I felt inclined to burst out laughing."

Georgina had a surprise up her sleeve for the beloved master. At the end of the final performance a huge and somber wreath of laurels was handed up onstage with a ribbon inscribed "From Gallia to G. Weldon." Gounod was horrified. "The meaning of it clearly is that *Gallia* is a *fiasco*, Charles Gounod is a *fiasco* and G. Weldon ditto! My poor child! What persecutions!"

Georgina explained. She herself had paid to have the wreath made up and presented. The funereal note was accidental: she had considered buying herself armfuls of flowers but settled on what she thought was a more appropriate tribute, in keeping with the solemnity of the occasion. About this there was no contradiction. Her "angelic old man" had made her a gift such as she could not have believed possible from anyone in the world. Only a year earlier she had toured North Wales playing to half-empty halls. Now she had done something for which all her life had been a preparation. She was a footnote in history.

The unlucky Gwen Jones died before Georgina's Academy of Singing could propel her to similiar stardom. After a bitter Mrs. Jones had withdrawn her other children, there were new pupils, though none of them well born. The academy was foundering. Talking to Gounod, Georgina had been fascinated to hear his stories of the Orphéon de la Ville de Paris. This was a school for child singers, drawn largely from the underclass of Paris, and supported in its work by a benevolent and sentimentally disposed government. It was a kind of showcase for the theory of trickle-down culture. Gounod had been its director for eight years at a time when Georgina herself was still a child. The idea of bringing culture to the unwashed began to attract Georgina more than sharing it with the daughters of those who had rejected her. The words *orphéon* and *orphelinat* began to conflate in her mind. What could be more appropriate than a choir not merely of children but of orphans, of which there were any number in London?

The underlying psychology of this seems obvious. A childless woman abandoned by her own class and with some revenge to take on the world as a consequence has hit on a dramatic way of expressing both her contempt for fashionable society and her love of music. But when these plans are undertaken by Georgina Weldon, the distinguished soprano and protégée of Gounod, edges begin to blur. Tavistock House had only so many uses. Was the academy to become an orphanage? Could it really be both, as well as the London address of one of the Queen's favorite composers?

At the end of November Gounod returned from Paris. Things with Anna had not resolved themselves, and he turned up on the Weldons' doorstep in a state of nervous collapse. "He fluttered into our nest like a wounded bird: he crouched down in his bed like a poor hunted animal, and there he lay for several days without moving."

The doctor was sent for and reported enthusiastically that the distinguished Frenchman was in danger of cerebral attack, as well as having eczema and badly congested lungs. He had found the smoker in Gounod, but maybe the eczema and cerebral dangers were misdiagnosed. Gounod was exhausted. Georgina herself, apart from that one problem with her womb, had the constitution of a horse, and mental depression was completely foreign to her. The poor hunted animal listened in alarm as his lover, her husband, and the doctor discussed what to do. Water, obviously: he must be plunged into more cold baths. But then he must learn how to sweat. He must be wrapped in furs and his body sealed with india rubber sheets.

Poor Gounod! He had fled Paris for the second time because he felt his wife did not love and honor him the way she should and was now a prisoner in a room heated to sixty degrees Fahrenheit, trussed up like a turkey and implored to sweat. Georgina would bathe him, lather him with the vigorous strokes recommended by the doctor, and then hurl buckets of cold water over him, before returning him to bed in his furs. He complained of colic and as a reward was visited over Christmas with dysentery. For once in his life, a woman had called his bluff.

Georgina had been raised by an expert in emotional tyranny, and this

was a very complex psychodrama playing itself out. With or without a physical content, it was a ménage à trois with a strong sexual character—the
complaisant husband, the besotted wife, and the tortured third party. Emis-
saries arrived from Paris to rescue Gounod: the abbé Boudier, Gounod's
confessor; Jules Barbier, a librettist with whom he had worked; and inevitably, Dr. Blanche. The psychiatrist at least may have seen what was
going on as not a struggle for the body of his erstwhile patient, but more a
wrestling match with the whole idea of genius. Like his operatic creation,
Gounod was flirting with the devil. What Georgina was fastening on was
what he was trailing before her—his talent, his genius. Of course, Gounod
had a much firmer grasp on it than she could ever realize, but that was the
nature of their tug-of-war. None of the Parisians who came to plead with
him could help him. He was enjoying himself.

Early one morning in 1872 there was an almighty quarrel with Georgina.
He dragged himself from his sickbed and dressed for the howling gale outside. If he was hoping to be dissuaded from sallying forth, he was disappointed. She said nothing. The battle of wills was conducted in stony silence.
Gounod pulled on his topcoat extremely slowly, with many a reproachful
glance. Still she said nothing. Finally, jamming her sealskin hat on his head,
he made an operatic exit and plunged out into the elements. He came back in
the early afternoon, by which time Harry had arrived home from the College
of Arms. Ernest Gye of Covent Garden was present, having been invited to
lunch. After a moment or two, and without explanation, Gounod left the
house a second time, in front of an astonished Gye. Harry ran after him. The
two men wrestled in the dark and smog of a London winter, Gounod clinging to the railings of Tavistock Square, Harry trying to dislodge him. At last
he was half carried home, Georgina's dogs yelping at the door.

Gounod had prepared in his mind a suitable climax to the scene. Rush-
ing to the desk where he kept his manuscript of *Polyeucte*, he seized it and
tried to throw it on the fire. Only now did Georgina play her part in the
elaborate drama:

> With strength lent me by the horror of despair, I threw myself
> on Gounod with all my weight. I knocked him down; I rolled on

him; we tussled violently for possession of the treasure. I tore it from him; I flung it upon the sofa; I suddenly picked myself off the floor; I sat up on it and screamed: "You shall kill me first, but you shall not burn Polyeucte!" My strength then gave way, I burst into sobs, I stretched out my arms to him—"My old man! My old treasure! Why are you so wicked to me?"

No librettist could have invented that last remark. The score stayed on the sofa, the fire crackled harmlessly in the grate, the moment passed. The element of transposition she had achieved—his wickedness, her embattled innocence—seems to have gratified Gounod. He had played a highly dangerous game, involving all three of them, and now disheveled, with wet boots, his arms blue with bruises from Harry's viselike grip, he was back where he had been, a prisoner.

Harry, who was present when they rolled about the carpet, was looking at two consummate actors, but he must surely have also recognized two very unstable people. Were the messiah of the new music to die of pneumonia from this and similar escapades, where would that leave him? Could he always count on the composer to draw back from actual physical violence toward Georgina or indeed anyone else in the household? Could such despair lead to suicide even? These were not idle questions. Gounod had already disclosed that he sometimes carried a loaded revolver. While what went on in the drawing room of Tavistock House behind closed curtains was purely their own affair, where was all this leading?

The scene Harry witnessed over the *Polyeucte* score touched on his own future. Should he ever wish to divorce Georgina on grounds of adultery, he had, he considered, enough evidence to bring an action. (The unfortunate party he had in mind was Sir Henry Thompson, whose incriminating letters to Georgina Harry had been careful to keep.) But if it could be shown she was mad, then his suit would be nullified. Such a thing had actually happened in a famous case only a year earlier, when Sir Charles Mordaunt tried to divorce his wife, citing members of the Marlborough House set and calling the Prince of Wales as a witness. Lady Mordaunt admitted adultery and even named the father of her just-born child as Lord Cole. The case created immense interest. Defending the action, the lawyers had Harriet Mordaunt examined by doctors and declared insane. She was removed to an asylum. Accordingly, her husband had no means of divorcing her. But Mordaunt had hired Sergeant Ballantine to act for him, and Ballantine, to the wrath of the Prince of Wales's set, contended that the lady was merely feigning madness, thus forcing into court all the evidence, including that offered by the Prince. In the event, the jury found Lady Mordaunt unfit to plead by reason of insanity, and the action for divorce collapsed. For Harry, this was a recent and notorious reminder of a key point of law. Too many tussles on the carpet like this and he would never be free to marry Annie Lowe.

Georgina, of course, did not consider herself mad. Quite the contrary: her abounding mental health was saving Gounod from going mad. She was his helpmeet and his salvation. What had caused this whole episode, of which Harry had witnessed only the climax, was really quite sinister. That morning, Gounod had received a business letter which Georgina had opened. When Gounod came upon her, she was framing a reply. Amazed, he asked what she thought she was doing.

"He asks when you can see him. As I know you do not want to see him, it is very easy for me to write to him to say you are unable to see him. You have only to sign the letter."

"I begin to think, my dear," Gounod responded angrily in rising cadences, "that my friend Barbier is right when he speaks of that unjustifiable influence which has set itself up to judge over my affairs, my works, my friendships, my life, my duty and even my conscience, over my letters, my answers, over every mortal thing."

Georgina insisted that she knew best. It had been for this reason Gounod stormed out of the house—to go and find the author of the letter and take his affairs back into his own hands. In March he wrote an extremely long letter to his wife, which begins:

Chère amie,
The state of moral and physical health into which I have fallen prevents me from returning just now to Paris. The too familiar atmosphere that awaits me there, an atmosphere poisoned by the most

odious wickedness, has become too noxious, too deadly, for me to expose it to the little strength remaining to me and the peace of mind which providence has spared me. Your lack of faith and tendency to believe evil without proof have for many years thrown into my life a poison which consumes and destroys it, and this has decided me to prolong my exile, perhaps to perpetuate it.

The surviving text of this letter is in Georgina's handwriting and was found among her papers at her death. Was it a copy or a draft? Either way, Anna Gounod could only conclude that she had lost her husband to the adventuress of Tavistock House. According to Georgina, Anna was telling friends in Paris that the Englishwoman would sleep with anyone for five pounds a night. Bizet, meanwhile, warned that Gounod should not be allowed anywhere near a school for young girls. Whatever tact and generosity had existed before, there was nothing now to stop the relationship from becoming public property.

5

*S*omehow or other, in the midst of all this, Gounod managed to work. More than sixty-three songs, two masses, psalms and anthems, and the scores of *Polyeucte, Jeanne d'Arc,* and *Georges Dandin* come from that period. In the afternoon and evening of most days his admirers and the plain curious called on him. Georgina inaugurated Sunday at-homes where the guests included Edgar Degas. In effect, Gounod had his London salon. He adapted to his surroundings sufficiently to cast off the brown suit in which she had first seen him at Benedict's and took to wearing a loose red shirt and on occasion a soft jacket and flowing necktie.

One visitor mistook him for Garibaldi. He smoked cigars, chatted amiably, revived all his old greenroom stories and was told some in exchange. In 1872 the Parisian cartoonist Petit depicted him as Paris imagined him to be. He is in red troubadour clothes, playing a guitar with only three strings and looking wet-eyed and troubled. In the bottom right of the design a tempestuous woman is attacking the piano. Staves of music rise to make a frame around the picture, falling at last on the protesting head of a roadsweeper crouching in the bottom left. Gounod could afford to ignore such things. The test of his time in England was whether he could create, and he found that he could.

"I internally approved every word, every gesture of Gounod's," Georgina wrote many years later. "I discovered that Gounod grew more and more like the ideal I had so long imagined him to be. I had imagined him just, without earthly desires, wrapped up in God and his heart full of love for his fellow creatures."

If it was not quite like that, perhaps the reality was better. The Gounod she had more likely imagined was someone not unlike herself—impetuous, untidy, and at heart deeply irrational. When he said God sent angels to dictate melodies to him, it seemed plausible to her that all art arrived in this way. In this she was no more ignorant than most people of her class. In her amateur career, ballads and songs had been either noble in a hearty sort of way or pathetic, enough to bring an audience to tears. She had the source of the second stream right there in the house. Cajoling, prompting, dominating by turns, she filled his day and he hers. If the results were sometimes unfortunate, he seemed to have suffered them with extraordinary patience. He was, for example, very fond of painting.

"Come on, old man," I would say to him, "your sands are very pretty, very sweet, very soft, but you have no distance. Put at the back on the line of the horizon to the left a little hill. Now then, old man, if you had a little sunset to the right, that would mark the horizon."

"There it is, the sunset. Don't you see that faint crimson line? There it is."

"No, it all seems sand to me, and you have little crimson dashes all over the place, so one can't make out the sunset at all. I can assure you that no one would dream of it being a sunset."

By degrees, when he was in a good humour I would get my sunset. That gained, I would say, coaxing him judiciously, "Now my dear old man, you must really draw something in the foreground—a few briars, a little brushwood, a little stream." Sometimes he would silently hand me his brush. I would then show him what I wanted.

In the history of the College of Arms, Harry's brief biographical note includes the statement that he once ran a circus. One wonders whether this wasn't a rather good joke at the expense of his colleagues. In many ways Tavistock House *was* a circus and Georgina rich entertainment. The people who came to visit were really more curious than friendly. If you were French—certainly if you were Parisian—you would want to see for yourself the woman who had abducted Gounod. Such visitors found Georgina not at all wanton but alarmingly forthright. She was without question eccentric, and she could be vindictive, but no one could deny she had colossal energy. Some of this was emotional fervor—she often spoke before she thought, or attributed good to an idea because it was in some vague way "worthy" or "elevated." But she also had a tremendous physical presence. Nothing daunted her. No challenge was too great. Part of her gift was never to see the absurd in life. It made her amusing to others, certainly, and a sense of humor might have saved her from some of the more irresponsible actions she took. But not to see the absurdity in things was more of a strength than a weakness. It absolved her from ever being wrong.

"Dear Mrs. Weldon," Charles Bulkely wrote to her about the academy:

What are we to understand? *In aid of the education of young girls?* Education in what? Spooning, learning to work the telegraph or perhaps a thorough education in the use of the Globes? Dear Mrs. Weldon, economy is everything. Don't remove from your present quarters or we shall have the expense of sending you back again. However, supposing you should have any pupils who might require what is termed a more finished education, please remember Charlie Bulkely's seminary where morals and calisthenics are combined with love and strong drink.

It was the kind of joke she needed to have explained to her. Whatever Gounod was to her, and whether or not they were actual lovers, he had unlocked something in her that Harry and his Beaumaris cronies had never done. With him in the house she was nearer to what she believed herself to be—talented, artistic, and, most important, sought after. This was a house of devotions, to each other and to music. It was nothing like the salon Sara Prinsep had created for Watts, though that comparison may have crossed her mind. There were too many crosscurrents, too complicated a cast of characters. Bewildered orphans she had found in the street mingled with the sons and daughters of those who believed she was running a respectable school of music. Gounod appeared from time to time from the upstairs study, his head full of music, his eyes full of sentimental tears.

One of Georgina's pupils was the young Danish tenor George Werranrath, whom Harry would one day come to cite in his adultery suit. Werranrath is treated badly by Georgina in the *Mémoires*, where she describes him as an illiterate baker's boy. However, long after all the muddle and uproar of those years had died away, he wrote a highly literate account of Gounod's work method while in residence at Tavistock House:

He would "think out" his theme sometimes in a house full of people. The noise and confusion would not disturb him, but on such occasions his friends understood they were not to distract him. In writing for the orchestra he would write each full chord for all the instruments instead of writing out each part separately. He rarely made alterations. Having thought out the subject for a few hours, he would sometimes make a few private marks, a kind of musical shorthand, over the words, and then played and sang the whole thing as it was in his mind. Even at this time the whole conception of the *Redemption* was in his brain and he frequently alluded to it.

In the spring of 1872 Gounod assembled a choir of twelve hundred voices and soloists for a season of concerts at the Albert Hall. The choir was formed into a society, an initiative of Gounod's himself, and joined forces with an existing and well-regarded choir under the direction of Joseph Barnby, which had been promoted for the past four years by Novello's. Gounod was given permission to call the new choir the Royal Albert Hall Choral Society (later the Royal Choral Society). The Queen accepted an invitation to attend the first concert. Gounod's new partner, Barnby, was organist and choirmaster of the fashionable church of St. Anne's, Wells Street. He had studied at the Royal Academy with Sullivan, where they had competed together for the first Mendelssohn Scholarship. He was by no means the junior or inexperienced partner in the enterprise, and his choir had been commercially exploited in a successful series of oratorio concerts.

Almost at once things started to go wrong. It seemed to Gounod only proper that since he had given his name and his energies to creating the society, the first concert should contain work almost exclusively by him. With some of Georgina's insensitivity, he packed the program. Along with new music for the occasion, he also wrote new settings for "The Old Hundredth" and "God Save the Queen." The management of the Albert Hall was understandably alarmed. Though Gounod was a valued client of theirs, the music publishers Novello's were also very uneasy. Under the energetic direction of Henry Littleton, the firm had branched out to become a highly successful concert promoter. Littleton certainly had an interest in Gounod's musical career, but he also bore in mind that Gounod might not be in London forever. The Barnby Choir, now in the belly of the whale that was sometimes called the Gounod Choir, had done very well for Novello's in its own right.

There was a second sticking point. Gounod had the uncomfortable job of telling Georgina that neither the Albert Hall nor Novello's wished to see her included in the program as soloist. Again, this was not solely an artistic judgment. The Queen had laid the foundation stone of the Albert Hall, and this opening concert was the first she would attend in a place so very precious to the memory of her husband. The whiff of scandal that hung over Tavistock House was more than either management dared ignore. When he

heard of this new condition, Gounod bridled. At first, he tried to stand on
the principle of artistic integrity. To suggest altering the program and attempting to dictate his choice of soloists was interference, pure and simple.
The two managements stood firm, and he had the unenviable task of going
home and explaining the situation to Georgina.

She was outraged. It is a sign of Gounod's infatuation that he could not
or would not accept what amounted to an ultimatum. At subsequent rehearsals he read out lengthy addresses to the embarrassed choir, as if they
were judge and jury in the affair. These were inspired by and may even have
been written by Georgina. It was, however, an argument the composer could
not win, and in his heart he knew it. The Queen's patronage of the first concert superseded all other considerations, and although Georgina may have
wished to take on the two managements, Gounod capitulated. Georgina's
name was removed from the billing. In the event, the music press savaged
him anyway.

Henry Lunn, in the *Musical Times,* which was owned and published by
Novello's, wrote, "If the first of a series of choral concerts given on the 8th
ult. may be accepted as a specimen of those which are to follow, it becomes
an important question whether the art which this grand aristocratic temple
was intended to foster (as we were positively informed by its promoters) will
not seriously suffer by its influence." Lunn noted the preponderance of
Gounod's own compositions and praised him with some sarcasm for not re-
working the "Hallelujah Chorus," which had been included in the program.
In September he returned to the attack, in a general review of the London
musical season.

> The Albert Hall, struggling against its acoustical effects and its
> amateur management has met the fate we from the first predicted.
> Had the aid of the highest professional talent in the country been
> sought to ensure the perfect presentation of massive musical com-
> positions . . . success would have been ensured; but the perfor-
> mance of a choir without orchestral accompaniment (to say nothing
> of the feeble programmes which were provided for each con-

cert) . . . were scarcely attractions to draw audiences from the West
End concert rooms.

In a fit of sulks Gounod turned the whole Gounod Choir enterprise over
to Barnby, who saw the project through to the creation of the Royal Choral
Society and continued with it until his death in 1896. (His bust, subscribed
for by the Royal Choral Society, can be found in the Albert Hall.)

Gounod acted in a very petulant way with the management of the Albert Hall and was convinced that his publisher and concert promoter, Littleton, had done him wrong. It was comforting to go back to Tavistock House
and rant and rage in French with Georgina, but it might have been wiser to
listen to others. Georgina was beginning to exhibit the first signs of a perse-
cution mania. She suspected Sullivan of orchestrating a campaign against
her. It had not gone unnoticed by either of them that Lunn had praised Sullivan's *Te Deum* at the Crystal Palace in the same issue of the *Musical Times*
that trounced the first Albert Hall concert.

In November Lunn wrote a long leader entitled "Paper Reputations"
which heaped scorn on people who styled themselves "Professors of
Singing" or advertised "Academies of Music" without having the slightest
professional qualification. Georgina was not mentioned by name, but the article was a swipe at her end of the music business. The modest sort of enterprise noticed with approval by the *Musical Times* was this sort of thing:
"A most successful Amateur Concert was given at the School Rooms of
Holy Trinity, Upper Chelsea, on Weds 26th April, for the purpose of establishing a Society for the Promotion of Window Gardening among the poor
of the parish. The programme included 'When the quiet moon,' 'Twilight is
darkening' and 'The Rose' (specially composed for the occasion)."

Lunn—and of course his proprietor, Littleton—were by no means
against the small and the amateur. That was their market. Their quarrel with
Gounod and by inference Georgina was straightforward. The critic and his
paper were reflecting a growing determination that the business should be a
business, and one in which the standards should be as professionally exact-
ing as anywhere else in Victorian England. It was all very well for Gounod

to bluster to Tavistock House visitors: "At the present day, vampires are said to inhabit only certain villages of Illyria. Nevertheless it is by no means necessary to undertake such a long journey in order to engage in monsters of this kind. They come across us in all parts of civilized Europe under the form of Music Publishers and Theatrical Managers."

In the autumn of 1872, and after an ill-advised series of more or less hysterical letters to Novello's, culminating in one signed by Gounod and published in the *Times*, Littleton found he had endured enough. He issued a writ for libel.

6

Georgina was delighted with Henry Littleton's action. To her he was no more than a "tradesman," an expression she had already used against Choudens, his French counterpart. She dismissed him breezily as "that little sweep." She and her dear old man would go to court and wipe the floor with him.

Harry sensed trouble, all the more so after learning from his friends at the Garrick Club that the proprietor of Novello's had engaged Sergeant Ballantine to act for him. Georgina scoffed at such naïveté—everybody knew lawyers were nothing but "curs." Harry was not reassured and roused himself to an unusually dramatic act. The night before the trial he packed an overnight bag and left the house. This should have put Georgina at least on the qui vive, for generally speaking Harry was afraid of nothing and no one. She derided him to Gounod as fleeing the scene "with death in his soul," as though he lacked the stomach for a fight. Harry knew what he was doing. What had hastened his departure was the knowledge of how much havoc was likely when Georgina went on the stand as a character witness, which she fully intended to do.

The sixty-year-old William Ballantine was among the bar's most skillful cross-examiners. He was a well-known and bonhomous Garrick Club figure who liked to count its writer and journalist members as his closest friends. Littleton could not have chosen counsel more wisely. By engaging such an eminent and popular silk he signaled his intentions to all his other clients. Like the trial itself, retaining Ballantine was a piece of shrewd publicity. Novello's headquarters in Berners Street rejoiced under the imposing title of the Sacred Music Warehouse, words blazoned across the building in Gothic lettering picked out in gold. Sacred Music must be above reproach and only the best engaged to defend its citadel. Once the case was won, as Littleton was sure it would be, he could rely on Ballantine's bluff and gossipy nature to send the story around artistic London. There was no particular personal animus against Gounod in all this, though the composer had behaved ungraciously and with much ill will in his dealings with his publisher. It was business. Littleton was determined to stop Gounod dead in his tracks.

Though she came from a family background famous for threatening litigation, it was the first courtroom in which Georgina appeared. The case was heard before Mr. Justice Denman in the Court of Common Pleas. It was a jury trial, and from the first Gounod found proceedings hard to follow. He gave his evidence in halting English and seemed bemused by the unfamiliar legal process. After a few exchanges he asked for an interpreter, and one was agreed to between the parties. The facts of the case were painfully easy to establish—indeed at law the composer did not have a leg to stand on. Gounod mumbled and blustered like a stage Frenchman, sometimes employing his interpreter, sometimes striking out on little arias of his own. He made a very poor impression on the jury. At last Georgina was called to the stand. She describes her evidence before Ballantine at considerable length.

> Ballantine wriggled like an eel, sniggered, pulled down his gown over one shoulder, put his leg on the bench, and said, "Now we are going to hear what this young lady has to say!"
> I looked at him, the picture of serenity, and gently murmured: "I am not a young lady, Sergeant Ballantine."

Ballantine looked at me—I do not think he had ever been so surprised in his life. Imagine a wild bull looking at a red rag for the first time! He then stooped over the desk and whispered to a solicitor sitting beneath us. The solicitor looked up. He nodded yes. I fancy Ballantine's question was "Is that impudent hussy Mrs. Weldon?"

He gave a little sharp cough.

"You are *Georgiana* Weldon?"

I began to feel a certain pity and said, "Sergeant Ballantine, would you like to know my name?"

I said so in the same tone I would have used to a child crying for a toy. "My name is *Georgina.*"

The judge was beginning to smile, the jury to titter. I was so calm, so candid, so innocent . . .

There was more of this knockabout. Was her husband Captain Weldon? No, he was not. He was *not*? No, he was *Mister* Weldon. Ballantine showed her a copy of the *Times* and asked her if she recognized a newspaper article in it: she said she did not. The paper was returned to counsel and a section marked in blue pencil. She allowed that she did recognize the indicated passage as a *letter*.

I turned to the jury: "Gentlemen, they do not wish to hear what I have to say. Have you ever heard anything more ridiculous? Neither party know what they are talking about. Mr. Gounod has been most shamefully robbed by these publishers, by all the publishers . . ." I could have run on forever. I thought I was doing the usual, proper, sensible thing!

That was the problem. What the court would and would not allow under the rules of evidence was of no consequence to her. She had discovered her stage. In the end she was forced out of the witness box "amid a universal din." Counsel on both sides were outraged—Ballantine, she says, shaking his fist at her as she left. According to her, Denman had tears of laughter running down his face. She, Mrs. Georgina Weldon, artist and lady, had ridden to the defense of the embattled French genius and musical messiah. It never crossed her mind that she had made a fool of herself. On the contrary, she had exposed the legal profession as incompetents.

There was only one small disappointment in such a day of triumph. Gounod lost the case, Denman awarding forty-shilling damages and £100 costs. The judgment was delicately nuanced: Gounod was guilty, justice had been done, and the size of the damages was a gentle indication to Littleton that honor had been satisfied. The publisher was quite content. There were ways and ways of getting satisfaction from the courts, and the learned judge had shown some shrewd calculation of the balance between guilt and ignominy. Gounod had been reproved at law, and that was an end to the matter.

Unfortunately, the parties who filed from the court reckoned without Georgina's taste for moral indignation. She now hit on a brilliant idea: Gounod could refuse to pay costs and thus force Littleton to have him sent to prison. This was a way of perpetuating the quarrel and returning the moral victory to him. Without too much hesitation Gounod agreed, signing away what goods and assets he had to her as payment of a notional debt between them, so preventing them from being distrained by the court. They waited to see what would happen. The answer was not long in coming. Littleton was not so forgiving that he was prepared to make himself look ridiculous—he wanted his costs. Georgina was thrilled when the ruse worked. After a few weeks bailiffs did indeed visit the house and were turned away empty-handed. Newgate now beckoned—the old man would be made a martyr to the English law. Gounod assured her he was quite prepared to go through with it. Indeed, he claimed to be looking forward to imprisonment: "On the 28th of the month [July] I shall go into my *convent*. In prison I shall orchestrate the imprisonment of Polyeucte and my Mass of Guardian Angels."

This absurd situation was unexpectedly resolved by a third party. At the last moment Hortense Zimmermann, Gounod's mother-in-law, paid the money into court, probably as a consequence of anguished representations made by his more rational English friends.

Mrs. Brown was the woman who had harbored the Gounods in their first days of exile, and now she came down from Blackheath to roundly accuse Georgina to her face of bringing the composer's name into disrepute. She had made a bad thing worse. Whatever the rights and wrongs of the case, it was never Littleton's intention to see Gounod in jail, as the Lord Chief Justice himself had observed. Mrs. Brown remembered Gounod as a quiet and sometimes annoyingly pompous man, very jealous of his reputation. She was staggered to see what he had become, with his quasi-bohemian clothes and confected outrage. Nor did Mrs. Brown like the way Georgina spoke for him as his legal consultant and artistic helpmeet. When she looked around more closely at Tavistock House, Mrs. Brown was even further disturbed. Who on earth were all these noisy children, trashing the garden and running helter-skelter through the house? Gounod was sheepish about that but otherwise stubborn. He knew what he was doing. If he said so without completely wholehearted conviction, that was because every last word he spoke was monitored by the watchful and interfering Mrs. Weldon.

For her part, Georgina was mortified that the costs had been paid, doubly so that the money had come from what she saw as a tainted source—what she described as the Zimmermann clique. In a midnight conversation with a friend of Gounod's named Franchesi, she revealed that she *wanted* to see the old man in jail. She explained why in very significant terms: "All the world would have known how Gounod was put in prison; all the world would have flocked to see him—the poor martyr! You think, perhaps, it is merit which attracts the public. Alas! I have learned quite differently; it is only absurdity and publicity which draw. Never mind what is advertised, people will speak of it everywhere, and they will be bamboozled into believing it necessary to existence."

This was true for her, but not for Gounod. Though he was fractious and took offense easily, he had never done anything so nakedly stupid as this. Very late in life, he wrote an anodyne autobiography. One would be hard-pressed to get an idea of who he was from what he wrote—but the work does include this passage, about the need the public has for artistic heroes: "To be brief, our houses are not in the street any more; the street is in our houses. Our whole life is devoured by idlers, inquisitive folk, loungers who are bored with themselves, and even by *reporters* of all sorts, who force their way into our homes to inform the public not only as to our private conversation, but as to the colour of our dressing gown and the cut of our working jackets!"

Some of this is an embellishment of the old cliché that the artist stands above the fray. It also excuses Gounod from revealing anything about himself of even a modest nature. The words were written at a time when the composer had become a national monument. By now his musical interests had dwindled to undemanding and unimportant church music. It amused him to pause and correct the tempi of certain works played on street barrel organs, explaining to the operators in a gentle, saintly way that he was the author of the pieces they were cranking out. Often, in more august company, he would express a sense of remorse at what had been in his life, tantalizing his auditors and leaving them to guess at what awful things he might be concealing. But there is nothing new here either, for Gounod had spoken like this since early manhood. It was part of his view of himself to half confess to dreadful deeds. In the autobiography there is no mention of Georgina or the rupture with his wife.

At the time of the trial, however, the critic Albert Wolff wrote a piece for the Paris paper *Le Gaulois* that expressed the French view of how he was perceived during his years in London:

> Was there ever a more singular history than that of Gounod and the Englishwoman? Since the woman Delilah, who cut off Samson's hair, never was seen anything so curious. Events of late years turned the composer into the London gutters. There he makes the acquaintance of an Englishwoman. At her feet, he forgets all—family and country! Passion had taken possession of the artist's brain and driven from it the remembrance of all that was decent . . .

There is much more in the same vein. Wolff supposed it to be a case of sexual obsession, which we can say fairly certainly it was not. Had it been, Georgina would have gone with Gounod to Paris when he was offered the directorship of the Conservatoire. Moreover, the lovers—had they been lovers in the way Wolff imagined—would have had to do something about

Harry. Not even the most complaisant Victorian husband could tolerate being cuckolded in his own home. The Rouge Dragon Pursuivant would have been forced to show his claws. If it had been a story of a sexually insatiable woman fastening on a man and dragging his talents and reputation to the bedroom, things would actually have been much easier to explain and resolve. But it was not like that at all. The strangest thing about the infamous Tavistock House ménage was how both men managed to be bewitched by her, without lust coming into it. What they were responding to was her manic energy. The whole time Gounod was preparing to martyr himself by going to jail, the first floor of the house was being noisily altered to make a second music room where Georgina herself might have a choir, the equal of the Gounod Choir. This was the real clue to her relationship with "the old man." Hero worship went only so far to explain it. She was in some way his rival, as well as his acolyte.

Shortly after Lunn's piece "Paper Reputations" Georgina published a flyer, intended as a reproof to her critics.

1. To those wishing to know if Mr. Gounod gives lessons in singing or harmony:

No, never, upon any consideration.

2. To those wishing to know Mrs. Weldon's terms for teaching grown up pupils or amateurs:

£600 lodged in the London and Westminster Bank to Mrs. Weldon's credit. In the case of a professional, the conditions are that he (or she) must remain for two years regularly training his (or her) voice under Mrs. Weldon's superintendence. The £600 being sufficient to keep any young man or woman respectably for two years in London; the balance of that sum to be forfeited by the pupil should the engagement be broken by him (or her). An amateur would not be accepted on any terms except £600 down, and Mrs. Weldon hopes she may never have those terms accepted.

3. To those wishing to ask Mr. Gounod's opinion as to their own, or any other person's musical capacity, voice, etc:

Mr. Gounod can see no-one on this subject.

4. To those wishing to know what Mrs. Weldon thinks on the same subject:

Mrs. Weldon knows that if anyone chooses to practise conscientiously for two years under her supervision, any one can make a good deal of his (or her) voice and style. But Mrs. Weldon, from experience, is of the opinion that it is impossible for a grown up person to practise patiently for the time specified, and recommends everybody not to try it.

The builders knocking bedrooms together, the orphans running about the house, the legal wrangles, and now the adult choir peering around the door. No sooner had the music room been established than she was forced to vacate it: Gounod, who worked above on the next floor, could not bear to hear the racket. It is dizzying to think of them all arguing, shouting, weeping, cursing. There seems to be nobody in charge, nobody to focus Georgina's energies. What Harry did from day to day is perfectly understandable—he went to the College of Heralds, thence to the Garrick or to wherever he had hidden Annie Lowe. At night he came home and viewed the wreckage of his house with that peculiar dispassion Georgina had for so long mistaken as indolence. Harry was not a saint, as he was to prove, but he did have one saintly quality—a monumental forbearance. To the limit of his interest (and his own sketchy knowledge of how artists actually lived) he behaved supportively to them both. When Gounod was ill, he nursed him. He found money for Georgina's ideas. On Sundays he suffered the company of people quite unlike himself and plied them with wine and refreshment paid for out of his own pocket. In this way, for example, he shook hands with the painter Degas.

It was not true, as Wolff and Gounod's other Parisian critics asserted, that Georgina had emasculated the composer's talent. No one can say what might have happened had he reconciled himself to Anna—had he never fled the war, even—but he worked quite as hard in England as he would have done had he never met the scandalous and ridiculed Mrs. Weldon. "Old man has rewritten his Paternoster again . . . Old Man has composed a most beautiful song on the words of the Song of Solomon, 'My beloved spake' . . .

Gounod composed a Biondina last night, lovely little Italian thing . . . Old man quite finished *Jeanne d'Arc*, three months and three days after he first saw the libretto . . ."

The real story of Tavistock House is what Georgina did. The saddest thing of all about her is that everything she attempted was for a more or less high purpose—art, love, God. She thought she knew about these things, but she didn't. She was an executant in an artist's world, a nanny in the world of love, a Tory when it came to God. There was a strong element of calculation in her efforts to keep everyone happy. For as long as Gounod stayed, she was saved from the outright descent into nonentity. Her aristocratic connections had vanished completely. Nobody came to the house from the world she had left behind her, and she received no invitations from the people she had once claimed as dearest friends. All those doors were closed to her forever.

The success she wished to make of her own talents was obstinately stalled. She was out of society but without the compensation of being accepted in the world of music. Over all that—all the frenzy and bustle of the last two years—hung a studious silence. Benedict, who had effected the introduction to Gounod, was mortified at the consequences. She had flirted with Clay, without ever understanding that his real loyalties were with Sullivan (they were bachelor friends), and of Sullivan she could not speak harshly enough. The few English musicians who came to the house—and they were few—came to see Gounod, not her. Nothing she did on her own account seemed to work. She was, in the eyes of her contemporaries—and now the courts—a willful and talentless woman who happened to harbor the rather aberrant French composer M. Gounod, but under such circumstances that it was impossible to speak of her in polite society.

In the spring of 1873 the remnants of the Gounod Choir, augmented by the Weldon Choir, gave six concerts at St. James's Hall, conducted by Gounod and once again comprising almost exclusively his own work. The promoter was a music publisher named Goddard. People came to these concerts because there was new work to be heard, of course, but the hall—on the site now occupied by the Piccadilly Hotel—was also the venue of two restaurants and a banqueting suite. The blackface troupe the Christy Minstrels performed in the second of the two auditoriums. Georgina was not the first person to travel west from Tavistock House to perform there—Dickens used it as a place to give his readings, the last in the year of his death, when he took his farewell of his audience amid scenes of frightening hysteria. The seats were hard, smells wafted up from the kitchens from time to time, and things were a long way from the opulent, but it was success of a kind, especially for her. Gounod was not so impressed. The choir was too small for the main auditorium, which seated two thousand, and Goddard insisted that it be spread wide on the stage to give the illusion of something bigger. Georgina took the solo soprano parts and her pupil Werranrath the tenor.

There was talk of moving on from the Exeter to the newly reopened Alexandra Palace with this choir, and so enter into direct rivalry with the programs of music at the Crystal Palace. It was a characteristic piece of overreaching on her part, for at Crystal Palace could be heard performances at which the choir and orchestra alone numbered three thousand and all the principals were drawn from the Royal Italian Opera. Fortunately, providence saved her from yet another fiasco. Sixteen days after Alexandra Palace was opened in May, a hot coal fell from a workman's bucket and the whole building was burned to the ground.

The first enchantments of the relationship had long fled. Gounod's towering rages, often followed by a headlong dash into the streets, came more frequently. The loaded revolver was referred to so often that on one occasion Georgina summoned the police to find him and fetch him home. They argued volcanically about nothing in particular: a hand of cards set them off on one occasion; in another month, criticism of the state of his trousers was the trigger. When they took *Gallia* to Spa, in Belgium, with Georgina as baggage master, she insisted that two of the dogs come along: Dan, the pug Harry had bought her when she lost the baby, and Tity, who was pregnant. They managed to get the choir to Spa without incident but then found they had left the dogs behind at the frontier. Georgina was distraught. Telegrams must be sent! Stationmasters must be alerted! The police must be mobilized! Gounod exploded.

Those brutal dogs. Why have you brought them? Why submit ourselves to such a nuisance? All the better if they are lost! You, you

can't live without your pugs! Is there a thing in this world more in-
supportable than a woman who cannot move without dragging after
her animals of all kinds, birds, beasts, parrots, frogs, tortoises,
hedgehogs? If they are found I insist on your opening their basket
and letting them run wherever they please! As for me, if those pugs
darken our doors again, I take the first train, I return to Tavistock
and you'll do the season at Spa without me!

*G*ounod was too selfish, Harry too indifferent, to channel all her
wild energy into a plan, a scheme, a campaign. Some of the
lesser lights of Tavistock House could not take it and left.
Georgina had been training up a young soprano, Nita Gaetano, who used
her time at Tavistock House to trap a certain Captain Moncrieffe. Shortly
after, she forsook the world of music for marriage without a backward
glance. In time George Werranrath left too, taking himself off to America.
Among those that remained, there were shocking and unsubstantiated ru-
mors that some of the orphans died and were buried in the garden, alongside (when old age at last claimed him) Dan the pug. The worst of these
accusations suggested that bowls of poison had been left out for the children
to eat like rats. None of this bothered her. She had an enviable capacity for
remaining deaf to what she considered petty and unimportant criticisms.
Unlike Gounod, she could not be depressed. Unlike Harry, she could not
play the waiting game. She had no understanding of music as an organized
profession and no inclination to acquire it. Like many people without a sense
of humor, she compensated for the lack of one by a joshing clumsiness. We
get the clear sense that she was driven, but only in the way a boisterous and

stubborn child might said to be driven by an obsession with some small aspect of life—a collection, say, or a desire to visit the zoo. Like a child's, her world existed outside of time. She was a woman without a real perspective of where she wanted to go.

Her unquenchable and scattergun wildness made her infuriating to deal with but did not necessarily indicate that she was mad. One of the niceties of nineteenth-century thought was that only God was held to be of sound mind. What was unsound about Georgina had lost her all her society friends—those that she genuinely had, as, for example, the good-natured Catherine Gladstone—and made her a laughingstock in the narrow world of London choirs. But what was that? There was a sliding scale of mental instability that certainly led in one direction to the private asylum, but included along the way every kind of quirk and oddity. The men who decided what was lunatic behavior were not doctors, but husbands. The laws of property and inheritance dictated terms. On the medical side it was commonly held that women were prone to lunacy through some connection between hysteria and the womb. What took the place of counseling and therapy in the case of many disturbed unmarried women was the speculum. A male doctor opened the cervix with a crude piece of stainless steel and looked for answers in the shadows of the womb. Among married women the husband was the judge.

All in all, Georgina was no more disturbed than Gounod. The difference between them was nothing to do with sanity, but talent. He could go away into a room—even a room without a piano—and externalize his feelings on a few pages of music paper. He was a maker where she was not. The whole house, the whole circus, was her arena, and in it no one thing was better than another. Else how could she be running an orphanage, organizing a choir, seeking individual pupils, *and* talking of a scheme to found a national training school? Ideas were drawn from a well that never emptied. One bucket was as pure and wholesome as the next. It all depended on how you felt when you woke up. Nothing was impossible. In her life, what was spilled or wasted could be refreshed without loss. She shared with Gounod an exasperation with other people and a deep sense of being unjustly persecuted. It had dragged them through the courts and led to explosive relationships with publishers and agents. However, in his case, vain though he was, he could admit at least sometimes that the fault lay with him. Such self-reproach was foreign to Georgina. It never entered her mind.

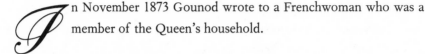

*I*n November 1873 Gounod wrote to a Frenchwoman who was a member of the Queen's household.

Dear Mlle Norele,

I have composed and written myself the poem of a great sacred trilogy, entitled *The Redemption*.

The music of this composition is the most important work of my life. I offer to dedicate it to Her Majesty Queen Victoria. I ask Her Majesty's gracious patronage and confidently await Her Majesty's commands for the first execution of *The Redemption* in the Royal Albert Hall.

I will now give my reasons for wishing this. I had hoped to found in this Hall, which is the most beautiful and magnificent one in Europe, and which is dedicated to the memory of a venerated and revered Prince, a great Institution devoted to Sacred Music. I have been shamefully expulsed, iniquitously turned out of the position of *Founder-Director* to which I had been appointed. I feel, and I know that I am truly inspired to say, that I am worthy of fulfilling this mission through my faithful and religious love for my divine art. I have the profoundest contempt for the illnatured plot of which I have been the object: but nothing will make me forget the great artistic fu-

ture of the Royal Albert Hall which has been my dream. I wish to re-
enter there with a work worthy of the place and of the name it bears,
and this must be by the Queen's own hand.

Every single note of this (which incidentally bears strong traces of
Georgina's composition) is falsely struck. Gounod was not turned out of his
post, but left it of his own accord. The "Institution" the letter mentions was
in greater part a commercial booking agency. "Gounod's choir" was at least
half, in terms of personnel, Barnby's choir. It would not need much knowledge of the London music scene on Mlle Norele's part to know that Joseph
Barnby had for twelve years been music adviser to the firm of Novello &
Co. and was now confirmed as director of the Royal Albert Hall Choir,
which Gounod had so lamentably let fall. The "contempt" Gounod felt for
the "illnatured plot" was hardly silent—the whole issue of the Albert Hall
and its musical policy was being vigorously aired in a paper called the *Cosmopolitan*, under the vitriolic pen of someone named Mrs. Weldon. When
this was pointed out to Gounod in Mlle Norele's reply, he denied all knowledge of it.

Georgina now wrote a letter to Mlle Norele under her own signature.
She confessed to having written the offending articles but indicated she
would be perfectly prepared to withdraw them in return for royal patronage
of a "National Training School of Music in South Kensington," of which
she would feature as principal director. Taking these letters together, both
written from the same address, we see a peculiar and murky picture emerge
for consideration by the Queen's advisers. The composer Gounod may well
have taken it into his head to ask permission to dedicate a work to the Queen.
That was a simple enough request, of a kind often made; nor was it completely out of the question that Victoria might graciously consent. The
soupier and more sentimental elements in Gounod's music appealed to her.
In his letter there were some disagreeable remarks concerning others that he
had no business to make, but that could perhaps be put down to his nation-
ality.

Georgina's letter was different. Leaving aside the veiled threat of blackmail, the writer of *this* letter seemed not to have been aware that a National

Training School had been mooted since 1854, nor that the Queen's second son, the gallant naval officer and passionate violinist the Duke of Edinburgh, had recently chaired a public meeting in which it was agreed to form one. Moreover, the writer of *this* letter describes Sullivan as "a little gentleman teeming with bad manners and impudence," not knowing—or not caring—that he it was who had already been offered the directorship of the new school by the royal Duke and his committee. Mlle Norele made some discreet inquiries about the relationship between Gounod and the mysterious Mrs. Weldon and was shocked enough by what she heard to bring the correspondence to an abrupt end.

Whether she was ignorant of the birth pangs of what in fifteen years' time would become the Royal Academy of Music or whether she knew of the baby and merely wished to replace it with one of her own, either way Georgina had caused Gounod's London reputation a further shattering blow. For as long as he remained connected to her in the public imagination, his standing would always be compromised. In Paris he was being spoken of by his colleagues as "the Englishman Gounod." The strain became too great. He started to suffer what Georgina called "cerebral attacks," which no amount of hydropathy could cure. In one of the more touching episodes of his stay in England, Harry took him off to the Royal Saxon Hotel, Margate, where they walked the promenade and took the sea air. Perhaps he, first among the three of them, saw that Gounod could not take any more. The Frenchman, bowed and elderly beyond his years, was exhausted, not by love, or even by work, but by endless niggling controversy. He had made it clear to Anna Gounod in terms strictly overseen by Georgina that he was prepared to live as man and wife again, provided it was in England and she accepted the Weldons as his friends. This she was not prepared to do. She saw that Gounod wanted what he had always believed possible—to remain a man of honor and at the same time enjoy the kind of quasi-sexual adulation that could only do him harm. She refused to accommodate him. She would not come to London; he must return to Paris.

Harry was sympathetic but noncommittal. He had his own secrets, which he was certainly not about to divulge to Gounod. It makes a pretty picture, the two of them with their canes and cigars, wandering along the promenade. In the end Gounod seems almost closer to Harry than to Harry's wife. Some of the exile's kindlier thoughts on the English applied as much to the husband as to the turbulent Georgina:

> The friendship of English people has the particular quality of not only being invariable in its constancy, but indefatigable in its activity. It is not a friendship which folds its arms, and is content with smiling at you when it meets you or when it wants you; it is a *certain* friendship which will not pay by a joke the pleasure of pulling you to pieces between friends; it is a courageous friendship which neither disguises its feelings nor its convictions, and with which one knows what one is about . . .

When he showed her these words, he asked, "Is that not a good portrait of you?," and she was touched and flattered. But they apply equally to the patient and good-humored Harry. And if that is so, they give a line to the way Harry suffered the wilder excesses of his wife. Georgina tells us in her *Mémoires* how Harry detested the world of artists. This does not ring quite true either. The amiable Garrick member knew as little about the interior life of art as his wife—but how they lived, what they wanted from life, the troubles they made for themselves, of all this he had firsthand knowledge.

In April when she came down to join them at St. Leonard's on the Sussex coast, the three of them sat on the beach more like two brothers and their sister than anything else. Gounod made her a last gift, copyright in a musical setting of Lord Houghton's poem "Ilala." He was ill, he was tired, and he could see no way ahead. The permanent exile that he had proposed for himself was much less attractive in fact than in fantasy. The failed priest in Gounod, which had grappled for his own soul and struggled with the world and the flesh, was looking for a benign retirement. L'Abbé Gounod, the much-loved, much-respected putterer, surrounded by his books and his scores, his pipes and snuff, was a more attractive picture than Gounod the firebrand, the martyr to love and the law. He made a very unsuccessful Englishman, as his wife and friends had always pointed out. L'Abbé Gounod, adored by his congregation, at peace with God, talking to angels, could only exist in France. Chaffing Harry for stretching out on the shingle "like a lizard" and studying her dear old man covertly, Georgina did not realize that he had already written to Paris.

Three days after her thirty-sixth birthday, the two of them set out from Tavistock House to visit Mrs. Brown at Blackheath. Georgina insisted on bringing two of her dogs, the decrepit Dan Tucker and a puppy called Whiddles. Along the way, the puppy began to scream frenziedly. It was having fits. They stopped the carriage and an anxious and angry crowd gathered, shouting, "Mad dog!" Georgina went to a nearby house to ask for a bowl of water. When she came back to the carriage, she found it surrounded by a mob. Inside, Gounod lay cowering against the cushions. The placidity he had shown in setting out was replaced by acute nervous excitement. She remounted the carriage and with the crowd battering on the doors, told the coachman to drive for his life. They arrived helter-skelter at the Browns', Gounod "more dead than alive." Before they could take lunch, ministrations had to be made of castor oil to Whiddles, who was locked up in an empty henhouse, and at the end of the afternoon Georgina drove away alone, leaving Gounod in the charge of Mrs. Brown. He was to stay the night to calm himself. But to her surprise and dismay, Gounod showed no signs of wishing to return home next day. After a week of anxiety and indecision she went back to Blackheath and found him in bed, "wandering in his mind."

The Browns were much upset, never having seen their friend in this state before. Georgina knew a great deal more about Gounod's capacity for self-pity than Mrs. Brown and tried to rally the poor woman. The master was ill but would soon be better, of that she was sure. Gounod cowered in his bed, feigning sleep. Even Georgina in all her aberrancy could not have been completely prepared for the enormous thing that was about to happen. She ushered the Browns from the room and lay down on the bed beside him. After a long silence she suddenly felt herself covered by "an immense net with great meshes of rays of lights" and saw written in the air the sentence "Woman, Behold Thy Son." These manifestations were as real to her as the jug and basin in the room, the wallpaper, the drawn curtains. They left her shaken but triumphant. She did not communicate the experience to Mrs. Brown.

On June 6 she returned to Blackheath to find a strange Frenchman in the parlor, a young man named Gaston de Beaucourt. When she asked to see Gounod, de Beaucourt positioned himself in front of the door. "No, madame, Gounod is better, but you cannot see him." She pleaded, she begged, she sobbed. She took herself off to a room adjoining the sick room and wailed at the wall, hoping to move the composer to call to her. Then she discovered that Gounod had been moved to another room altogether and she had been wasting her breath. She came back downstairs and pleaded with the company. Mrs. Brown was especially disturbed, and after an hour or so of entreaties de Beaucourt relented. Georgina might see him for five minutes. At this very moment, arriving pat upon cue like a character from one of his operas, Gounod appeared at the doorway, shocking her by his haggard appearance. His clothes seemed to hang from him.

" 'My Mimi,' said he folding me in his arms and kissing me over and over again, 'what a long time it is since I have seen you! Why do you desert me?' I gave M. de Beaucourt a look. He was sitting just behind Gounod, and he was making signs to me to leave, pointing at his watch. I, stupefied, confused, agitated, pulled from behind by the two women, said suddenly to him—'Goodbye, my dear old man.' "

She left the house with a heavy presentiment of the end. The next day Dr. Blanche arrived from Passy. It at last became clear to Georgina what had been arranged. Gounod was leaving for Paris and would never return. In her heart she suspected he was not so much being spirited away as fleeing: she knew him well enough to see that his feeble protestations to the contrary were a pretense. With Blanche and de Beaucourt in the house, responsibility for his own actions had been nicely delegated and he could play the part of the wandery invalid. On Monday she returned to Blackheath and gave him a letter she had written, stained with her tears. He did not read it but put it in his jacket. They then sat at the piano and in a grotesque parody of what they had been together, he accompanied her in this:

Watchman, what of the night?
Do the dews of morning fall?
Have the Orient skies a border of light
Like the fringe of a funeral pall?

Right to the end farce was mixed with real emotions. The two French-men bustled him to his feet. Gounod jammed on a panama Harry had once given him and took tearful and repetitive farewell of Mrs. Brown and her daughter. His bags were put into a carriage along with those of his two keep-ers, and he drove to Charing Cross, followed by Harry and Georgina in their victoria. On the platform of the boat train, where four years earlier German students had sung and chanted *"Nach Paris!"* on their way home to fight for the fatherland, the composer orchestrated his feeble farewells, into which were mixed protestations that they would meet again within the month.

I did not shed one tear, nor even had tears in my eyes. Gaston de Beaucourt must have seen that I was able to "control myself." The railways clock marked 1.20. Gounod was in the carriage: my husband and I both stood near the door.

He sobbed, he yet held our hands tight in his, without being able to utter a word.

"Come, my dear old man," said my husband to him tenderly. "Don't cry so much. I promise you that Mimi shall rejoin you in ten days!" The guard came up—"Take care, sir—the train's off."

Georgina went back to Tavistock House and slept for four hours. As surely as if he had been Moncorvo, she knew she would never see him again. What made it all the more poignant was that in the house were the pitiable relics of a three-year relationship: the rest of his clothes, his pens, his pipes, books and manuscript papers, his evening dress, the bits and pieces of a man's wardrobe that in the absence of the man himself become ugly some-how, and foreign. In a drawer downstairs was the only copy of his *Polyeucte*. Even that had been sacrificed in the absolute necessity for him to get away.

Tavistock

hree years on, Georgina published at her own expense *The Story of My Orphanage*, a rambling and sometimes incoherent background to the Gounod years. The house is suddenly peopled with minor characters like the brazen orphan Rosie Strube, whom she seems to have picked up in the street when she was eight, and the four children of the Rawlings family, who had been fathered by a blind man from over the river in Lambeth. He formed them into a bell-ringing act and then sent them to live with Georgina with his best wishes. The number of actual orphans in the house from day to day, week to week, is difficult to establish, and Georgina herself ducks the issue. To the question of exactly how old the youngest children were, she answers blithely that when a child loses its first teeth, one can form an approximate idea of its age. In one case, she is more certain. Katie, for whom she had a special affection, could read when she was two and a little later "converse with people in three languages."

The children ran about in bare feet. The idea for this had come originally from orphan Tommie, who asked her politely if he could take off his shoes and a day or so later whether he could also dispense with socks. Soon everybody followed suit. She saw some advantages in this and commends the children for using their discarded shoes as toys, pushing them about the lawns and filling them with mud. Bare feet made the house quieter and saved work for the maid, who would otherwise have to dress the younger children. Orphan Dagobert, who wore a brace made for him by Pratt's of Oxford Street, was an exception to the shoeless regime, but brought home from Mr. Pratt the welcome advice that there was no harm in the other children going without footwear.

The children addressed her by command as "Grannie." Every morning, prayers were conducted, including an orison from the Dominican rule, something very scandalous to those Protestants who heard it. It was followed by a quarter of an hour's organized yelling, to get the naughtiness out of their systems. There was little formal instruction in anything other than music, though when she was away from the house, Georgina did demand of those who could write that they send her a daily letter, to which she invariably replied. Every child, no matter how young, was part of the Monday evening concerts she arranged for them at the Langham. They were transported to and from these engagements by a typical piece of Georgina improvisation. For £25 she bought and had converted a milk float, painted it brown, and with the words "Mrs. Weldon's Orphanage" emblazoned down the side, sent it out into the teeming streets. On Mondays it took the children to their performances, heaving through the fog like a toy omnibus. The concerts, and the name "Weldon," were also advertised daily by sandwich men patrolling in Oxford Street and Charing Cross Road. The point of performing in public, their patroness insisted, was not to exhibit the children like freaks, but to raise money. This happened seldom, and the orphanage ran at a considerable loss, even under the austere management Georgina employed for it. Nevertheless, it was an accusation made by some who went to the Langham that the children were in effect participating in organized beggary. The whole enterprise was poised between laughter and tears.

Alfred has been very ill these two days he has a very bad stomachach and todays dinner was lovely only the meat was salt and Ernest liked the opera very much indeed and Willie has his too ears bad Ernest has his heel so bad and his big toe His bad and Margret's finger is much better it broke last night and all the matter came out but she cannot use it well yet the children are playing in the dining room Willie is playing at clappers and Johnnie with the top of the House-Maid's box and Ernest and Willie is playing at dinners now they are pretending to cry and Ernest is crying because he has a nock on the nose and Katie is taking the books from the bookcase I remain yours affectionate pupil Rose Strube.

The adults who came to the house to participate in the Gounod Choir were understandably surprised to find, as well as the master, this tribe of orphans scattered about, yelling and banging, chasing the dogs, and kicking up mischief. An intelligent and willing young girl named Marian Westmacott was a sort of liaison between the orphans and the choir, the grumpier members of which were quick to relay the shocking things they encountered. They had plenty to complain about, for it was a music school like no other in London. Each member of the adult choir paid two guineas for a seasonal subscription for the honor of being conducted by M. Gounod, but did not always see him, except at performance. When they did, they discovered he reserved his cooing, affectionate side for more distinguished company. On one occasion he stormed into a rehearsal in the new music room to insist they were singing out of tune and the noise was driving him mad. Georgina calmly handed him the baton, returning only when his exasperation had reached combustion point and all his English was dissipated.

Life in the choir was not all Exeter Hall either. For one engagement Georgina laid out £50 in publicity and got back £2.50 in receipts. Sometimes they found themselves engaged to sing out of town, but without rail tickets to get there. Georgina explains frankly that she was running both the choir and the orphanage from 1870 to 1874 on the £100 sent to her by her mother for clothes and makeup. Gounod had no money of his own other than royalties and for a long time paid nothing toward his upkeep. Harry had yet to formalize any agreement with his wife about the use of the premises. As a business venture, Tavistock House was a mess. What hurt most of all was that part of the bad publicity she received came from those very people she intended to benefit. What was worse—to have a child wet herself onstage, or to have it broadcast to the world by an indignant Gounodist who really could not care less what the Evangelist was instructing Mrs. Weldon to do with some very disagreeable children?

In the pamphlet she published about the orphanage, Georgina says little about her charitable purpose. Nor does she explain how she acquired the children, though it is possible that some at least found their way there by their own efforts and others were left on the doorstep or abandoned in the overgrown gardens. There is the hint that one or more were sold to her, not as orphans, but as the bastards of rich people evading a scandal in the family. Nobody came to inspect what was going on; contrariwise, none of the staff of the house rebelled enough to go to the police. Harry was once again the pivotal figure. The master of the house was indirectly a member of the Queen's Court and by day went off to trace the genealogy of the greatest in the land. If at night he came home and could tolerate the presence of ten or so squalling brats, who were they to raise a voice against them? Georgina found no problem with the children either; she claimed she raised them much as she would have done her own. For the servants it was more entertaining to speculate about her relationship to the gloomy French gentleman. Quite in keeping with her personality, Georgina did not feel the need to justify to servants what to her was a perfectly ordinary state of affairs. One of the people one would like to talk to across the grave is the Tavistock cook.

My Orphanage has nothing to say about the children in any detail. They are not the story. Instead, Georgina first puts into words her disillusion with the world she had left behind and the difficulties she has in understanding the music business she had joined. She advises her readers to grasp the concept that the music press is not objective, but led by a desire for profit and tied to the fortunes of a very few artists and performers, whose fame it has helped create. She admits that she had never before considered things in this way, any more than she has asked the very pertinent question of why her former society friends never patronized the popular concerts, which were now the battleground for her own exertions. Taken all together, she has blundered into a dark room without knowing the exact position of any of the furniture. She invents some characteristic reasons for having got into this situation. She is incurably shy, enough to blight a professional career as a solo vocalist, and that has driven her back into choirs, where there is safety in numbers. In this way, her light is always hidden under a bushel. Her husband is too concerned about his social position to be of any real help to her. Gounod's ill health and lack of business sense force her to give up her own voice. And so on.

The question arises: who would read such a book and with what result? Georgina's sense of justice sprang directly from her perception of what had befallen her as monstrous examples of ingratitude and vindictiveness. The jury in the case—the ideal reader of *My Orphanage*—was someone she had never met and probably did not exist. Nowadays we would call the work a green ink effusion: addressed blind, filled with excruciating and obsessive detail, deaf to humor, lacking in self-reproach, and grindingly self-justifying. It is a view of the world where only the writer is marching in step. The tone wobbles badly.

> Certainly it is my opinion, which I have never hidden—Mr. Weldon should have been made to horsewhip M. Gounod. My feelings as to what honour is are perhaps exaggerated, but I believe I would deserve to be calumnified and despised if I lived with a man who was not anxious to protect his wife and himself against the most atrocious public gossip; and that, if I had abandoned my School, I would have given the right to those who said (M. Gounod himself said it) that Mr. Weldon closed his eyes to my dishonour in the hope of getting rid of me and receiving large damages from M. Gounod as *co-respondent*. M. Gounod, counting on my despair, has hurried to say on every occasion that this Englishwoman lured him into her net under the guise of charity; that her orphans were myths; her School a swindle and the *children* (of whom he has spoken in his own published letters) were no more than three little pug dogs who made messes everywhere in the house.

If Georgina was looking for revenge on Gounod by means of press publicity, she was disappointed. Nobody picked up in any detail on Mrs. Weldon's story. Some of the reason for that was the perception that if there was an injured party in the affair, it was surely Harry. If there was a reputation to safeguard, it was his and not hers. The Garrick, which was patronized by many journalists and editors, was his bastion and refuge in this respect. Squire Bancroft was one of the most assiduous and popular Garrick members of the period, an actor manager with a genius for social networking. It could be said of Bancroft that he only ever met the right people. He was put up for membership by the editor of *Punch* and counted as one of his earliest friends in the club the Marquis of Anglesey. In his memoirs Bancroft had no hesitation in describing Harry as his wife's dearest and closest friend. In Bancroft's hail-fellow-well-met view of the world, a man who could have his French chum Gounod elected to membership of the Royal Yacht Club, which Harry had done, was hardly likely to be a bad egg. (Harry's own membership is a curious and intriguing detail in his biography, until we learn where his illicit second home was. For more than twenty years he kept Annie Lowe on a moored houseboat on the Thames at Windsor.)

All this in a house once owned by Dickens. Whirled about the rooms, even after Gounod had fled, was the undigested content of a satirical novel, plot and character jumbled together, but a book, were it ever to be written, now sadly out of fashion. It was a picture composed in broad strokes, lacking shape and focus. Trollope, who to some extent had inherited the mantle of Dickens and Thackeray, was far too fastidious an ironist to portray anyone like Georgina. Tavistock House was unkempt, disorderly, lacking in comforts. There was dust in every corner and an overpowering smell of dog. People who came there were shocked by Georgina's careless attitude to the normal duties of a wife and homemaker. She dressed erratically and had begun to interest herself in vegetarianism, a sure sign of eccentricity. After the vision she received in the bedroom at Blackheath, spiritualism also occupied her attentions. She was disappointed to find she was not herself a conduit for spirit messages and would never make a medium. She was merely a person of importance to whom the dead wished to speak.

Many of her former devotees in the choir began to panic. The Ballin family, who had girls under Georgina's care, actually went to Paris to inter-view Gounod under the guise of offering him a testimonial and when they came back, tried to hold a secret meeting with other choir parents. Georgina immediately threatened a lawsuit. But the rot had set in. "Some people called Hinton prevented their daughter from belonging to my choir because of ru-mours concerning me and Gounod. As a consequence I lost not only Miss Hinton but her fiancé, Mr. Johnstone. Mr. Maskelyne made some publicity for his business and scandal for me by putting about the fact that I was a spir-itualist. As a consequence the Alexandra Palace turned me down!!!"

The Maskelyne she mentions was John Nevil Maskelyne, a professional stage magician and illusionist who was also an unmasker of mediums. It is a shame he of all people did her in because they had much in common. Like Georgina, Maskelyne had appeared at St. James's Hall. He had made his name by exposing two fraudulent mediums called the Davenport Brothers. With his partner Cooke he ran a magic and stage illusion show at a venue called the Egyptian Hall in Piccadilly. With only a little alteration, and with-out the curse laid on her of an aristocratic background, Georgina might have done very well as a showman. She had the unquenchable self-belief but lacked the common touch. Father Rawlings, who foisted his scruffy and im-pudent bell-ringing sons on her, had a better instinct than she for what the general public wanted.

It was now twenty years since she had made her play for fame at Little Holland House. So much had changed, and not just in her own life. Some-one who knew Dickens and Tavistock House was Thackeray's eldest daugh-ter, Anne. She had been invited to the little theater in the garden to attend the first night of Wilkie Collins's *The Frozen Deep*, a play based on the last expedition to look for Sir John Franklin, the arctic explorer. As a much younger child she had seen her father and Dickens at their very liveliest at Christmas dinners in which the children were passed boisterously from hand to hand like little squealing parcels.

Born within weeks of Georgina, Anne Thackeray had grown up much more in the mainstream of Victorian life. The day Thackeray caught Georgina buying her wedding ring in Cockspur Street, *his* daughter had just published her first novel. Of course it helped to have a father like Thackeray, not because he was famous, but for the benefits of his teasing, affectionate nature and bearlike possessiveness. Thackeray loved his two children, and though their upbringing was highly unconventional and at times painfully lonely, he taught them the true shape of the world. Georgina, who could claim to know or to have met many of the people Anne Thackeray had met, might as well have been on another planet altogether now. For all the trademark pandemonium of Tavistock House, it was a lonely and unpopulated place.

O nce Gounod was gone, the degree to which their financial affairs had mingled became apparent. A fortnight after he took his farewells of her at Charing Cross, repeatedly begging her to visit, standing at the window to his departing train with tears running down his cheeks and wetting his beard, she received a reply to her anxious inquiries after his health and well-being.

My dear Mimi,

I can no longer hide from you the profound and bitter grief which your letters since I have been here have caused me, they have upset all my heart and brought the height to the trouble of my existence.

I have lived three years near you: in your hands, under your guardianship. What I have accomplished of work you know, you have been the witness of that which I have expended in strength, acceptance of anguish, endured of suffering of all kinds.

That you have wished for and looked for my good I feel assured, but you have pursued the realisation of it by generous devotion to an absolutely chimerical end: many times, you know, I have attempted to oppose a resistance and my objections; I have been obliged to renounce to them each time if I dared say a word.

To re-enter into this life of anxiety, of submission to the terror of saying the least word, of the sacrifice of my own thoughts so as to feel myself paralysed, is beyond my strength . . . Since you have desired my peace and my tranquillity, do not dream of reopening for me an existence which can bring neither you nor us peace. All that which is admirable will never destroy your instinct for command, nor my repugnance to this entire annihilation of myself and my child, the thought of which terrifies me. The part which I am now taking is imperiously commanded to me by the feelings of exhaustion produced by the struggles of these last years. To attempt to argue against this decision is useless and can but aggravate what I suffer. I know that the wish for my repose and the re-establishment of my health passes in your eyes before all—the cares you have taken of me when I was ill have sufficiently proved this. May God keep you

Your dear old man who kisses you,
Charles Gounod

However clumsy the translation Georgina made of it into English, the meaning was unmistakable. She already knew that he was never coming back, but there was more to it than that. Gounod wanted nothing more to do with her. This was devastating. In her eyes at least she was his musical associate and there was money as well as art involved. She was his English apologist and historian, as well as being the holder of several important copyrights. She was his muse, his Pauline, the next great soprano in his life. It was perfectly true she had prepared for this last role in a very unusual and maladroit way, but she was shrewd enough to see that without him she was nothing. She sent a man named de la Pole to Paris to act as her agent and find out what was going on. Gounod responded by asking her to send in a bill for the time he had spent at Tavistock House, just as though she was a common lodging-house keeper. At the same time he asked her to make an inventory of all his possessions left in the house, which she was to pass to the French Embassy, which would then arrange to have them collected.

This was mean and unfeeling at the personal level. It was also an attempt to divest Georgina of any commercial undertaking made between the two of them. For it now came out that far from being merely his landlady, there had in fact been such undertakings. She considered the copyright in some of the works he had composed in London to have been gifted to her, most particularly (and unjustifiably) the score of *Polyeucte*. Moreover, she was prepared to remind Gounod that he had once agreed that after setting aside a dowry for his daughter of 100,000 francs, the residue of all his future royalties would be devoted to the orphanage. Her view of his stay was that she had acted as "agent general" to him, going the rounds of the publishers, writing his publicity, doing his secretarial work, and fearlessly facing the vampire business world of music he affected to despise. She said, with some justification: "I had played the devil so that he might appear an angel." The results might have been unfortunate, but there was truth in the remark, which she further refined as this: "I had been the monkey among the crocodiles."

It was a mistake of Gounod's to ask for a bill—Harry could have warned him what would happen. She sat down and itemized every last expense. The first section throws useful light on his stay.

In the first place, Mrs. Weldon only wishes he would refund to me

the sum I have spent on the engraving of several of his works	£282.0.0
M. Gounod's pension for 7 months, washing, carriage, wines, etc	£140.0.0
Solicitor's account	£110.0.0
Subscription and entrance fee, Royal Yacht Club	£8.0.0
English translation, Joan of Arc	£16.0.0
Doctor's bills and medicines for 2 years	£45.0.0
	£601.0.0

All of this money had been expended by Harry in the first place, and for three years in London it does not seem an unreasonable amount. But she was merely warming to her task; these were the trifles of the account. "The first thing which I consider undoubtedly due to me by M. Gounod is £3000 as compensation for having prevented me from carrying on a profession by which I was earning money for my orphanage." This was much more contentious and must have left Gounod with his jaw on the table. But there was a greater sum yet to be subtotaled:

Damages as compensation to some extent for the injuries
    done by infamous calumnies, lies and libels   £5000.0.0

The grand total came to £9,791.13.9, a sum she must have known she could never recover. Gounod did not have that kind of money, and no court in France or England would entertain damages of £5,000 for hurts it could be easily proved she had brought down on her own head. She was a woman scorned, and it brought out the vindictive streak in her. A concert of Gounod's music in Liverpool was canceled because she would not release the copyright in some of the works, and there was a particular piece of pettiness with the score of *Polyeucte*, which she had wrestled for on the carpet in such a thrilling way and which she now absolutely refused to surrender. Gounod had a very strong case against her for theft but seems to have balked at the thought of bringing her to court. Enraged, he set about rewriting the entire score from memory. Whether she had wind of this or not, he had only just completed the task, which took him almost a year, when she sent him the original, every page of which was slashed through with blue pencil.

Gounod was by now fully rehabilitated in Paris. In March 1875 he attended the first performance of Bizet's *Carmen* at the Opéra-Comique. Massenet and Saint-Saëns were also in the audience. The master displayed his usual capacity for duplicity when it came to the careers of others. After hugging and kissing Bizet repeatedly during the second intermission, he sensed the production was going to fail. In the third act he leaned back in his box and murmured, "That melody is mine! Georges has robbed me: take the Spanish airs and mine out of the score and there remains nothing to Bizet's credit but the sauce that masks the fish." Those who heard him smiled wryly. The London years had not altered him after all.

In June he attended Bizet's funeral at the church of La Trinité in Mont-

martre. Claiming to have come direct from Bizet's widow, who was prostrate
with grief and unable to attend the funeral, he began to read from a speech
scribbled on a scrap of paper. With a trembling voice he quoted Geneviève
Bizet's words, entrusted to him as one of the composer's most cherished
friends. " 'Those six years I spent with him,' she told me 'there was not a
minute, not one minute that I am not proud and happy to remember.' "

Gounod paused, bit his lip, and then burst into tears. Everyone knew
that Geneviève had granted no such interview to Gounod and the words she
might have spoken had been stolen out of her mouth by this master of self-
dramatization. Gounod was back in the bosom of his reputation.

*I*n the winter of 1875 Georgina went to lick her wounds in Rome.
The French Embassy had collected Gounod's possessions, and
the elaborate account she prepared and sent him disappeared into
the maw of what she now conceived of as "the Gounod clique," a set of
silent but inveterate enemies centered in Paris. Harry was invited to accompany her to Italy but declined, giving as his excuse his duties with the College of Arms. He agreed to join her for Christmas but in December wrote
that his mother was ill. Georgina had no way of knowing whether this was
true or not, but she must have had some anxiety about his general state of
mind, because before leaving London she arranged for the bell-ringing
Rawlings children to keep an eye on him. Her spies duly reported no particular cause for concern. She was uneasy all the same. What was at risk was
not her honor, but the house. She had lost practically everything she thought
worthwhile when Gounod left, and all that remained—the orphanage, the
remnants of her singing career, her inextinguishable sense of social posi-

tion—depended upon having Tavistock House as a base of operations. For ten years she had wandered England singing for her supper and retreating only when it was necessary to the cottage in Beaumaris. In half that time the house in Bloomsbury had become the touchstone of her existence. It was the museum of her real self, every stone of it. Harry might scoff, and there were certainly things wrong with Tavistock, never a light and happy home, too ill proportioned to be the most desirable property. Nevertheless, it was generally accounted hers and not his. He paid. She created.

It was true that when in Rome her thoughts turned to other possibilities, such as a life of retreat in the Mediterranean where she could bring the children and live according to her other idea of herself, as a name written on an international register, the world as a Grand Hotel. One of the jokes she did understand was this: a man loses a sixpence in a dark alley and looks for it under a distant streetlamp, as offering more light. Plenty of the minor Italian aristocracy were cruising the Roman hotel lobbies in search of attractive but lonely Englishwomen to give this idea more than a theoretical base. Indeed, even while she spied on Harry, she was considering a proposition to live in Sicily with a shadowy but enthusiastically amorous count and forget her woes forever. There, it would rain blessings, the children would grow straight and strong, and she would spend her time traveling Europe with her voice. A stick to poke in Gounod's eye.

Harry was unfortunately telling the truth about a sick mother. Hannah Weldon died suddenly in January 1876, leaving a will that revealed some disheartening facts. The other Mrs. Weldon's thoughts and wishes strongly favored her sister's family. The will had been drawn up in 1865 in the Wynnstay Arms Hotel, Wrexham, and some of its many legacies fell to "the eldest son/eldest daughter of my said son" at a time when it was almost certain she knew of Georgina's inability to conceive. Were Harry to be childless, the legacies would revert, but not always to him. She is described in the will as still being "of Beaumaris in the County of Anglesea" and her bequests favor nephews and nieces who sprang, like her, from the North. Georgina, who had been married to Harry for five years when the will was made, was gifted £100 and none of the jewelry, plate, or pictures. What other wealth Hannah had to dispose of, which amounted to no more than

£3,000, she tied up in a trust fund, and there are many provisions for the distribution of the profits of this among the Rawson family. Harry benefited, but by no means as generously as he had hoped. This was the testament of a cautious, modest, and unfashionable woman of average means, who had skewed her charitable wishes to her sister and her family.

It was a disappointing moment. Harry was bequeathed a few boxes of uninspired plate and china, books and pictures he did not particularly want, and—once the trust was divided among all the parties—next to no money. The reading of the will hardened his attitude toward Georgina and her plans. As she had begun to suspect, he was growing tired of Tavistock House. As an experiment in living in the grand style, it had proved disastrous. There were other options open to him. If he left Georgina or sold the lease and moved into smaller accommodation, what was lost? His post at the College of Arms afforded bachelor rooms, his club was as good as a home to him, and Annie Lowe waited patiently on the houseboat at Windsor.

It was true that in business and money matters he was no more experienced than Georgina, although only a few years later he was made treasurer of the College of Arms. The thing he had that she lacked so conspicuously was the ability to think things through. He may have seen, long before his wife, that Gounod's defection had been more than an emotional blow. It really signaled the end of all her schemes and the snuffing out of her music career. It was all very well for Georgina to insist, as she did, that a true musical orphanage of the kind she envisaged must, absolutely *must*, have fifty children in it, but Harry could see what effect ten already had on his patience and goodwill. And it escaped no one that these ten had been left in the hands of servants while their patroness and music director took herself off to mend a broken heart in Rome. Without Gounod's name and reputation to give some credibility to the ideas Georgina dreamed up, they were worthless. For as long as she was in the house, goading and urging, it was perhaps just possible for Harry to tolerate the children, the noise, the relentless self-advertising, and never ask where it was all leading. But when she was away, as now, the absurdity of what she wanted to do was apparent.

Georgina claims that she sensed all this and had offered to place all the orphans back where they had come from—whatever that meant—live quietly, and be the model wife of a Herald. In her version of life after Gounod, she says that Harry recognized the good she was doing, disliked her absenting herself from the house for such long periods, but wanted to give her every chance to succeed. She wrote to him from Rome suggesting a pure piece of Georginaism. Her family considered him a blackguard. But he was not all bad, and she had thought of a way out of their present unhappiness. He liked Freddie Warre, and Warre had a whole floor to let in his house. Harry could go there. In three years' time the trust allowed for in his mother's will would mature, and if in those three years she had not made a success of the orphanage, "the ugly moment would have passed" and they could be as they were. Meanwhile, she would not ask for more than £1,000 a year from him and, imperatively, the house. Harry replied that he didn't give a fig what the Trehernes thought of him but that he was in agreement "and he did not say a word to make me suspect he did not think my plan admirably diplomatic." Fortified by these remarks, she packed her bags, said good-bye to her crestfallen Sicilian count, and set off from Rome, not to come home, but to stay with her uncle and aunt at the Schloss Hard.

She had been away since November, and she did not return to London until the following July. The choir, the students, the plans for a national college, and all the rest of it vanished from her mind as surely as the winter snows. The orphans were not so easy to dispose of. The advertising cart gathered leaves in the garden, the sandwich men had given up their boards, but the children still had to be fed, cared for, dosed with medicine, and kept disciplined. That was not Harry's job. But whose job was it? It seems incredible that she could abandon that responsibility and get away with it. However, though she did not know it, the long vacation she took from her rejection by Gounod was beginning to have repercussions wider than what to do about the children.

There were new players coming onto the scene, one of whom was Georgina's mother. The timorous Louisa had shown no wish to meet her daughter after the marriage to Harry and its disastrous effect on Morgan Treherne. After her husband's death she still kept her distance, salving her conscience by sending Georgina a small allowance every Christmas. The accompanying notes were vague and noncommittal. It was her duty as a woman to defer to a man, and that man was now Dal. Louisa learned with alarm that unforgivable Harry had begun to exchange letters with Dal in his role as head of the Trehernes. Their purpose was brutal and businesslike. Behind Georgina's back, the most awkward question of all was being put: could her actions be described as those of a mad person? Or perhaps the question was differently nuanced. How would the Trehernes react to such an assertion, and would they stand in Harry's way?

Georgina arrived in Switzerland in March, still firing off letters to Tavistock House and getting back answers signed by Harry—phrased, she thought, in rather more stylish terms than was customary with him. It at last occurred to her that he might not be writing them himself. When she got the chance to subpoena documents in the divorce action that eventually resulted, she found copies of these letters. They had been drafted for him by his lawyer. Moreover, she discovered that all the correspondence, including her suggestion that he move out as far as Freddie Warre's, had been shown to her mother and the rest of her family

> to make them believe I was a terrible woman and that "I had chucked him out of doors!" . . . One will appreciate that in spite of my (legal) flair, I could not have suspected something as Machiavellian as that, but I did imagine there might be a woman at the bottom of it, because he ended up by giving me the idea he had a grievance at this arrangement to live apart, and that he wished thereby to pay court to some woman that he wanted to seduce, given there is nothing that does seduce a woman more easily than the pity she feels for a man abandoned by his better half.

All these thoughts occurred to her in her walks beside Lake Constance, seven months after last seeing Harry, the house, and her orphans.

She did at last come home, not without a little Machiavellian plotting of her own. She wrote to a man she knew named Alfred Nodskou, who had been a dilatory and minor member of the Gounod Choir, a property developer who let furnished apartments. The idea was to enter London secretly, stay a few days with him, and spy out the land. The blind old man who was father of the Rawlings children was summoned to the Nodskou address and confirmed to Georgina that there was indeed a woman in the case. He was naturally unable to describe her. Nodskou, meanwhile, had contrived a scheme that she should buy a house he owned. He was very persuasive. It would be a fallback if things turned out badly. With her usual capacity to be duped by plausible men, she agreed, signing away £1,000 for a house worth maybe a third of that.

Early on Tuesday morning, July 4, she set off for Tavistock House, arriving a little after nine. She found Marian Westmacott and the children coming down to breakfast—"a little late, in my opinion, but there was my big difficulty—not the children, but the grownups on whom I was obliged to depend." Harry was in the habit of rising late, and while she waited for him to show himself, she snooped around. She found the name she thought she was looking for—someone named Amy Oliver. She seemed the most likely candidate for Harry's attentions. (It was not for another ten years that she realized she had been barking up the wrong tree.) She crept about on the ground floor, looking for more evidence. With a stroke of genius, she called for the housekeeping accounts. Someone, for some reason, had ordered twenty pounds of veal the previous Sunday, not one scrap of which remained by Tuesday. It was the kind of detail that was conclusive: Harry had been enjoying himself while she was away. It seemed to her unfair.

At half past twelve the unsuspecting Harry came down to breakfast and—as well he might be—"was visibly knocked sideways, but I leapt into his arms and embraced him with all my heart." She found him uneasy and unresponsive. He refused to compliment her on her new costume, bought in Paris a few days before, and explained that he had to go out after breakfast and had engaged to dinner that evening three of his Garrick friends, Freddie Warre and the artists Sandys and Alfred Thompson. Georgina felt a migraine attack coming on. She went to bed and did not come down again that night. In the detailed account she gives of this fateful Tuesday, the children are not mentioned once. The one piece of remorse she felt was at the condition of her pugs Dan Tucker and Jarby. One was paralyzed, the other blind. She felt bad about being away from them so long.

Harry's use of lawyers to draft his letters was the first step in divorce proceedings. He had to move extremely cautiously. He was fairly sure, after consultations with his solicitor, Neal, that under the terms they had agreed, if he left the house now, she could not subsequently sue him for divorce on the grounds of desertion. He was in fact quitting because he could not stand it anymore, but in law the arrangement was a separation and nothing else. There remained the matter of her adultery. This was a way of ridding himself of her altogether. The most recent of his suspicions concerning what was then called criminal conversation fell on the unfortunate George Werranrath, whom he believed to have slept with his wife in a Strand hotel room the previous year. But Werranrath had gone to America. The much more obvious candidate for any action of this sort was Gounod, but that made difficulties for Harry, since it could be easily proved that he was complicit in most of what went on between the Frenchman and his wife. There were other candidates, some going back six years, but here he risked alienating his new allies, the Trehernes. Mrs. Treherne did not wish to see her daughter in court on charges of adultery, or for anything else. Her concern was with Georgina's sanity.

So much was made by Georgina of her mother's treachery in what was to come that it bears examination here. Louisa was far from the action (if one counts a train journey of two hours or more), insulated from the world of real events by invalid retirement in her daughter Emily's house near Worksop. The image one has of her is of someone sitting more than moving about. She found even the smallest problem too much to contemplate, and her capacity for giving family advice on any subject was compromised by the long shadow Morgan's madness had cast over her life. It was all very well for her children to scold her now, but Louisa had gone along with things another wife and mother might have rebelled against much earlier. This she had not done for the sake of keeping up appearances, and despite her heroic self-abnegation, things had ended in the ugliest way possible. Thirty years of excusing Morgan to others had come to the point where he was unable to recognize her and was as mad as anyone could be. Nobody and nothing could palliate the simple truth: the M.P. for Coventry was insane in the way such things are represented in the most sensational books and plays. In the last years of his life he had gone to live far, far away, beyond the reach of anyone's compassion. A second experience like that was more than she could contemplate.

As for Harry, when Georgina came back that Tuesday and shocked him so much, it is really the last time he is seen in the story with any clarity. Many another man would have jibbed at living with her under the terms she set, especially since their arrival in London. The enigma in Harry was his easy-goingness, his laconic good nature. As he approached forty, he had endured—and often enjoyed—fifteen years of an extremely rackety marriage. In the conversations he was having nowadays with his brother-in-law, Dal must have struck him as the most colossal prig. Harry was no angel and not especially complex or sophisticated, but he knew Georgina as well as anyone else on earth. What was sad about her unexpected return was that his interest, his curiosity, and his compassion had come to an end. He had been her support, her chiding critic, a long-suffering friend to her genius. Now he had nothing more to give. The week after she returned he quit the house and went to live with Freddie Warre.

Menier

1

One of the uninvited guests at Tavistock House in the days when Gounod lived there was a compatriot of his, Anarcharsis Menier. Menier first called in December 1873. He introduced himself as from a small commune near Bordeaux and more recently Paris, where he had spent the Siege and Commune. In his native village, he assured his fellow countryman, the family name was so well respected that men removed their hats at the mere mention of it. There had been distinguished Meniers in the Year One, friends if not intimates of the revolutionary heroes. But he was not there to brag about his republican credentials, which in truth he had been forced to refurbish a little for the present circumstances. He came as an artist. He explained how he had written a play that Gounod might like to use as the libretto for an opera. An accompanying note, clipped to the text, summarized the situation: "I sent M. Valnay a three act comedy which he has given back saying: 'the characters are too naturalistic; the piece lacks the grotesque; the characterization is well sustained: wit is absent; as a consequence I will not play it.' "

This meeting took place during the time of the much-publicized Littleton libel case, and it may have been the newspaper accounts of it that drew Menier to Tavistock House. Menier shrewdly ended the cover note to his play with this familiar complaint, as from one embattled artist to another: "These general criticisms, if I accepted them without examination, would lead me to think that the skies of England had boiled my brains."

It was a crude but bold pitch. Wasn't Gounod himself a victim of English perfidy? The skies of England shone as fiercely—perhaps much more fiercely—over the Court of Common Pleas as on the head of Anarcharsis Menier. Perhaps Gounod, a fellow artist, would do him the honor of reading the work? Unfortunately, Gounod found the idea very resistible—Menier was asked to leave his manuscript and wait for a considered reply, which as the composer explained might be some time in coming. He was very busy; M. Menier would of course understand; yet the work looked promising, etc.; something might come of it. Menier noted that the bouncy and buxom Englishwoman at Gounod's side was more encouraging. Not having read a word of the text, she was quite sure it was eminently playable. The problem, as he had correctly identified, was England, always an enemy to talent. Menier heartily agreed.

There were, however, many things working against the author of *The Spidder and the Fly*, not all of them to do with the title. Menier was extremely unprepossessing, an overweight and unhealthy man of about Harry and Georgina's age, with lank hair and a pale, even a bloodless, complexion. Georgina noticed how dirty his fingernails were, and how stiff with cigar ash his waistcoat. His manner with Gounod had been wheedlingly intense. The note attached to the manuscript was written on letterheaded notepaper from the offices of a journal called *La Liberté Coloniale* which he and his brother ran. He signed his name above the title "Editor in Chief," and while it was true that the Paris office was in the rue de la Victoire, an irreproachable address, Gounod was forced to excuse himself from knowing anything at all about this particular journal. Menier explained only too willingly.

The purpose of *La Liberté* was to resettle the poor of France in her newest colonial possessions where they might find God and make a new start in life. All that was required was capital, and the shrewd investor who also had an eye to the spread of civilization and the French language might make a fortune. In other words, the newspaper was a thinly disguised stock prospectus. Through their contacts, Menier and his brother had managed to secure a deal to develop what he described as several thousand hectares of prime farming land on the Pacific island of New Caledonia, without troubling to explain to investors that the territory had only recently been brought under civil control and its backwood ravines (which was where the land was situated) were occupied by extremely restless natives. Negotiations had proceeded admirably, and he and his brother were arranging to charter a ship for the first colonists when the Franco-Prussian War began. Patriots before they were capitalist entrepreneurs, they at once gave up their plans and joined the National Guard. But, as Menier explained hastily, in view of Gounod's own position on this matter, that was another story.

The play he had entrusted to Gounod was part of the detritus the composer left behind in his flight. Three years passed. Then one day the sharp-eyed little crooks of the Rawlings family, who were in the habit of reading tidbits out to Georgina from the newspapers (she kept a particularly close eye on wills and bequests), happened to see the forgotten Menier's name mentioned in a case at Bow Street Magistrates' Court. He and his wife were implicated in some cloudy business about a case of child stealing.

Georgina at once sent the Rawlings boys to Bow Street to try to discover where Menier now lived. Their task was an unexpectedly easy one—he lived a few doors down the street from the court. He replied to her note with a welcome promptitude. It gave him and his wife great pleasure to accept an invitation to visit Tavistock House once again. Georgina had recently discovered the missing manuscript while dusting in the library, and it was arranged that M. Menier should come to tea, take back his property, and tell her what had brought him to his present sorry state. The story turned out to be a gripping one.

Menier's wife was named Angele. Her sister Gabrielle died in the Commune, leaving two children, one of them a little girl nicknamed Bichette. The father, who was the plaintiff in the Bow Street case, was a terrible man named Duprat. For his many crimes and misdemeanors during the Commune and after, Duprat had suffered what the French call *la mort civile*, removing from him all legal rights. Angele now wished to adopt Bichette and bring her up as her own (her motherliness did not extend to the older child). With this in mind she had snatched Bichette and brought her to London. But thanks to the ignorance of the English courts, the poor creature had been taken from her and returned to her father. When Georgina asked where the child was now, the answer was unexpected. She was in Brussels with her grandfather, where, of course, English law did not apply. It would be the simplest thing in the world to sort out the legal niceties there and restore Bichette to her loving aunt. That is, the couple added significantly, for anyone who had the fare to the Continent. Quite by chance—or was it chance?—Angele provided the clinching detail. Her eyes cast down, she confessed that she herself could not have children, and that had made her especially sensitive to the fate of this particular child.

Georgina reached into her gown, and her hand closed on the only money she had there, which happened to be a £50 note. She gave it to the Meniers, bidding them to find Bichette and set to right the wrongs done to the family by English justice. Their protestations of joy were wonderful to behold, and Georgina felt a special bond with Angele Menier that she hardly bothered to hide. The two women had hit it off in an instant. The Frenchwoman was roughly her age and height, a short and dumpy blonde with dark eyes and an appealing eagerness. She was also a natural sentimentalist, and Georgina, who completely lacked this attribute in her own makeup, found herself entranced. People who wore their hearts on their sleeves confounded her as much as people who made jokes or wore other social masks. Nevertheless, she felt she had met a soulmate.

Angele Menier was the kind of woman whose eyes filled with tears and whose lips quivered at the merest suggestion of cruelty and injustice. It was true that when she laughed it came out as a raucous smoker's cough, and her husband let it be known that in matters of appetite she was regarded as "the human cormorant," but that was part of her charm. Angele had been cheated by the world of men, and so had Georgina. The one thing men were good for—to give children—had not happened to either of them. Angele (and this at least was genuine) indicated by sighs and glances that Anarcharsis was a sorry disappointment in bed. Measured by his essential scruffiness, his wife seemed contained and even chaste. He wanted to talk about business, the iniquities of the legal system, and the stupidity of Mr. Flowers, the police magistrate. She wanted to talk about Bichette.

A few days after their departure for Brussels, there was bad news. Some minor complications with the lawyers meant they must ask for more money, as much again. Georgina sent it.

Angele came originally from Clermont Ferrand, where she had left long-suffering peasant parents and hopes of a small inheritance from an ancient family relative—a house without a roof and half a hectare of land. There were three sisters in the family, and they had all left for Paris as soon as they could. Angele wanted to be a dancer but soon found herself on the streets, where she was picked up by Menier. Since that time she had lived a kind of fantasy life with the two Menier brothers, flitting from one apartment to another in Montmartre. She was tough in the way that whores had to be, but also hapless in the way they sometimes are. For her, even having the shambling and unkempt Anarcharsis as her rod and staff was a step up. With him, although many times sinking back into hysterical self-recrimination, she could reinvent herself. She genuinely adored her niece Bichette, to the point where she drove her husband mad with exasperation: the desire to have the child as her own was an obsession.

Menier, on the contrary, cared very little for other people. He merely wanted to be rich. The Second Empire had failed him, but the Third Republic was the same gold mine waiting to be dug. Angele disgusted him. She was clever, in a narrow streetwise sense, but vacillating and vague. She was also much more interested in women than men, something Anarcharsis bore with complete indifference. What he looked for in a woman was a workhorse. Love and romance did not come into it. What his life required was a clean shirt and the loan of a few sous. From time to time, as now, it helped to have her with him as his dutiful wife, to add color to his fraud. They were partners only in crime.

Which of these two first saw financial salvation in the strange setup at Tavistock House it is difficult to determine. It could not have escaped Menier's keen eye that on his earlier visit there had been two men on the premises, living in a cloud of cigar and pipe smoke, and now there were none. This was all the more noticeable because Georgina never employed a male servant of any kind. By the time Menier saw Tavistock House a second time, it had become a ménage of women and children. The faithful Marian Westmacott's mother was cook, there was a maid of all work named Tibby Jordan, and Georgina kept up a personal maid named Villiers. It was hardly a rich person's house, although it was by Menier's unexacting standards well appointed. It was better than what he was used to. In most ways he was hardly more than a petty criminal and thought like one. Although his more major schemes were awe-inspiring (he and his brother were now working up an idea to sell colonists plots of farmland in the most southerly dunes and wastes of the Sahara), his immediate problems were always more pressing. He was one of those men who dress and act as though millions are about to pass through their hands, but whose gloves are patched at the finger ends and who dare not cross their legs in a chair for fear of showing the holes in their boots. As for Angele, though she was without doubt what the French would call *une sournoise*—a sly devil—she was also a woman without a home to call her own. Menier's sharp eye might dart about the room valuing all the readily portable items. Angele, weary and dispirited, saw a haven.

In the end, using Georgina's money, they recovered Bichette and took her back to Paris, putting up "the house in Clermont Ferrand" as collateral for the loan. Angele proved not to have the practical skills that went with a mother's instincts. She liked dressing the child and taking it for walks, but was easily depressed by her own many failures and shortcomings. Bichette's frequent minor illnesses gave her panic attacks: if the child ran a temperature, it was her fault because she had been such a wicked woman. The poor girl was shuttled to and from Brussels and Paris like a railway parcel. Meanwhile, Anarcharsis worked up his new scheme to sell the Sahara to people looking for a little adventure with their savings. However, selling sand dunes to the credulous was proving even more difficult than selling them jungle ravines. *La Liberté Coloniale* kept up its offices and letterheads yet published

Georgina Weldon in 1857,

from a painting by J. R. Parsons

after the portrait by G. F. Watts.

à ma chère amie Georgina Weldon.
Ch. Gounod

❧ Gounod's photographic calling card—

perhaps, under the circumstances, a little too

laconically inscribed. ❧

Georgina

and Harry

in 1873.

Georgina, Gounod, and some of the older orphans

in the gardens of Tavistock House.

Sitting next to Gounod is probably Marian Westmacott;

standing (second from right), Rosie Strube.

Frederick Clay.

Georgina

with Bichette, 1877.

With Angele Menier, 1879.

Note the almost identical

clothes and bags.

Georgina in her

stage prison clothes.

As Serjeant Buzfuz

(Mrs. Bardell's

blustering and

unpleasant lawyer in

The Pickwick Papers*).*

Expropriated by

Georgina in 1884.

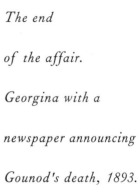

The end

of the affair.

Georgina with a

newspaper announcing

Gounod's death, 1893.

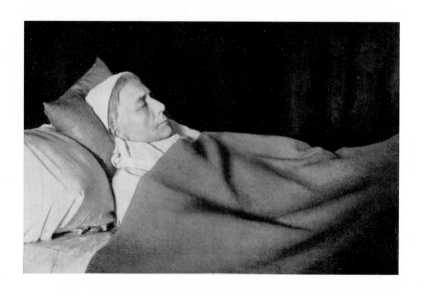

The "deathbed" photograph of 1913.

less and less frequently. Soon there was nothing left but the office stationery. Anarcharsis's brother Auguste did not conceal from him his opinion that Anarcharsis had married an idiot. Things were getting black. Then something wonderful happened. In August 1876 the Meniers received a letter from Georgina asking Angele to come to London and live with her there. She would pay her keep by helping in the orphanage.

Angele jumped at the chance, bringing Bichette with her. Once again the house resounded to cries and alarms in French, for Angele, though she was willing enough and dutiful as much as she knew how to be, found it hard to follow the ways of the orphanage. What struck Georgina as normal upbringing for children scandalized her. The plump and unhappy Bichette sat in the middle of all the chaos, dressed like a doll, unable to understand a word of what was going on. It was just as well. Georgina detested her and said so. Angele was mortified. Maybe she had made a terrible mistake. However, one could not live with Georgina long before one's hold on ordinary reality began to slacken. Like Harry and Gounod before her, Angele felt herself seduced and then overwhelmed by the sheer animal exuberance of her employer.

Slowly, inevitably, the two women fell into a pattern relationship. Georgina cut her hair short and became the dominant force, Angele assuming the role of the blonde with bewildered but bewitching eyes. After a while, she began to ape Georgina's style of dress. The two women dressed in black, their clothes cut with almost military severity. For walking out, they wore coats with coachman capes faced in dark silk. The relationship gradually deepened. They began calling each other Minette and Noireaud (Blackie) interchangeably. In speaking French Georgina habitually used the familiar form to her new assistant and in writing notes to her, and speaking of herself, adopted the masculine gender. They shared the same bed.

In February 1877 Menier came to England for a few weeks and discovered much had been going on in his absence. The first morning of his stay he was startled to see Georgina walk from room to room naked. It was also very marked that when he demanded to sleep with his wife in a bed appropriate to his needs, it threw his hostess into a rage. He later embellished this by claiming that he was several times forced to repel her own advances, a

charge Georgina hotly denied. The children scurried about, their feet blue
with cold, their misery a sorry contrast to the pampered Bichette on whom
Angele lavished her love. Meanwhile, the plaster was beginning to fall from
several of the ceilings, the taps leaked, the garden was overgrown, the main-
tenance that might normally have fallen to the direction or overseeing of a
butler or manservant was neglected. There were no fewer than twelve pianos in the house, and one by one they fell out of tune. It did not help that
the Duke of Bedford's other properties on that side of Tavistock Square
were equally run-down. Perhaps only now did Menier begin to consider his
wife's lover—for what else had she become?—a bird ready for plucking.
The swindler in him sensed there was urgency in the matter.

He was right. Since leaving Tavistock House, Harry had made no effort
to keep in touch with Georgina. He was hardening his heart for a dreadful
and irreversible course of action. On March 19 he wrote to a devastated
Louisa Treherne in Sparken:

> About three weeks ago I received a visit from Major General
> Sir Henry de Bathe: he had been to see Georgina at her urgent re-
> quest. He told me he regarded it as the duty of a friend, given his
> friendship for her and for me, after what he had seen on this occa-
> sion and heard from her own lips, to make her visit one or two spe-
> cialists of the first rank, like Munro or Forbes Winslow: for the
> impossible schemes she poured out to him; the filthy state of the
> house; the childish running of it absolutely convinced him that in
> her own interest, mine, that of her family, as much as that of the
> poor things she is trying to look after, at the very least a responsible
> opinion might be given to the state of her mind. Before deciding
> what to do, I would like if possible to have your consent and that of
> Dal, to whom I would have written had I known where to find him.

Calling Henry de Bathe to the house was an extremely reckless thing for
Georgina to have done. He was another Garrick Club crony of Harry's, a
Dubliner of ancient family reckoned by his generation one of the most good-
looking men in England. De Bathe had fought in the Crimea, was said to

maintain three separate households, and had quite recently married a seventeen-year-old girl, younger than his own daughters. No house in London would receive him, according to Harry, and Georgina had been pressed to do so when they first came to Tavistock Square. For this she had the general and his lady's warmest thanks.

Whatever "urgent request" called him to the house on this occasion, it was a peculiarly ill advised cry for help. De Bathe, though he was styled a major general and had recently inherited his father's title, was no longer on the army active list. Though he did not disclose this to Georgina and she seems to have been sublimely unaware of the fact, he was the new governor of St. Luke's Asylum. It was this that gave him the license to suggest signs of mental instability in Georgina. Whatever was said between the handsome Irishman and his formerly helpful hostess, he did not stay above half an hour. Harry's explanation of events—that he had "received a visit" from this concerned family friend—was a way of couching things in a suitable fashion for Louisa. She did not know that the two men and Freddie Warre were almost daily drinking companions. By asking de Bathe to the house, probably to complain about Menier's behavior, Georgina had unwittingly dug a trap for herself and fallen into it.

De Bathe was not an especially intelligent man, but neither was he wicked. The thing likely to have shocked him as much as anything else was the presence of the Meniers, people with no clearly defined role yet apparently on terms of extreme intimacy with Georgina. (Quite recently, Anarcharsis Menier had sold two enormous wardrobes to Georgina for £40, without mentioning he had a day or so earlier stolen them from a house in the Minories, where he kept an office.) The house was filthy and in poor repair, and Georgina talked to her friend de Bathe in an odd, torrential way that genuinely alarmed him, but he must also have mentioned to Harry the shady French couple as people likely to do Georgina financial harm.

The sensible thing to have happened was for Harry to have roused himself and gone to Tavistock House to see for himself. That he did not do so is an indication of his general way of avoiding a crisis by ignoring its existence. However, this time there was more to it. De Bathe had given him the opportunity he needed to start lunacy proceedings. He needed the support

of Georgina's family if he was to rid himself of his wife by these means.
Louisa Treherne replied to Harry a week later:

> Your letter coming like a clap of thunder—though not entirely
> unexpected—has grievously surprised me. I've sent it to Dal, who
> will have it in four days more or less, perhaps three. Dr. Blandford
> would be an excellent man to consult but it seems to me this would be
> premature. I hope very much you will not do anything precipitately. I
> feel really too unhappy. I had prayed to God to let me die before this
> terrible thing came to pass. You have precipitated this sad event by
> leaving your house at her behest.

The presence of Anarcharsis Menier and his wife at Tavistock House
had certainly not helped matters. Georgina, though she did not know it, was
dealing with crooks. Menier was a professional trickster and fraud, a type she
had never before met. Servants might turn out to be dishonest, in which case
they were dismissed. They stole wine or inflated grocery bills. They gave
money that was not theirs to canoodling soldiers or men they met in the
park. Combs and brooches might sometimes go missing or laundry come
back an item short. These crimes were more often than not impulsive and
amateur—a good cook or a trustworthy butler was expected to police the
household and keep some sort of order as part of the terms of his or her own
employment. Many times in the past Georgina and Harry had left the house
in Tavistock Square in charge of their servants for weeks and sometimes
months at a time, without trouble. Only a fool of a servant would mistake
Georgina's torrential lifestyle for weakness. Nobody knew better than she
how to make lists and keep accounts. The house might be unkempt and the
mistress of it eccentric by the neighbors' standards, but there was always
enough of the grande dame about Georgina to command respect from her
women servants, and in little things she was pernickety to a fault.

Menier was a very different kettle of fish. Who he was, what he wanted,
was hidden behind layers of imperturbability. He was deep. It pleased
Georgina to deride him, and she too readily assumed that Angele hated him.
When she caught him in minor acts of theft, she treated him like the grubby

little opportunist that he was. She had never met anyone whose mind-set was wholly criminal, and she underestimated him. His plan was to make both himself and Angele indispensable to Georgina, and despite the almost daily volcanoes of indignation and outrage, this is what happened. In fact, the storming arguments helped. In a grotesque parody of the Gounod years, she was tricked into believing that she was in charge of her life, simply by exercising the force of what always seemed to her a superior personality. She had taught Gounod how to paint. Now she would teach Menier how to behave.

This attempt at education and everything else she set her hand to at Tavistock House were costing Harry dearly. She never asked whether he could afford to keep her in this fashion, or for how long he could continue. Annie Lowe was discovering his natural indolence just as Georgina had done before her. He made no move to shift her from her Windsor houseboat, although she was clever enough or grateful enough not to ask for it. She may have noticed something unusual about him that had escaped Georgina. Harry was one of those rare Victorians who showed no interest in property or furniture. For a man who had lived in such a famous house he showed a decidedly un-Dickensian lack of enthusiasm for the Tom Tiddler's ground of a quiet study or a well-designed conservatory. He was in temperament an almost perfect bachelor and held a single man's view of material possessions.

Nevertheless, the present arrangements had begun to cause him concern. Quite as disturbing as de Bathe's report of his wife's state of mind, which he already knew of as well as anyone, was the condition of the house he had left her in. The lease had been drawn up under the old Duke of Bedford, but the eighth Duke, who inherited the title in 1872, was showing a much more active interest in his properties, and his London agents had begun to look askance at the uses to which Tavistock House was being put. Harry knew very well that an orphanage of fifty children was a fantasy and would never reach fruition. He could not be sure that under the existing terms the new Duke would tolerate even ten children, all of them unrecorded by age or birth. Nor did it do His Grace's reputation good to have one of his properties advertised up and down Oxford Street on the side of a converted milk float. Harry was being edged ever nearer to a decision. The Georgina problem was—by his own lackadaisical arrangements and failure to keep an eye on things—also the Tavistock House problem. Something had to be done.

Now that the word "madness" had been spoken, they were all of them on a road that had no turning. When Harry mentioned the doctors Munro and Forbes Winslow, and Louisa countered with the pitiful suggestion of George Fielding Blandford, they were not talking of medical men who might help or cure Georgina. They were talking—and they both knew it— of three men who made a business from consigning their patients to private asylums. They were in the language of the day mad doctors. Blandford owned an asylum in Long Ditton, and Forbes Winslow was the proprietor of Brandenburg House in Hammersmith. However sympathetic to mental illness they might be personally, their business was grim and unforgiving. People who went into madhouses seldom if ever came out. Incarceration was itself the cure. Broadly speaking, you went into a madhouse to learn to behave yourself, live there quietly, and die. Louisa's hesitation—"I hope very much you will not do anything precipitately"—was an acknowledgment of the irreversible nature of any decision they might take. Practically, nothing could be simpler than to commit someone to an asylum. All the application required was the signature of two doctors.

Anarcharchis Menier had come back to England with a brand-new moneymaking idea. As a veteran of the Siege of Paris he was well placed to observe the worldwide interest shown in the balloon ascents from the beleaguered city. The most famous of these had been that of Léon-Michel Gambetta, on his way to organize resistance from outside the capital. Setting off from the Butte de Montmartre in light airs, and trailing a massive pennant declaring *Vive la République!*, Gambetta had twice nearly fallen into Prussian hands. Though he had gone aloft with the intention of reaching Tours, he had landed near Amiens, a generous 180-degree error of navigation. Narrowly avoiding death after crashlanding in the canopy of a wood, his hand grazed by a Prussian bullet, he had staggered away from the most famous balloon escape of them all. By such slender threads had hung the Third Republic!

Anarcharchis Menier had pondered this and come up with the solution—the self-steering balloon. And the business had progressed beyond an idea. He went back to Paris to fetch the prototype, which was subsequently stored in the front garden of Tavistock House while he tried a sales pitch on the Woolwich Arsenal. No matter that he knew as little about ballooning as he did about small Pacific Islands or the Sahel: all that was required was that the British Army run trials. He would soon be rich beyond his dreams.

That summer, the Duke of Bedford's agents asked Harry what a balloon was doing in the front garden, something for which he did not have a ready answer. It was Georgina's idea to design a sash around the belly reading "Mrs. Weldon's Orphanage," which was actually fitted, and mystified the army on the few field trials they made. Things were going from bad to worse. De Bathe, the gallant veteran of the 89th Regiment, did not fail to add this to the list of dangerous improprieties he had discovered. But Georgina now capped all. At this moment of greatest danger to herself, she asked Menier to take charge of all her affairs and act as her agent and steward, sending him off to the bank, whence he returned, incredulous, with eight £50 notes. Without the slightest effort on his part, he had been given the power over her that he had been plotting all along to acquire. Some of this was sheer stupidity on her part, but there may have been an unconscious vanity in it too.

Georgina knew by bitter experience that it was a man's world. Harry's complaisance, his lack of expostulation, and, since her return, his stony silence would have sent warning signals to any other Victorian woman. In an age where women had very few property rights, the freedom he had offered her by turning over Tavistock House was an illusion. What he gave he could as easily take back. However, she had been used to men giving way before her, and this she supposed Harry had done. Asking Menier to take control of her finances was a thoroughly idiotic thing to do, but she supposed, at some deep level, that he, too, was hers to do with as she liked. To get, you had to give. She did not want Menier physically, but she did desire his obedience (and complicity in what was going on between her and his wife). Unaware of the difference between a fool and a crook, she gave him too much.

It was a disastrous summer for anyone wishing to protest one's sanity. One afternoon a strange face appeared at the ground-floor window. Standing in the garden were a young man named Richard Waddy, his wife, and

their two young children. They wished to know, as so many did who came
to the house, whether this was the place where Dickens had once lived. Conversation took place through the open window. Waddy was the son of
Samuel Danks Waddy, M.P., Q.C., a man of irreproachable rectitude.
Richard was, it very quickly became clear, mildly deranged. He introduced
himself to Georgina as Cadwalladwr, Prince of Wales, "someone with as
much if not greater claim to the title than the present Prince." Mrs. Waddy,
who was heavily pregnant with her third child, watched and listened helplessly. While Georgina humored him, he went on to say that she, too, from
her ancestry and evident beauty, was very worthy to be his Princess. She
laughingly told him she was old enough to be his mother. After more of the
same, she closed the window on him, and the little family trooped off
through the shrubbery. Watching with keen interest from the shadows of the
room was Anarcharsis Menier.

The next afternoon Waddy called at the house alone, and a startled
Georgina told Villiers to say she was not at home. He came again in the
evening, leaving a white rose and a red one bound together in a ribbon. Soon
an avalanche of letters began to descend on the house. In spite of herself, she
warmed to him. This was the sort of thing Georgina considered herself
good at: Waddy was someone she could control. The message in the correspondence that rained down on Tavistock House almost daily was simple
enough. Georgina was the woman of the Welshman's dreams. He was in
love with her the way Dante loved Beatrice and Tristan Iseult. They were
destined for each other. He conceived the plan of running away to India,
where he would make Georgina Queen of the Orient.

The last letter from England was written in Liverpool on the eve of embarkation. Georgina should come to him, bringing with her £100 for the
one-way ticket and the necessaries of the voyage. Unable to budge her, he
set off alone, writing from every port of call along the way. Mrs. Waddy retreated to her parents in Plymouth, from where she sent piteous letters to
Tavistock House. With the peculiar cruelty of which she was capable,
Georgina made a most horrible reply: "I understood at last he was a poor
madman. I gathered together all the letters he had sent me and which lurked

in every corner; I made a little packet of them and sent them to his poor little wife . . . telling her his letters would help her rid herself of her husband."

The runaway, who had never worked in his life, pitched up eventually in Madras. He had scouted out a French hotel that might suit the Queen of the Orient from the point of view of cuisine, though he strongly recommended they move up into the backcountry, where the weather was cooler and the scenery might remind her of Camarthen. He dwindled: his voice grew fainter. In the last of the letters he wrote to her, he had been turned out of European society and was living on the beach without shoes and in the rags of his London clothes.

Whatever might have happened between them, Georgina showed him no mercy now. Waddy was clearly mad. Pity was wasted on him. Even the smallest sympathy was misplaced. To be mad was to be incomplete, and what happened to him from now on was inalterable. It was true she had flirted with him, or given the appearance of encouraging him, though it is very unlikely their relationship was physical in any way.

In the *Mémoires* she deals with him magisterially: "I have published the letters of this poor 'Cadwalladwr' as well as those of Mrs. Waddy as a way of giving the reader an idea of the difficulty my poor dear husband must have faced in finding an excuse to have *me* locked up as a madwoman." However, in a letter to her mother in 1881 she mentions Harry's other purpose, which was to cite Richard Waddy as her lover in the divorce action he was bringing. The story has been suitably abbreviated: "By this post you will receive the tale of one of my lovers, Cadwalladwr Waddy. Have you ever read anything more absurd? This is a man to whom I spoke *literally* once and once only through a window, in the presence of his wife and children and others who could, if the need arose, witness the truth of what I'm saying." The others she mentions were Menier and Angele, by whom the episode was remembered very differently.

Cunning and manipulative, for the Meniers every single thing that Georgina said and did was a source of potential blackmail. Angele understood, no less than her husband, that the real purpose of friendship was to discover and exploit weakness in others. She might look demure and flatter

Georgina with her adoring glances, but she was playing a different game. As for Menier, he grasped that things could not go on in this rackety way much longer. Harry was closing in. What cards the Frenchman had in his hand he must play skillfully. It was true that Georgina quarreled with him daily and derided him to his wife, but this he bore with equanimity. He could sense Georgina's restlessness: her situation was worsening, and nothing new was coming into the house to spark her explosive energies. As the summer sunlight gave way to lamps and fires, and the gutters overflowed and plaster broke off from the walls, she found goading Anarcharsis just too easy. He was common, vulgar, ugly. He had no culture, no ideas. She failed to realize that what he did have were the keys to the house.

In October 1877, at exactly the right moment, Angele came up with what Georgina called "a luminous idea." Angele's sister Marie Helluy managed an old people's home in a small village called Argeuil, a few kilometers to the west of that country where Flaubert had set *Madame Bovary*. It was in rolling landscape dominated by the Epté Valley and could be reached from Paris via Forges-les-Eaux, which was on the main line to Le Havre. The proposal was to take all ten children and Bichette to Argeuil, where Marie and her companion, Victoria Claisse, could run the orphanage, while Georgina and Angele went to live in Paris. There they would train orphan Katie—who was three—to accompany Georgina in her quest for an international singing career.

Georgina jumped at the idea with her usual enthusiasm. Anarcharsis Menier, for whom this sort of thing was his bread and butter, drew up a prospectus in which his sister-in-law was nominated matron and Georgina director. The names of the superintending doctors were left blank, but the whole thing was handsomely printed as from the offices of *La Liberté Coloniale*. On paper it looked well. Georgina insisted that Menier, who was still trying to sell his balloon, should stay in London. The two women—soon to be four women—did not want him near them, not now or ever. He pretended to take his dismissal with suitable amounts of hurt and disappointment. His role, he supposed, with a resigned shake of his head, was to continue to handle the money and keep an eye on Tavistock House. Yes! Georgina replied triumphantly. What else was he fit for?

Once an idea had been put into her head, Georgina always acted on it with the greatest speed. Now nothing else would do but that they transfer the children to Argeuil, a place she had never visited, to the care of a woman she had never met. It had to be done now, immediately: passports for the children had to be obtained, travel arrangements made, letters exchanged between France and England. Maps were consulted and timetables checked.

A few further refinements crept in. She and Angele would live together in Paris without servants, the better to save money. Menier suavely recommended the Montmartre district as being suitable to their needs. Angele agreed to live with Georgina and act as a housewife while the singer went out to conquer all Paris with her voice, but she put her foot down about one thing: Bichette must come with them. Georgina had become accustomed to Angele's maddening irresolution on the subject of this miserable human shuttlecock. The Frenchwoman's capacity always to see herself as a victim made her a bad guardian of others. She loved Bichette when she was good, but the slightest upset or reverse in her relationship with the child sent her into frenzies of self-hatred.

This notion of woman as victim was almost completely foreign to Georgina. Women were wronged, but when they were, it was their duty to set things right. Retaliation was much better than recrimination. Angele may have been driven into prostitution, but she wasn't walking the streets now and would never need to again. If there were wrongs left in her life, she should kick someone's shins. All the vaporing about Bichette was annoying. Angele should do as she did and come to a decision. While they squabbled, trunks were packed and piled up in the hall. The children were warned against being sick, either in the train or on the boat.

Menier kept up the pretense of being aggrieved at the prospect of being left behind. It cost him nothing to be scorned, for as soon as the orphanage decamped, he had the run of a large house with a cook and three servants to look after him. At the last moment, Georgina had a rush of common sense. She entrusted her set of keys to a young couple named Lowther, with an invitation to live in the house rent free in exchange for looking after it. The Lowthers were only too happy to accept, and much might have been avoided if they had taken up residence. They turned up on the day of Georgina's departure in good time to wave off the cabs bearing the orphans to Charing Cross. Then they went inside to explore the huge and suddenly silent house. To their surprise nothing had been packed away—the pictures still hung on the walls and china was displayed in every room. With characteristic feck-lessness, Georgina had hardly bothered to put aside her personal jewelry.

The boat train had not left London before there was the sound of a key in the lock. The Lowthers went into the hall to discover who had access to the property in this way, expecting to find Harry. Instead they were greeted by Menier, whom they had never met, brandishing a piece of paper that he said was an agreement between himself and Georgina that made him her sole agent. The unfortunate Lowthers protested they had given up good lodgings to take up their new caretaking duties here. Menier waggled the paper under their noses, and they were thrown out even before they had un-packed.

Argeuil and Paris

rgeuil is a surprise. It is a handsome lopsided village on the road south from Forges. On the left is a handsome *manoir* and to the right the church, the *mairie*, and a little terraced hotel called Le Lion d'Or. What makes it so pleasant is a large sandy square, surrounded on three sides by tall farm buildings and two- and three-story bourgeois residences, some of them eighteenth-century. It was in one of these that Marie Helluy had her failing business, now to become the Weldon Orphanage. The village is light and airy, partly as a consequence of the church grounds having been absorbed at the very end of the nineteenth century. The cemetery, which had straggled into the main square in front of the church, was moved up to a knob of land three hundred meters away. The view from there is of rich pasture, though the Fôret de Lyons is just over the horizon, extending southward toward Rouen and the Seine. Argeuil is by no means *la France profonde*. The church is small and unimpressive, the hotel cramped and ancient, but by the standards of many another commune in neighboring *départements*, Argeuil is now and must have been then a sturdy and well-heeled place.

Angele had the gift of saying and doing what she thought people wanted to hear. During the London months she had begun to speak about the orphanage in the same high-flown way as Georgina herself, with more emphasis on the power of music in the upbringing of young children than the usefulness to them of soap or three hot meals a day. Her sister Marie Helluy was a shock to Georgina. Tall, skinny, and bad-tempered, she was distressingly down-to-earth and practical. She swore like a trooper, cooked uninspiringly, and often had to be rousted from her bed in the morning, which she shared with her friend and lover, the younger and more moody Victoria Claisse. The curé and the other communal dignitaries had never had much time for Marie Helluy and her ill-managed nursing home, but were utterly astounded to see its transformation now. Lallygagging about the streets and besieging the bakery for their morning bread, a handful of Protestant English children broke the peace and calm of Argeuil, none of them clear as to where they were or what they were doing there.

They were children unlike any seen before in the village. Their experience was bounded by Tottenham Court Road as far as Oxford Street. They had seen trees before and in those trees rooks and pigeons, squirrels, even. What they had not seen was a hundred head of cattle being driven down to milking or the utter dark of countryside after sunset. Having lived communally in Tavistock House, they had an elastic sense of property. Georgina had taught them to walk with their arms swinging, and now they marched about like ungainly marionettes, bellowing at each other, shouting and thieving. Argeuil folk quickly learned to despise them. There was a small community of Carmelite nuns next door to the hotel, to whom matters of charity were normally entrusted, and the villagers had—like all French men and women—a keen sense of propriety. *C'était pas propre, cette galère.* They were also highly suspicious of the voluble directrice whose principal point of interest in the life of the community was the post office, to which she repaired daily. A rumor grew that this was a man dressed as a woman, probably someone from Paris. To be from Paris was the ultimate opprobrium.

It might have been different if the orphanage had descended on Argeuil at another season of the year, when the days were longer. But they came when the village was battened down for the winter and women in particular hardly left the house. If they did, it was to buy vegetables they had not grown themselves or to walk to church. It was startling to see, looming out of the rain, children with a London pallor, dressed in oddments and shouting in jagged and ugly English. The more bourgeois families kept an aloof silence. Their farmhands were puzzled. To all of them, it was completely inexplicable why anyone should want to bring an orphanage to their doors. Used to charity as an outward expression of religious devotion, it troubled them that this establishment had no connection with the church. For women used to obeying their men, as well as working alongside them in the fields, it was equally shocking that the children were in the charge of four women, with no man to make the ultimate decisions. How could that possibly turn out for the good? If Angele and Georgina were married, as they said they were, then where were their husbands?

At first, Georgina found Marie Helluy's strength and acerbity refreshing. There was certainly nothing namby-pamby about her. She slogged her way through the day, cooking and cleaning, bellowing warnings at the startled orphans, wagging a spoon in their faces. With no children of her own, and little English, she nevertheless soon let it be known who was boss. At night she had the habit of playing cards and smoking, a bottle at her elbow. The table talk was uninspired. Marie and Victoria had never heard of Gounod and made it clear they did not give a fig for music, art, or anything else. Their preferred topic was money. Like their neighbors, their day was made up of work, hard physical work that in London had been undertaken by the Westmacotts and Tibby Jordan. Here, there was no mistress and servants—the four women mucked in together, Georgina proving the least resourceful, Angele the most accident prone. The children were smacked and beaten and threatened. On occasion they were ceremonially thrashed. They fared badly at meals. A village rumor was that Helluy bought horse oats for a household that had no horse, with the implication that the children lived on them. All of them—and all the women—were infested with lice. There was never enough hot water and no plumbed bath. At night, with nothing to do but drink and smoke, the stories began to come out.

Angele's background was soon laid completely bare. She had been seduced by a married man in Soissons when she was sixteen, by whom she had a stillborn child. This man made her a small allowance and gave her some sticks of furniture. Anarcharsis had not taken her off the streets and made an honest woman of her overnight: he had pimped her for seven years before he married her. It was in vain for Angele to protest that she had danced at the Folies Marigny under the name of Mlle Lucienne: Marie knew it all.

Georgina disclosed some of her own adventures. She told them how the elderly and utterly respectable surgeon Sir Henry Thompson had come to her in the guise of "the Moth," helplessly attracted to her flame, and how letters signed by the Moth had been discovered by Harry, who threatened to use them against him. He had also found the Moth and the Flame in the bedroom of a house they rented from time to time in London before Tavistock came along. This was greeted by ribald laughter. But her most reckless confession was one that, if true, throws new light on the Florence years. She claimed she had been abused as a child by Antonio, Morgan's butler. She told this story perhaps to impress, perhaps because there were few topics of conversation other than sex. For the other three women it was a scandal, yet a familiar and unexceptional one. For us it leaps out of the story like a tongue of fire. This was a family secret with a vengeance. At some point in her childhood, Georgina had virtually the power of life and death over a grown man, for had she told her father of what had passed, surely Morgan would have given his butler up to the authorities. An even darker possibility is that he was told and did nothing.

When the fire was banked and the lantern turned out, these four women would go to two double beds, to whisper in the dark and all but Georgina to plot. Marie had already formed an opinion of her employer as far as the orphans went: "For her they are marionettes to show off and if their health suffers, it's nothing but a detail. What do you say to what she told me: that since grown ups enjoy playing around with each other, she could not see why one stopped children doing the same thing?" Marie's solution to these sexual explorations was a version of the straitjacket in which the hands of the children were separated one from another in canvas cuffs held apart by a rigid bar.

The children's general health was poor. Nobody came to the house, and no doctor had been appointed to be the medical supervisor of the orphanage, any more than there had been one in London. The ten orphans were underfed and disoriented. While the older ones experimented with sex, the young ones incurred Georgina's wrath in particular for failing to get up in the night to totter to the lavatory. There were huge rows about this, and dire punishments were meted out—the most incontinent children were shut in cupboards for their shortcomings. The gossip came back from the outraged commune that what was going on here was not a charitable work, but some sort of secret cult. Otherwise, why would the unhappy orphans bear such ridiculous names—Sapho, Baucis, Dagobert, Mireille, and Merthyr?

After only eight days, Marie tested her new employer's willingness to be parted from her money. In her capacity as a trained nurse she tried to persuade Georgina that Angele was tubercular and the only possible solution for her was to go to Bordeaux. Georgina was startled. Angele had always seemed to her to have disgustingly good health. Bloody handkerchiefs were produced. Angele skulked behind doors and refused to answer straight questions. Marie chided Georgina for her heartlessness and brushed away her objections. It came down to a matter of generosity. Who was going to pay to save Angele? If money could improve her lot, who would be so heartless as to refuse it? She pressed on Georgina the urgent need for the patient to go to Paris at the very least and there have a thorough chest examination. Maybe, if things were as bad as they looked, Angele would have to go away into the country and languish there. But, Georgina asked, were they not already in the country? They were, but it was the wrong kind of air. Bordeaux was the only possible place, the choice of which bewildered Georgina, though it was probably the most distant city Marie could come up with on the spur of the moment. Questioned further, Angele was evasive and shamefaced.

Georgina took herself off to Gournay, a few kilometers farther south, to complete her translation of Gounod's *Jean Dacier* libretto and ponder what to do. Gournay, she found immediately, was more to her taste. She put up at the Hôtel du Cygne and found the proprietor, M. Bournisien, very sympathetic. She even discussed with him the idea of bringing some of the orphans there, and in this she was undoubtedly influenced by the comforts on offer. The little town had paved streets and real shops. Its broad square was lit by the windows of cafés, and, though she was a celebrity of a kind, there was none of the impudent curiosity of village life. Nor were there any of the chores associated with the orphanage: it was pleasant to have servants again and a decent table d'hôte. She sent Angele the menu.

As Marie Helluy was discovering, Georgina was easily hooked, but an extremely difficult fish to land. She came back to Argeuil with this plan: she and Angele—and the odious Bichette—would go to Paris together forthwith. Even a few weeks in Gournay had convinced her that her best contribution to the success of the orphanage was to shine on a large and well-lit stage. She would go to Paris with a new name—Valerie de Lotz, international soprano—and put the rest of her ambitions on hold. Angele would go as her companion and servant, or not at all. All talk of doctors was scotched, and there was to be no more mention of Bordeaux. Enough money was set aside to keep the orphanage in its present unsatisfactory premises, but once in Paris, when singing engagements began to pour in, she would settle them all in happier circumstances. Marie and Victoria accepted this plan with gloomy resignation: they had been outflanked and were stuck with the children. In early December Angele and Georgina set off with Bichette by farm cart to Forges, where they caught the train to Paris.

They came as fairly respectable-looking women, but without money. The Paris of the boulevards was out of the question, although Georgina did suggest they stay to begin with at the Grand Hôtel, an establishment of the highest rank, beloved of English tourists and right next door to the Opéra. Angele—cunning Angele!—led her instead to the Café Rocher in Pigalle. After a while a man sidled up to them. Were they by chance looking for somewhere clean and respectable to stay, in which case he could recommend the Hôtel d'Alexandrie in the rue Lafitte? He could, if they wished, take them there now. The proprietor of the Hôtel d'Alexandrie was a man named Marx, and it turned out that their young guide was his son-in-law. Marx, act-

ing out of apparent disinterest, soon introduced them to an elderly couple
named Mayer, very sympathetic to their situation and lovers of music and
the arts. Georgina was delighted. It only sank in later that all these people
were already known to Angele—they were all part of the Menier gang. In
fact, Mme Mayer was Bichette's godmother. The offices of *La Liberté Coloniale* were around the corner from the hotel.

There was a larger Paris, and she made some acquaintances on her own
account. She met and entranced an old roué, Edward O'Sullivan, former
U.S. ambassador to Portugal, whose mistress was a society medium by the
name of Mme Rohart. It was perhaps through this last contact that she ran
across the mystically minded Edward Maitland again, the man who advised
her to find the woman in herself and discard the boy when she was twenty.
He had come to Paris to be with the extremely beautiful Anna Kingsford,
wife of the vicar of Atcham in Shropshire, but far too clever for him. Mrs.
Kingsford was training to qualify as a doctor, a profession not open to
women in Britain yet. Both Maitland and Anna Kingsford were interested in
esoteric religion, a subject, happily, Georgina did not attempt.

There were other distractions, slightly less lofty than the company of
Edward Maitland. On one occasion Georgina was taken to a store and had
an oriental shawl bought for her by the agent of an Indian prince. On another it was a rich Egyptian pasha who declared himself overwhelmed by
her charms. This was all more familiar and agreeable social territory for
Georgina. She describes carting Angele around to these and her other new
friends. One night she took her to a reception at the impresario Charles
Salazar's house. He was the man she had engaged to promote her concerts.
"All there were shocked; it made no sense that a wellbred woman allowed
herself to be accompanied by a creature who had absolutely nothing to recommend her ... Poor Menier was penniless and ugly and myself, I attributed this furious reaction against her to prejudice." She met the great
tragedienne Sarah Bernhardt, who did not impress her, and took her favorite
orphan, Sapho-Katie, to tea with a dyspeptic and bored Victor Hugo, an old
and wandery man in his seventies who said nothing of any interest but
seemed not to share her opinion of the child, even though she was made to
recite a few lines of the master's oeuvre.

At the back of all this socializing was, of course, the Gounod question: did he know she was in Paris, and if he did, what was he going to do about it? At one of Mme Rohart's séances the shade of Gounod's mother, Victoire, spoke to her. Georgina's main interest in the spirits of the dead was to have their opinion of the living. The life to come was far too distant to interest her: what she appealed to in the spirit world was a sort of High Court ruling on the world below. Madame Gounod did not let her down. The view she held of her boy Charles was much the same as Hannah Weldon's opinion of *her* son, which was a proof of the Other Side's perspicacity. Mère Victoire gave a warm endorsement of Georgina's plans: "Unite and work, and you will accomplish the devoted mission that the Almighty blesses; and the dead souls of all those young beings will follow you and bless you in their turn. Hope! In six weeks, not a day more or less, you will accomplish your mission." This was held by all present to indicate New Year's Day of 1878.

Meanwhile, Gounod himself was hiding behind his lawyers and being obstructive and unforgiving. He refused to release copyright in his own works for a concert that Salazar had arranged for Valerie de Lotz. *L'Evénement* carried the announcement that the concert had been canceled "by a superior order"—that is, suppressed. Salazar failed to advise those who had already bought tickets and refused refunds to those who complained. Georgina hardly noticed. The bitter blow for her was to realize that Gounod, at whatever distance, could still be mean and vindictive in this way.

Five days after the cancellation of the concert, Angele went out to do the morning's shopping. They had moved from the Hôtel d'Alexandrie to unfurnished rooms in the rue de Luxembourg, and as she set off, Angele was approached by a man right outside the door. He was well dressed with a ribbon decoration in his buttonhole. He asked her if she was Georgina Weldon. Angele said no, she is up there on the entresol. You have only to knock and she will answer. "Ah," the mystery man said, changing tack, "you must be Madame Menier and it's *you* I really want to talk to." He suggested they walk together a little, and Angele agreed.

"After a few idle remarks he asked me if I had it in mind to return to England," she explained to Georgina. "I replied that I couldn't leave you. 'Oh, you could very easily leave her for a few days, couldn't you?' "

Angele was terrified, the more so when the mystery man outlined a proposition to her. They would go to a bank, and for any sum she named, they would leave at once for England. She immediately thought of Menier, supposing the scheme "some unhealthy idea of his." She agreed in principle, saying only that she must tell Georgina and—an appealing touch—prepare lunch for her. Ah no, he said, that was the sole condition. They must leave for England now, this instant. Shouting that he gravely mistook the person with whom he was dealing, she turned on her heel and fled, followed down the street by an elaborate and ironic salute as the man lifted his hat and made a sweeping bow after her.

When she heard this, only moments after it happened, Georgina collapsed in a chair. Her reaction was very significant.

"Don't you see? It was a terrible ambush . . . They would have got you away from me, then come to tell me there had been an accident, that you were in hospital and calling for me. I would have left without suspecting anything, and ended up in Blanche's asylum!"

This is the first clear indication that Georgina herself realized that others might think her mad. The séances she had attended suddenly took on a new and dangerous meaning. A belief in spiritualism was looked on more askance in England than in France and the rest of Europe, where the celebrated example of the Edinburgh-born Daniel Dunglas Home was held to be a baffling instance of supernatural powers. Home had recently followed the Prussian Army from Sedan to Versailles and been consulted by the Emperor of Prussia in the Hall of Mirrors. Home received an elaborate gift of jewels from him, just as he had done over the years from the Emperor of Russia and many others. It was considered an indication of Home's probity that the medium never asked for a fee. It was true that Robert Browning had tried to denounce him twenty years earlier (in the less romantic venue of a house in Ealing) as "Sludge the Medium," but that was only because Elizabeth Barrett Browning believed in him with such unsettling conviction.

Though many in England were as disgusted as Browning by table rapping and disembodied hands and spectral mist, an interest in spiritualism was not thought in itself a symptom of insanity. John Brown, the Queen's servant, was widely believed to act as her spiritualistic medium in the search for the dear departed Albert. If true, that might make Brown a scoundrel, but it could hardly be held to indicate the Queen was mad. Nevertheless, belief in spiritualism *was* very often thought a contributory factor to more marked delusions. It was, so to speak, a dangerous game to play. As for Georgina, she always believed her interests in spiritualism and phrenology were as rational as her enthusiastic embrace of vegetarianism or her support of anti-vivisection campaigns. As she saw it, it was ignorance and envy in others that led to accusations of insanity. People who dared to be different were forced into a form of internal exile.

She knew her sudden and peremptory decision to remove the orphanage to France might have been considered an irrational act. However, though she had left London in ostensible high spirits, her diary revealed another, more realistic mood: "I never felt so profoundly sad to leave my home—so uncertain, so upset and discouraged. It's the first time in my life that I've resolved to do something or taken a single step without attempting to foresee the outcome."

One of the reasons for leaving that weighed with her was the continual theft of small objects and sums of money at Tavistock House, for which Rosie Strube was blamed more often than not. Though the results of the move were so far disappointing, the wish to put the orphanage on a new footing was justification enough for uprooting everybody. Even so late as this, it did not occur to Georgina that it might be the Meniers and their Paris cronies, not the children, who were systematically robbing her. She was perplexed not to hear from the Lowthers but no more than usually suspicious of "the imbecile" and "cretin" Anarcharsis, as she styled him. When Angele rushed in to tell her of the stranger met in the street, Georgina had a ready and to her mind much more obvious explanation. Who else could the mystery man be other than an emissary of the Gounod clique, and what motive could he have had other than to remove Georgina Weldon from the Paris music scene by the surest route? This was a story about someone trying to blight her music career. It was not Menier who was doing her wrong but Gounod.

Her elderly American friend O'Sullivan was summoned to the house, and the advice he gave was highly practical. He recommended she apply to the police for protection. She promised she would think about that. On Christmas Eve, however, the hotel proprietor Marx came around to say that no less a dignitary than the *commissaire de police* had been to the Alexandrie to ask a few questions. Georgina's worst fears were realized. This *must* be Gounod's work. Like a good swindler, Marx picked up the cue immediately. According to him, the composer had indeed been to the police, complaining that "the Englishwoman" was without means and quite mad, and should be taken not to the clinic at Passy, but to the much more sinister public asylum of St.-Lazare. O'Sullivan was sent for again, and he pressed her strongly to go to the police and ask for an interview, which she did. The unfortunate Commissaire Brissart was made to listen to an hour and a half's harangue, at the end of which he ushered her from the office, promising to make Gounod leave her alone. But on New Year's Eve Marx was back. The police had been to the hotel a second time, making inquiries.

There are question marks hanging over all this. The only description of the stranger in the street came from Angele—neither Georgina nor the concierge saw him and he never returned. The police already knew something about the two strange women of the rue de Luxembourg, because earlier in December Georgina had hired a maid, a young girl named Emilie who turned out to be a runaway. At Christmastime her irate stepfather came to fetch her home. Nettled, Georgina accused him of wanting her back in order to debauch her, and he went straight to the gendarmerie. It does not therefore make sense that the police should inquire for her at the Hôtel d'Alexandrie when they already knew where she lived. While it is probable that Gounod would have been only too pleased to see the back of her, it was completely out of character for him to go in person to the Ninth Arrondissement to talk to Commissaire Brissart. When it came to accusations of mental derangement, Gounod was like a man standing in a glass house with a stone in his hand. Furthermore, apart from trying to steal copyright in his work (for which he had the Salazar concert suppressed), Georgina had done him no wrong.

There is certainly an element of conspiracy about all this in which the sly and shifty Marx played a part. Yet Marx was acting for others. The hub of any conspiracy must have been Angele herself. Their apparently friendly and supportive neighbor Prosper Mayer, whom Georgina had not known from Adam in October, and who had never visited Argeuil, felt himself perfectly able the following March to accuse her of murdering Freddie, one of the orphans. This had to have come from Angele. Desperate to be loved, hopelessly incompetent in all the little things, Angele was undoubtedly the real traitor, but also the only one of them who ever really respected Georgina. She loved her. "You, I *hate* you," she cried out once in exasperation. "You are so *good!*"

The word "clique" was one of Georgina's favorite borrowings from the French language. The term was only mildly pejorative when used by native speakers, but Georgina widened its meaning to indicate criminal conspiracy. If in this way the Menier clique was more dangerous to Georgina than Gounod and his supposed myrmidons, there was an immediate reason. On one of her social forays in Paris she had come across a Miss Leigh, who with her sister ran a refuge for fallen women. Miss Leigh had a property for sale in Neuilly which Georgina saw at once would suit very well as the final resting place of the orphanage. Overeager as always and long before the lease had been signed, Georgina began to lay down rules of behavior for Angele when they took up residence. She was to mend her ways and behave more circumspectly. They would no longer live as lovers, but as mistress and servant. The test of Angele staying would be her sobriety and circumspection—Georgina's beauty and talent could no longer be compromised by some Parisian lowlife.

An injured and apprehensive Angele told Marie Helluy of the planned purchase, and on January 9 she came from Argeuil to see the place for herself. (She, after all, was destined to do the donkey work.) Miss Leigh could perhaps stomach Angele, but Marie in a foul mood was something new to her experience. "The great beanpole rejected it with utter disdain," Georgina wrote, adding bitterly that Gounod's rich friends had in any case poisoned all Neuilly against her. The devoutly evangelical Miss Leigh consulted with her sister and then revoked the contract that had been drawn up.

Georgina had written to Menier in London a few times but had no answer. Now Angele received a letter from her husband which she scanned hastily and then threw into the fire. To someone of Georgina's way of thinking this was unimaginably stupid. Letters were to be saved and filed and, if necessary, used against their authors at some later date. She tried to find out what Anarcharsis had said to upset his wife so, but Angele refused to tell her. It was a very unwelcome reminder of Tavistock House nevertheless.

Georgina had written to her mother with a jocular account of the threat to have her committed to the St.-Lazare, and Louisa had replied in terror, begging her to come home. Georgina tut-tutted, saying she had a tongue in her head and was perfectly capable of outwitting the Paris police. But her resources were stretched to the utmost. Maybe she already knew she could not trust Angele—but on the other hand, she could not live without her. Meanwhile, she had made her mark in Paris in a demimondaine sort of way, but not as a singer. Bernhardt disappointed her; Hugo, for all his encouraging interest in spiritualism, was a bad-tempered old fool. The most interesting musician she met was someone named John Urich, who stubbornly refuses to rise from the biographical dictionaries of the period. Angele had the sulks. In Argeuil Marie Helluy was simmering like a boiling washpot, and in London Menier's grubby hands were beginning to meddle in some way she could not quite determine.

2

The catastrophe that had been quietly incubating for seven years now occurred. At the end of January there was an outbreak of measles in Argeuil that left the local children untouched but laid low the entire orphanage. On February 2 Marie ran through the rain to the post office and cabled Georgina: "Come at once. Mireille died at 7 this morning. Letter arrives tomorrow. See consul for birth certificate." A whole day passed before Angele replied to her sister, and that was only to say they would arrive on the fourth. Georgina scribbled a note to go by post, saying she would catch the train that left Paris at four in the afternoon.

Marie sent a second anguished telegram on the morning of the fourth: "Catch the 11 oclock train. Merthyr close to death. Dagobert very ill. We are desperate. Don't bring Katie. Measles. Epidemic. Reply." Marie Helluy was not the village's favorite citizen, and even though the children had been treated with cold contempt, only the stoniest heart could fail to be moved by the horrors of the house. Georgina's telegraph reply read, "Will arrive this evening alone. Angele ill. We are desperate. Above all anxious for you two."

By the time she finally arrived it was nine at night and there was hardly a light left in the village. Mireille's corpse—she was only fourteen months old and a particular favorite of all the women—lay in the house wrapped in a shroud. The curé had agreed to conduct a burial service the next day but insisted she be interred in unconsecrated ground, in the part of the cemetery reserved for suicides and victims of the guillotine. Marie and Victoria were almost too exhausted to speak. It would seem that no doctor had attended and no help had been given by the neighbors. There were comparatively rich and educated people who lived in Argeuil who might have helped, but they did nothing. The Carmelites stayed inside their gates. The surviving orphans lay in their dormitories much as if they would soon enough follow Mireille. It was a disaster.

Georgina knew then, if she ever knew, that she had failed these children utterly. Neither Marie nor Victoria ever forgave her for being so dilatory. Though the orphans were in their day-to-day care, the legal responsibility for them lay with Georgina, who had fetched them so blithely from London. The orphanage—all the lofty aspirations for a revolutionary music education founded on Mrs. Weldon's unique talents—now lay in the dark of a small French village mired in shit. The two Frenchwomen listened in horror as Georgina, in a blaze of hysterical rage that all the children could hear, blamed the incontinent and pigeon-chested Dagobert for the death of the beautiful and angelic Mireille, whose tiny body had not even been furnished with a coffin.

She was buried the next morning, a furious Georgina waving in the face of the curé copies of telegrams sent to the ambassador and consul in Le

Havre. She wasted the rest of the day ordering a piece of monumental statuary from Paris. (Today Mireille's grave and—if it ever arrived—the little pink marble angel Georgina commissioned have vanished. Touchingly, if Mireille is still there on the hill outside the village, she shares the ground with another solitary Briton. In the debacle of June 1940 a sergeant of the Black Watch was killed on the road to Argeuil and is buried in the cemetery's only Commonwealth war grave. Before the Germans left in 1944, they torched the *mairie* and destroyed the last official traces of the orphanage.)

Georgina's practical contributions to the measles crisis were negligible. She was prevented by Marie and Victoria from employing her sovereign cure for all things and plunging the children into cold baths: on the contrary, she was made to suffer while the two women heated the house at what she considered reckless expense. She wrote rambling letters to Paris, in one of which she asked Angele to send down a large kettle (*une bouilloire*). Angele wandered around Pigalle, confused and distraught, before buying and sending a hot-water bottle (*une bouillotte*).

In a fit of pique—and having spent ten francs on telegrams trying to place the unlucky Dagobert in a hospice or asylum—anything to get him from her sight—Georgina decamped once more to the comforts of the Hôtel du Cygne in Gournay. There she felt free to write to her mother that "the French are the vilest, most dishonest people in the world." Louisa had good reason to agree with this. She counseled her daughter to return to England immediately. She knew, although she did not disclose, what had already been set in train. She did mention for the first time that Harry had talked to de Bathe. "If I had the temperament or the willingness of flesh and spirit—or the means—I would do all in my power to get you out of there," she wrote. "But I am powerless! Good for nothing, incapable of what's needed. I can do nothing but despair and there is in my life enough to make me like that."

It was unhelpful, as was her opinion expressed in the same letter that Georgina was a great teacher and devoted to the welfare of children. Louisa believed in the fiction of the Gounod clique even more fervently than her daughter. Like the whole family, she believed what Morgan had taught her, that the world was comprised of dark and inimical forces and that the evil far outweighed the good. During his life Morgan had done her thinking for her, but he had been dead ten years. Louisa had since dwindled to the feckless, uncertain creature she had been when he married her. It was true she was elderly (though by no means frail) and lived out of London with Emily and her stodgy husband, Mr. Williams. But she might have done more. She knew very well that Harry was preparing the ground for lunacy proceedings, and she knew in full what that meant. For Georgina to come home, as she pleaded with her to do, would be to see her immediately taken up in a coach at Charing Cross and sent to a private asylum.

﹡ At Argeuil things were completely out of hand. Rosie had begun to terrorize the other children. She had been seen shaking Mireille the night before she died, she punched the boys black-and-blue, made Pauline drink her own urine, lied through her teeth to Marie and Victoria. Perhaps more clearly than Georgina, she could see the end coming. The house was filthy, the weather outside was vile. Rosie, like the others, was trapped. It was a fond boast of Georgina's that if you gave her a child, any child, she could in three months transform its character. She added, with unconscious irony, that if she broke the routine for more than a day or two, the child would revert to what it was. Rosie was the evidence. She had only to look at Marie and Victoria (who liked to be called Valentine) lolling in bed and drinking tea while the children howled in hunger to recognize the world from which she had come originally. She could be slapped, even whipped, but she had identified the weakness at the heart of things. This was a childhood not much up from the life of the tenements from which she had come.

It was in trying to find a place for this termagent that Georgina discovered Gisors, farther south than Gournay and much larger. Gisors is ancient. The Epté River runs through the town, which is overlooked by a castle called the Château Fort. Since medieval times there had been a charitable endowment to care for the sick, and this had now devolved to an order called Les Dames de St.-Thomas de Villeneuve. To Georgina's surprise and delight, she found that only ten or so years ago, a brand-new hospice had been erected on rather a noble scale to care for twelve men and twelve women of the town, as selected by the sisters. Of these good women, Sister Françoise turned out to be an amiable and levelheaded Irishwoman, who very soon knocked the recalcitrant Rosie into shape, though it might be truer to say that Rosie had at last found a reliable adult to help her. The change in the teenager was so dramatic that Georgina opened negotiations to bring all the children there. This plan required the nuns and their lay administrator to bend the rules of admission and in particular find extra accommodation—though there was some, if one counted the outhouses and stables. It was a question of money. Georgina, they realized, had money.

The hospice was sited in ample grounds not far from the market square, and by the standards of the nineteenth century, its provisions were generous in the extreme. As a building it was not less grand than Tavistock House itself—in fact, it was rather better suited to its purpose. A branch of the Epté ran through the grounds, which were laid out for the cultivation of vegetables. When they weren't digging, the hapless menfolk fished. For the care of only twenty-four indigents, most of them the victims of cider drinking, it was a quite spectacular endowment. Taking nine Protestant orphans into care was clearly outside the immediate remit of the order. Rosie, who had been set to work in the sewing workshop the hospice organized, had made a very good impression, and Georgina herself turned on all her charm. The deciding factor as to whether the orphanage transferred to Gisors or not was, of course, Harry's money. Georgina did not mention that Marie and Victoria had washed their hands of the Argeuil arrangements and that the only other alternative was that the children would be sent to Paris and dumped.

On March 8 Harry's solicitor sent Georgina a letter in which he announced his client's intentions to sell the lease of Tavistock House. A London friend, Lise Grey, had been to the house to discover what had happened to the Lowthers. She reported Menier in occupation with his drunken cronies and an impudent English mistress. Louisa Treherne wrote once more to beg Georgina to come home. Still she vacillated, trying to settle the future of the orphans. At last came the letter that spurred her to action. Harry had finally lost patience with her, thrown Menier out, and repossessed the property. No singing career, no famous orphanage, and now—if she was not careful—no house. She left at once for London.

The Mad Doctors

On April 4, 1878, after a millpond crossing from Le Havre, Georgina ran into the hall at Tavistock House to find boxes and chests of her own belongings done up in stout cord and standing over them a man who introduced himself as Mr. Bell. Harry had taken legal possession of the house, and Mr. Bell, as he explained in his phlegmatic way, was there to see fair play. Had he any knowledge of this luggage? Georgina asked, bewildered. Why, yes, he had helped pack and secure it. That was his job, to be a bailiff. But what was in it? Stuff—in the technical phrase, goods and chattels. Meanwhile, Bell added with a heavy significance, she would find the French gentleman in the cellars. At which point, Menier emerged, cobwebbed and flustered. With him was a heavily pregnant woman, the mistress Lise Grey had mentioned in her letter. Voices were raised, sneers and jibes exchanged. The young woman, Olive Nicholls, laughed in Georgina's face. "You won't be here long," she taunted.

Georgina ran frantically from room to room. Menier's dogs had fouled every corner and up and down the uncarpeted stairs. The floors were unswept and the mirrors filthy with grime. Even at a cursory glance, much that she had left on display six months ago was now missing. She ran down to the cellars and found an Ali Baba's cave of portable objects, some in chests and cartons, some yet to be wrapped. Menier, meanwhile, had hastily found his coat and summoned a cab. The truth at last dawned on Georgina. She had caught the Frenchman on the very morning and in the very hour he intended to decamp. Though she appealed to Bell to help stop her own property from going out the front door, the only suggestion he could come up with was to send for the solicitor involved in the matter, Mr. Neal.

Neal was acting for Jeavons, Harry's Liverpool solicitors. He, too, had only a modest grasp of what was going on, though he did produce a signed agreement made between Harry and Anarcharsis Menier. The Frenchman had been given a fortnight to quit the property and permission to take goods to the value of £178.1.1 in payment of wages owing to him by Georgina. She was incandescent with rage. Menier was never even on a wage! To sums owed, then. But, she cried, Neal did not understand. Menier owed *her* money. And then a strange and sinister thing happened. Neal recounted to Georgina how he had "sucked in the following tales, which he gravely informed me were compromising, if they got bruited about: I had put poison bottles about the house in various corners, which the babies sucked, died, and were buried in the garden. I got one thousand pounds for each baby— no questions asked. Menier had the most compromising letters from me proposing all sorts of dreadful things."

For Neal to know this—particularly about the provenance of the children—was to have been told by Harry. It makes an unusual picture. Neal could not prevent Georgina from occupying the house, though he could and did insist that Bell remain on the premises. But he felt it his duty to warn her that Harry intended to get her out. When she taxed him with why he had made these other accusations to her, he was perfectly frank and straightforward. They were not his accusations but Menier's. He had advised Harry it would be better to let Menier take goods at his own valuation rather than risk exposing Mrs. Weldon to such damaging revelations. He told her this with all the pointedness he could muster. What he was trying to say was that Harry had bought the Frenchman off. But Georgina did not understand this at all. Neal was to join a long line of men flattened by Georgina's typhoon energy. If Menier had fled with her goods, he was a thief! He must be sought out and destroyed! The solicitor was dismissed from her presence, and Georgina loosed herself on London like a hound from hell.

The first thing to do was put a spoke in Olive Nicholls's wheels. Her parents lived in Cambridge and Georgina cabled them: "Come at once. Your daughter is dying." Mr. Nicholls and his wife arrived only two hours after receiving the telegram, having had the train journey and the dash from Liverpool Street to prepare themselves for a deathbed farewell. They met instead a short and plump woman with retribution written on her brow. "I told them, morally their daughter was dead anyway," she comments offhandedly. So much for the imprudent Olive, who had dared to sauce her in her own home. The enraged Mr. Nicholls went away, looking for the man who had despoiled his daughter.

By midnight Georgina had tracked Menier down to a hotel room in Golden Square. Accompanied by P.C. 50 and a detective from Vine Street named Uriah Cooke, she lay in wait for his return. If it had been true once that she had flirted her nakedness before Anarcharsis, her portrait of him as she saw him now is a masterpiece of invective:

"I remember his filthy appearance, the dirt, his nails in perpetual mourning, the three hairs at either side of his upper lip, his hook nose with two dirty holes which seemed like tunnels at the other end of which you could see his brains, two huge eyes hidden behind perpetual spectacles— someone told me he slept in them—teeth like mediaeval battlements steeped in ink . . ."

When toward midnight he came back to his hotel to find his room filled with the posse drawn up by Georgina, she at once stepped forward, pointed with arm outstretched, and declared in ringing tones, "Detective, I give this man in custody for the theft of these things."

Menier replied in excitable English with a stage French accent, "Yes and I give this woman in charge for murder, for the murder of little children." Little *sheeldren*.

Cooke, who had previously established to his own satisfaction that some at least of the goods were Georgina's property—that is, as distinct from Harry's; otherwise how could she bring a charge of theft in her own name?—arrested Menier and, hiring a four-horse coach, had them all driven back to Vine Street. Whoever was duty sergeant that night could tell a hawk from a handsaw and promptly rerouted the carriage to Hunter Street, where he correctly surmised the lady might be known to his colleagues there.

Shouting, reviling each other in French, dragging up the bitterest accusations, the child murderer and the thief gave the Hunter Street officers something to think about. It was really no contest—Georgina was a lady and Menier a scruffy foreigner. In the small hours of the morning, and after volleys of bitter French had been exchanged—*grédin! putain! crapaud! tasse de merde!*—Menier was charged. Barely had the ink dried on the charge sheet when, on being searched, a letter signed by Harry was found on the accused, constituting him "a proper person in charge" of Tavistock House. Menier danced on the floor in delight. His triumph was short-lived. The desk sergeant had him sent down to the cells anyway, to appear next day at Bow Street Magistrates' Court. Georgina went home believing she had won a great battle. The faithful Villiers had prepared her a bed in the middle of all the squalor, and though Bell was still up and about, she was back in occupation.

On the following morning, Menier was put up before Mr. Justice Flowers, the very same magistrate who had found against him in the child custody case. Flowers was approaching seventy and looking forward to an honored retirement from the Bow Street court after twenty-two years of distinguished service. Georgina found him grave and courteous. To her delight he remanded the prisoner in custody for a week but tempered this—wisely and humanely—by passing the papers in the case to the Treasury Solicitor, with a view that he should represent the plaintiff's interest. Frederick Flowers had heard enough to realize, like the Hunter Street officers, that there might be more to this than met the eye.

Neal was present at the hearing and was, of course, relieved that not too much had come out in open court. But the prisoner, of whom he had an opinion quite as low as Georgina's, seemed to him a tricky cove, and when it came to trial, Menier would undoubtedly repeat his accusation of child murder, already heard by half a dozen people. As for Mrs. Weldon herself, he could not see how even the Treasury Solicitor could save her from an absolute passion to say more than the law required. Of Menier's potential testimony she wrote:

> He forgets I kill little children, that Freddie's death had preoccupied me; that I was a lunatic; that I was a forger; that I was looking to poison *him;* that I had him arrested from jealousy of Olive Nicholls and because he would not sleep with me; that I appeared stark naked in front of strangers; that I scandalised Paris; that the police chief made me leave; that I had a nervous breakdown if he slept with his wife; that I was demented, a maniac, and riddled with debts.

If she spoke even half these whirling words aloud, Neal was right to be alarmed. The Treasury Solicitor was not an individual, but a government department. Whoever was briefed to appear for Mrs. Weldon would need a clear head and a certain degree of brutality if he was to hold her in check and keep back the most damaging of her self-incriminations. Chief of these was the fate of the orphan Freddie. The truth was that Freddie (the orphan whom Rosie Strube's letter, quoted earlier, mentions as having "a very bad stomachach") *had* died in Tavistock House at some time since 1875, after Harry left. No death certificate was ever issued, and although Georgina never fully confessed to burying him in the garden, that was almost certainly where he lay. He could have died of any of half a dozen causes, of which the least likely was brutal murder, and his burial under the mulberry tree could be put down to panic and ineptitude.

Neal never asked her what had happened. His main purpose was trying to contain the story so that it did not come out in court. In this, coming from someone acting for the other party in possible divorce proceedings, he shows a rare compassion. Georgina describes him as "simple-minded," but he seems to have been a kindly and intelligent man. Something really terrible had happened out in the garden one night, enough to have Georgina committed, if not for lunacy, then for a full criminal trial. If Neal chose to hunt down what happened to Freddie, finding witnesses and corroborating statements, Harry could certainly secure the divorce he wanted, but his wife might find herself behind bars. Georgina owed Harry's solicitor more than she ever realized.

All the same, Neal knew more than he was letting on. The vacillating Louisa Treherne had been brought to the moment of decision. She and her son Dal had at last expressed their complete agreement with Harry's plan to bring in the doctors. To these three, it was more than ordinarily vexing that in only twelve or fourteen hours since her return, Georgina had succeeded in dragging the whole sorry mess out into the open. Harry understood his solicitor's advice only too well: let this grubby Frenchman take what he wanted, so long as he cleared off, went back to France, and kept his mouth shut. The stupid man had not even done this properly: some of the goods stolen—jewels, watches, a christening mug—were Georgina's private property and not for Harry to dispose of as he wished. In short, she was free to bring an action against Menier in her own name. Meanwhile, in his remand cell the prisoner had called for pen and paper and was preparing a lengthy rebuttal of the charges. He alerted his brother Eugène, who set off from Paris to help him, pausing only to heap abuse on Angele.

In Argeuil, Marie and Victoria had packed up shop, and finding the plans to move the children to Gisors to be so much hot air (though Georgina had painted a glorious word picture of them traveling through the Fôret de Lyons like medieval troubadours), sent them by train to Paris. Angele was horrified.

*W*hat Georgina should have done was to find Harry and ask him what he thought he was doing. Her silence was the expression of a catastrophic pride. In the next few days there would be events so grave as to change the rest of her life. Through choice and circumstance, she faced them alone. She realized one thing clearly enough: there was no one she could trust. In a drawer of the desk on which Gounod had composed—in so sacred a place as that—she found three letters from Eugène Menier, written from Paris the previous December, plotting with his brother to do her harm. (Was *he* the mystery man who had accosted Angele in the street, and had they together concocted the story she had told Georgina?) Whether she ever really understood that all the people she had met since moving to France were fleecing her is hard to determine, even from reflections written thirty years after the fact. In the short term, an old habit kicked in. Attended by a sympathetic Bell, she toured the house and made a detailed inventory of what had been stolen. She made no attempt to contact Harry or anyone else.

What had always been lacking in Georgina was any sense of her own history. The past did not linger for her. Whatever happened that was awful was at once erased and replaced by what was going to happen—better still, what she would like to have happen. It is the gambler's mentality. Her brother Dal dissipated his entire inheritance in this way—and before him, the youthful Harry had done the same. Men did that: they ruined themselves on the turn of a wheel or the fall of cards. They gave up their wives and their children for sex, for the promise of something just beyond their reach, the dream of riches or the ideal woman. It was true her father had been different, plotting and planning, risking nothing. For Georgina to have run away with a penniless Hussar was offense enough with him. Had he lived to see

her in bed with Angele at Argeuil, stroking a head from which lice fell, and
spending days and even weeks unwashed, wiping up the children's shit from
the floors, his reaction would have gone beyond disgust, but he would have
seen it as the inescapable outcome of her original defiance. For him,
Georgina had fallen once and once only. She had disobeyed him.

This was also Louisa's view. It was true she and Harry and Dal wanted
Georgina committed because they were afraid of what might be disclosed.
It makes no difference that many of their worst nightmares had already been
realized. If Georgina was heading for an asylum, she had only herself to
blame. She had been a bad daughter and a worse wife. She could not be
saved now. She could only be silenced. Neither Harry nor Louisa made the
slightest attempt to talk to her face-to-face, nor did they ask for a full account of what had been going on with the orphans and how the Meniers became involved. The hunter does not ask the rabbit in his sights what he feels
about it.

Nor did it matter that Georgina herself made no effort to justify her actions. It was a very foolish thing not to have seen her husband at all for two
years, and though she harangued her mother in hugely long letters about
Harry's awfulness, imagined and actual, Louisa's advice was always the
same. "In my opinion, you have only one path to follow though it may seem
very disagreeable to you," she wrote to her daughter. "The law obliges you
to live with your husband and no matter what his wishes might be in regard
to your orphanage, it's your duty to comply." Louisa had touched the heart
of the matter as it was seen by the age. Georgina was to be excluded from
the Victorian woman's paradise of calm and measure and a quiet life not because she was special or exceptional. It was simpler than that. She had failed
to show obedience to the wishes of a man.

Angele aside, she had no friends and confidants. There was no one to
argue with her or plead with her. She lived without the healing properties of
contradiction, upon which most relationships are founded. She most certainly did not consider herself mad, or likely to go mad, and there is something heroic in the way she sat and occupied the ruination of Tavistock
House, pleased only that Menier was behind bars and looking forward to

making her second appearance in court. Valerie de Lotz had vanished, and Mrs. Georgina Weldon was back in the saddle.

One of the things that puzzled Victorians was that the greater the number of public asylums, the greater the number of lunatics. It was almost a commonplace that when a new asylum was built, on however grand a scale, it was within a year or two insufficient for the needs of the community it served. It only gradually dawned on the general public that empires were being built by the medical officers in charge of asylums and that maybe many of those locked up had no real need to be there. Today this would seem to us to be obvious. But in the nineteenth century there was very little analysis of the categories of mental illness and no neurological basis by which it could be described. Disturbed patients were seldom treated by general practitioners in any methodical way, and individual psychiatry was practically unknown. Meanwhile, in any large community in Britain, up on the windswept hill somewhere out of town could be found that cross between a prison and a workhouse, the general asylum. It was true that the great and inglorious days of asylumdom were coming to an end and that the workings of the lunacy laws had yet again been widely investigated by a recent parliamentary select committee.

The picture was a bleak one. Paupers, alcoholics, pedophiles, patricides like Richard Dadd, baby stealers, blasphemers, shoplifters, religious maniacs were all lumped together under one category. They were mentally deranged, but much more to the point, they had disturbed the moral order. Henry Maudsley, the most famous alienist of the day, whose sardonic and pugnacious critique of the system had already thrown the mad doctors into confusion, was at least sure about that: "The so called moral laws are laws of nature which [men] cannot break, any more than they can break physical laws, without avenging consequences . . . As surely as the raindrop is formed and falls in obedience to physical law, so surely do causality and law reign in the production of morality and immorality on earth."

According to Maudsley's brutally materialist analysis of mental illness, Georgina was mad because her father was mad. In cases where inherited traits could not be established, there was a simple rule of thumb that all alienists applied: if the patient was likely to be a danger to himself or others, an asylum was indicated. Just as "in the body morbid elements cannot minister to healthy action, but, if not got rid of, give rise to disorder, or even death; so in the social fabric morbid varieties are themselves on the way of death, and if not sequestrated in the social system, or extruded from it, inevitably engender disorder incompatible with its stability."

The very term "alienist" for what would nowadays be called a psychiatrist reinforced this idea that mental illness was foreign to the common experience and had to be dealt with by methods other than those of general medicine. Maudsley was a savage critic of the system but believed as fervently as the most reactionary asylum keeper (but possibly with less Christian compassion) that lunatics were by definition inferior beings—"a new or abnormal kind which being incapable of rising in the scale of being, tends naturally to sink lower and lower." This from the lecturer on insanity at St. Mary's Hospital and Professor of Medical Jurisprudence at University College, London.

⇗ The mad doctors called for Mrs. Georgina Weldon on Sunday, April 14, the day after Menier was remanded for a second time. The house was in a turmoil of spring cleaning, Georgina atop a library ladder wielding a feather duster, her servants at more basic tasks, when two gentlemen called Shell and Stewart sent in their names. She scolded Villiers, who had surely meant Messrs. Duff and Stewart, small-time music publishers of her acquaintance. (They had quite characteristically gone bankrupt, and she supposed it was this they had come to discuss.) Before she could completely descend her ladder and get out of her apron she was astonished to see ushered in two complete strangers.

"Mrs. Weldon, you do not know us but we know you very well, we have often seen you. We are spiritualists. We have read your letters on The Education of Children in the *Spiritualist* newspaper and we are very desirous of placing some children with you."

She came down; tea was offered and accepted. While they talked, she took note of their appearance. Though they spoke like gentlemen, they were miserably unappealing specimens. One was an old man—"the very ideal of the lean and slippered Pantaloon." His companion was about thirty, "all blinks, winks, and grins, and looked like a washed Christy Minstrel." The discussion, which had begun with spiritualism, ranged over topics close to her heart, and she was soon prompted to disclose some of her own mystical experiences. As professed spiritualists, they asked a great many elementary questions, mostly to do with mediumistic powers. For example, how far did she believe in the physical manifestation of the departed spirit? Her answers were uncontroversial. She had never attended a séance in order to see the table fly to the ceiling or a ghostly face appear from behind the curtain. What she sought from spiritualism was a better opinion of herself. As to whether she thought her dear dog Dan Tucker had a soul, which was one of the questions these two then asked, the answer was self-evident. Such a loyal and faithful friend deserved an afterlife, as much as and more than many people. Was he in heaven, then? She supposed so. As to the rest, yes, she had received visions and heard voices—who hadn't? Why, only a month or so ago she had been talking to Victor Hugo about these very things! Her visitors must surely concur that from the Other Side came insights and wisdom wholly beyond the grasp of mortal beings, as well as providing glimpses of a higher moral order. She really could not spare the time to discuss these things, though she commended to her visitors the interest in psychic phenomena shown by many distinguished men of their generation, including some doctors. But, they persisted, wasn't much of spiritualism a fraud practiced on the credulous? She replied succinctly that she knew all about fraud.

Georgina's experience of spiritualism was much less dramatic than these two gentlemen wished to suggest. She liked the medium Towns best of all because he set her what seemed to be such entertaining riddles. A good example was his insistence that she would one day be threatened by a man with one eyebrow. This seemed such a bizarre possibility that she puzzled over it without success, until at last she realized Towns was trying to indicate Charlie Rawlings, the eldest of the bell-ringing brothers. (A friend of hers, Mrs. Adamson, quite disgusted by the bushy blackness of brows that met in the middle, had once insisted to Georgina that the pubescent Charlie shave a gap over the bridge of his nose, else she would never come to the house again.) At another sitting, Towns indicated danger from the friend of a man in uniform who died with a ball in his head. Nobody in her family or acquaintanceship could be made to fit the bill, until at last Menier, walking into the room on some other errand, mentioned offhandedly that a friend of his in the Garde Nationale had been shot in the head by a Prussian bullet. Spiritualism was always a roundabout way of telling her what she already knew.

Mr. Bell watched the visitors leave. They walked through the ruined and overhung gardens in high spirits, laughing and joking.

"Aren't they hugging up to each other as if they had a fine prize?" he mused thoughtfully to Villiers, who was with him.

The two men were in fact Dr. Winn and his son-in-law Forbes Winslow. Bell's independent testimony that they were laughing as they left is especially interesting. Dr. Forbes Winslow had made a parlor trick out of a parlor trick by attending society séances in London and at the critical moment leaping up and exposing the medium. On one occasion he flung a pot of red ink into the face of a spectral visitor that was decorating the face of the medium when the lights went up. He was the son of a much better known—and very much more sympathetic—doctor specializing in the insane who had died four years earlier. Lyttleton Stewart Winslow inherited his father's Hammersmith asylum in 1874 and changed his name by deed poll to ensure a continuity of brand image—in Georgina parlance, he had already been materially helped from the Other Side. He was ambitious, hardworking, and completely unscrupulous.

The conversation Georgina had with him was never disclosed to her as a medical consultation, or anything like it. Indeed, no case history of

Georgina's symptoms was ever taken by a doctor of any kind. Armed with the knowledge that her father had died insane, Forbes Winslow had only to prove in her a hereditary disposition to madness. This would manifest itself by the exhibition of suitably irrational behavior. It happened that an interest in spiritualism seemed to the unlikable Winslow just that. In the Mordaunt case, a telling piece of evidence had been that Lady Mordaunt sat down upon a gravel walk in the grounds of the Crystal Palace and pushed a fallen sprig of fir into the top of her boot. No person of quality in his or her right mind would do such a thing. Talking to angels—or being duped by mediums—was hardly less aberrant.

That afternoon, just after lunch, Villiers announced Major General Sir Henry de Bathe. In the circumstances, this was a piece of brazen effrontery on de Bathe's part, though of course he was there at Harry's bidding. He was appropriately uneasy and only stayed ten minutes. He had come to welcome Georgina back to England and commiserate with her on the theft of her belongings by the blaggard Frenchman Menier. The unsuspecting Georgina pressed him to stay longer. This was a family friend and she had much to tell him. In fact, he could have no idea the troubles she had experienced. De Bathe waved all this away and made the pitch he had been sent to make. Concerning this theft business, did she not see that it would only increase her woes to drag some worthless wretch through the courts? She was at a loss to understand him. Why, de Bathe said, wasn't it clear as day that a lady of quality could and should let the prosecution drop? It was beneath her to trifle with this man. Georgina was astonished. She had been *robbed*. Did a lady who had been robbed decline to prosecute—was this the advice of a veteran of Talavera? De Bathe fled shortly after.

At half past eight in the evening, Bell admitted two men again claiming to be Shell and Stewart, alias Winn and Winslow. They were in fact yet two more doctors, the "short and tubby" Semple and "the dark, taciturn, evil looking" Rudderforth. They explained that they were associates of Shell and Stewart, with the same high purpose of placing children with the orphanage. Georgina gave them an hour of her time in the drawing room and once again allowed the conversation to turn more upon spiritualism than philanthropy. This meeting was more cordial than the first, and she rather fancied

Semple had taken a shine to her. As a reward, she told him about the rabbit that had materialized at a séance with all the corporality and bodily functions of an actual rabbit before disappearing back across the earthly divide. Semple asked where this farewell had taken place, and Georgina freely told him: in the garden. One day the rabbit was there and the next, gone. The two men were greatly interested.

After they left, a cold wind of doubt began to blow. She had found it exhilarating to speak about the orphanage, even in the last minute to midnight of its existence, but two inquiries after it in a single day were either heaven-sent or sinister. A huge reaction set in.

"Oh Tibby," she cried to her maid, "I feel dreadful. Something awful has come over me. What can these men be? They are Menier's men. All is prepared. They want to get me away from here."

Twenty minutes later she heard the large piece of masonry that held together the ruined gates of Tavistock Square being moved, and a landau was driven through. The timing would seem to indicate that all four doctors had met out in the dark in order to have a pavement consultation, for the landau was from Forbes Winslow's asylum and the three occupants of it were a keeper named Wallis-Jones and two female nurses. There was to be no more shilly-shallying or deception. Nice Mr. Semple agreed with his colleagues and did not need reminding that the referrals he had made to Forbes Winslow in the past had always been profitable. If he had the fleeting sensation they were behaving like burglars, it was something he must put from his mind. They were doctors and Mrs. Weldon was unwell. Now they had come to fetch her.

Inside the house all lights had been hastily extinguished, and after an agonizing pause there came a hammering on the door. With Georgina and Tibby clinging to each other in terror, the phlegmatic Bell went to parley with the unknown parties gathered in the courtyard. Standing in pitch-dark, the door on the chain, Bell refused to allow Winslow's servants into the house. It is evident from this he had been kept in ignorance of his employer's intentions toward his wife, and this in turn suggests that only the threat posed by the upcoming trial had forced Harry into such urgent comings and goings.

Though Wallis-Jones did not identify himself, Bell could read the situation as well as anyone. More than a few times, in his capacity as a bailiff, it had been he who had stood out in the cold trying to gain access to a property. Now, with some gallantry, he held his ground. Mrs. Weldon was abed and could not be roused. He refused a bribe to open the door. It was a sorry piece of work, this, and the honest and bighearted Mr. Bell had begun to take a dislike to the voices blustering on the other side of the woodwork. Their way was not Bell's way, oh no. But there was something said that certainly made him think, if the significance of it did not immediately strike Georgina.

"You are here for *Mr. Weldon*," Wallis-Jones explained with heavy emphasis, not once but twice. Bell was being told which side his bread was buttered on. It may be that he put two and two together at this point, and if he did, the stubborn defense he made of the front door does him even greater credit.

After a while, Georgina heard the landau pull away, and Villiers, who was returning to the house from her night off, saw it pass her, driven by a coachman with a cockade in his hat. Unseen, but surely somewhere close by in the shadows, was her former master in a huddle with the four doctors. It was nearly midnight.

The true identity of those who had attacked the house was still unknown to Georgina. Late though it was, she sent her maid back out to ask any beat policeman the maid could find to patrol the grounds. Villiers was then to run to Hunter Street and ask for the appropriate senior officer to call in the morning. Then Georgina did what seemed to her most natural. She sat down and wrote to Mr. Gladstone. But Gladstone had more than enough on his own plate. The government was in a war crisis over Russia and Turkey once again. Gladstone's London house was being stoned by his political opponents, and he and his wife hustled in the streets. It was a poor time for Georgina to call in favors she may have believed she was owed from him—favors that were in any case now ten years old. Nor would he have been particularly pleased to know that her other calls for help that night were addressed to the editors of the *Spiritualist* and *Medium and Daybreak*.

Her mind was seething, and as so often happened with her, she chose the wrong target to lash out at. It seemed to her that in some way or another, Menier was reaching out from his remand cell to do her harm. There had already been an indication of this. In the newspaper reports of the Bow Street remand proceedings against Menier, both the *Standard* and the *Daily Telegraph* had included this remark by his counsel, a Mr. Grain: "The sole fact of having established an Orphanage in a house owned by Charles Dickens without the sympathy or even the co-operation of her husband tended to prove that Mrs. Weldon suffered from hallucinations." She was quite certain Grain had not said these words in open court. They were an interpolation by interested journalists. In short, there was a clique at work in some way controlled by the hideous Menier.

As soon as the post offices opened, she sent this pathetic telegram to de Bathe: "Come up at once. It is a matter of life and death." De Bathe did not reply. During the morning an inspector arrived from Hunter Street, and she made a statement. She fired off a further volley of letters to anyone from the past who might help her, though their memory of her was likely to be exceedingly dusty. She chose the library as the fortress keep within the house and fortified it with a police rattle and two brass rose syringes, each containing three liters of water. Bell's position in all this was highly ambiguous, for it was no job of his to fight for her freedom with a rose syringe. Neal came by at half past eleven and advised her once again that it would be "a great pity to stir up muddy waters." It was a badly chosen phrase.

"Muddy waters! It isn't muddy water that's stained me! I don't know what you're talking about! Explain yourself!"

"Menier says that you owe him money, that you made contracts with him and that he has the most compromising letters from you."

"Menier can tell as many foul lies as he wishes," Georgina yelled in outrage. "It's he that owes *me* plenty of money. I have not made a single contract with him and since I have never been able to stand the sight of the dirty beast it's not very likely my letters have been compromising. That lot! They're a gang of idiots."

Neal was sent off with a flea in his ear, though before leaving, it is beyond belief that he did not speak to Mr. Bell and instruct the bailiff to open the door to the doctors when they next came back, and not to be such a damn fool.

Then, at two in the afternoon, a small miracle occurred: Mrs. Louisa Lowe sent in her card.

The elderly and garrulous Louisa Lowe had given damning evidence to the select committee hearings in 1877. She was one of the few educated women ever to have overturned asylum committal proceedings. Sent to Lawn House in Chiswick by her adulterous husband, she had escaped and, on the evidence of an independent medical examination, been judged perfectly sane. The case was an interesting one, not least because Lawn House was the property of Henry Maudsley, the archenemy of asylumdom. Even though he had not himself signed the committal order, he was sufficiently embarrassed by Mrs. Lowe's revelations to divest himself of Lawn House, which he was in the process of doing when she pitched up on Georgina's doorstep.

Mrs. Lowe was a woman somewhat in Georgina's own mold. After her release, she at once founded the Lunacy Law Reform Society, which she ran from an address in Berners Street, a short way from the Sacred Music Warehouse. Her main target was the chief commissioner of lunacy, Lord Shaftesbury, though there she was pushing on an unlatched door. Lunacy law reform was in the air (though not likely to proceed from Mrs. Lowe's understaffed and ad hoc offices, which opened only two afternoons a week. In this she was completely sister to Georgina. Louisa Lowe thought it was she and she alone versus the establishment, an idea that gave her preternatural strength of purpose).

How had she got wind of Georgina's particular circumstances? It would seem that Georgina herself had not fully understood what was afoot until Neal's arrival. He was not acting for her but for her husband, yet not even the most devious solicitor could avoid answering two very obvious questions: what was happening to her, and who were the people trying to force entry to the house? Had a sympathetic Neal secretly sabotaged his client's wishes to see his wife sent to an asylum by summoning Mrs. Lowe? The two women had never met, and Georgina had never even heard of Mrs. Lowe and her good works. If no one—neither Neal nor just conceivably Bell— had a hand in it, her arrival was truly providential. The one woman in London who could delay proceedings at least long enough to give Georgina good advice had appeared in the nick of time. On coming to the house Mrs. Lowe had seen the landau drawn up in the square with Wallis-Jones and the nurses peering out. She understood at once they were there to take Georgina in the street if she left the house. Georgina might have spiritualism on the brain, but her visitor thought of nothing but asylums. Only a little while after they began to talk, an ashen-faced Bell put his head around the door.

"Them three of last night have pushed their way into the hall and declare they won't leave. They want to see you. I told them you were out, but they said they'd wait until you came in."

Bell had done his duty—"you are here for *Mr. Weldon*"—but clearly did not like it. While Louisa Lowe ran from the house to summon the police, Georgina retreated to the library, where she barricaded herself in with a wall of bound musical scores. Villiers, Tibby Jordan, and at least one of the Westmacotts, together with Bell, were left outside. Again, it seems certain that all these knew by now exactly who Wallis-Jones was, and his business, though he persisted in saying he was there for "something about an orphanage."

Mrs. Lowe returned with the first two policemen she could find, who happened to have been patrolling the Euston Road. They were completely unprepared for the impasse they discovered—seven people milling about in front of the library door, from behind which the lady of the house was demanding to know what was happening.

Mrs. Lowe advised Georgina to come out and ask Wallis-Jones his business. This she did. The asylum keeper declined to answer. Then, Mrs. Lowe told the police, he should be taken up for trespass, at which point Wallis-Jones made a lunge for his patient, bellowing, "Take her, take her!" There was a scuffle and Georgina scrambled back behind her barricade, Louisa Lowe shouting to her, "Give them in charge: they are assaulting you!"

Georgina slammed the door, built up her wall of scores again (which assuredly included many by Novello's), and, her ear to the woodwork, tried to piece together what was happening. With a howl of anguish, she heard the constables confess they were not from Hunter Street, home to so many Weldon dramas in the past, including searching for Gounod in the fog when "the old man" had plunged out on one of his suicide missions. These policemen were large and comforting, but they were strangers to the Weldon saga. They were from the Tottenham Court Road station. Georgina yelled at Villiers to run across Woburn Place and fetch men from Hunter Street. And then she heard the hubbub subside and a question-and-answer session begin with the usual and agonizing slow-wittedness of the police. Hunter Street arrived and there was more confusion, more repetition of the facts.

At last there was a knock at the library door, and Mrs. Lowe whispered the awful truth. Wallis-Jones was armed with an indisputably legal order to commit a lunatic at large, one Mrs. Georgina Weldon. She hesitated and then broke the news: the signature at the foot of the document was that of William Henry Weldon.

Georgina's response was magnificent. She found pen and paper and composed a draft telegram. It was addressed to Harry at Albert Mansions in South Kensington: "Come at once. Some villains sent by that villain Menier have got into the house with a forged signature of yours." She pushed the slip of paper under the door and watched it disappear. Mrs. Lowe read it in silence before showing it to the police. The two men from Hunter Street and their colleagues from Tottenham Court Road mulled it over with maddening slowness. For Georgina's servants trying to peep over their shoulders, it was a heartbreaking moment. From their point of view, their mistress had at last been brought down. Below stairs, one might speak lightly of doolally-tap, one might marvel at the risks Georgina had taken and the thinness of the ice on which she had skated, but this was just too awful a way to end it all.

Wallis-Jones tried to talk the police around. He had his order to serve, it was all perfectly above board, they had all surely seen similar sad occasions. The lady was without question a lunatic at large. Rubbish, Mrs. Lowe said, pointing at the mute door to the library. How could it be held she was at large when she was in a treasured room of the family home? She was, presumably, where her husband desired her to be—at home, and quiet, and, though frightened, very obviously not deranged.

Maybe the telegram Georgina had pushed under the door made the police hesitate, or maybe they knew of the identity and reputation of the formidable Mrs. Lowe. Or maybe the two Hunter Street constables knew and liked Mrs. Weldon for her past instances of pluck and her invariably cheery greetings to them. This was the lady whose famous milk float had trundled past them on the beat, bearing the nippers off to the Langham Hotel, the singer whose house had twelve pianos. They declined to satisfy Wallis-Jones, and he was sent packing. The policemen from Tottenham Court Road left to resume their patrol of the Euston Road. Only then did Georgina emerge.

It had taken two days, but at last she understood the enormity of the situation. She could not bring herself to believe Harry would do such a thing. Mrs. Lowe was in no doubt, and kneeling on the carpet, stroking her hand, the faithful Villiers agreed, crooning, "It is! It *is* Mr. Weldon."

Louisa Lowe proposed the immediate next step. Georgina should leave Tavistock House at once and outrun the committal order, which was only valid for seven days. If she was sane, she should fight. But if she stayed where she was, she would be taken up anyway, sane or not. Georgina looked beseechingly at Bell. "I'd go with the lady," he murmured. The Hunter Street constables, who were still there, nodded. "Do go, ma'am," one of them said.

She was handed a bonnet and a cloak and, still in her slippers, ran from the house, followed by "a puffing and panting" Mrs. Lowe. On the east side of the square was a hansom, attended by a young policeman. He offered to help them up. Louisa Lowe was momentarily suspicious, but the constable turned out to be on their side. "I have not taken the number of the cab," he muttered helpfully, and the two women shouted to the cabbie to drive on.

They clattered out of the square and were swallowed up in the afternoon traffic. It was not much of a headlong flight—Mrs. Lowe had lodgings in Keppel Street only a few hundred yards away.

Forbes Winslow's daughter was married to the *Punch* contributor Arthur A'Beckett, and it amused him to pitch up outside the house in Tavistock Square late that night. A'Beckett stood in the dark shouting, "Mrs. Weldon is a dangerous lunatic! A thousand pounds to anyone who will help me take her tonight!" However, those that were left failed to see the joke.

A'Beckett had come into the square in the same sinister landau that he used to pay a bumptious visit to the Lunacy Law Reform offices the next day. He seems a particularly irritating young man. Women and madhouse keepers were funny in the same way women and gamekeepers might be, or women and stationmasters: the joke was about rules. These rules were an expression of the male world. Women, too, had their rules, chief of which was not to interfere in the world of men. But this haw-haw dundreary-whiskered kind of humor was pretty old-hat. Were it ever truly believed that Harry had offered a bounty of £1,000 on his wife's head, the crudity of the thing would do him irreparable damage. There is little question that to lawyers like Neal, the whole business had been botched from beginning to end. De Bathe seems to have been the first to have realized this. He fled to Baden-Baden with his daughter Mary, under the pretext of visiting friends.

Georgina's mother had, of course, stayed out of the way in Worksop, but when the news of the debacle reached her, she sent Emily's husband, Bill, to go and look for Harry Weldon in London. Louisa Treherne was in a position very common to many women. Having left it to the menfolk to plan and execute a delicate business, she now realized she—even *she*—could have done it better herself. She wrote to Dal: "Poor Harry: he is, as you say, a confounded idiot, if only for having chosen his moment so badly. But I'm sure he has a good heart and without a doubt suffers terribly, above all from the vexation of having been the author of such disgusting fatheadedness."

Georgina had no difficulty in evading Forbes Winslow's servants until the order expired. After a day or so in Keppel Street, the good-natured Lowthers hid her in Fulham and then in a room in Whitechapel. How wholeheartedly was she being pursued? Her brother Dal, writing from

Cox's Hotel in Jermyn Street, let the cat out of the bag: Harry had given *him* full powers to parley with her. The moment she heard that, she knew Harry's determination had begun to falter. Nobody with any sense would employ Dal as an intermediary. Joyously, she made mincemeat of her brother's gloomy unctuousness. She told him she needed no moral lessons from a drunk and gambler, charges that stung because they were so close to the truth. "You, you've led a worldly and dissipated life: me, I've lived in a sober and unfashionable way." Dal could never think quickly enough to rebut this sort of thing.

Georgina had been swift to get medical certificates of sound mind and good health from two doctors of her own, one of whom, Edmunds, gave what we might see as a modern opinion. "Eccentric? Certainly. But mad, no." (He had been especially impressed by her account books, in which she meticulously recorded every expenditure.) She even wrote to Gisors and got the lay registrar, with whom she had shared such pleasant thoughts and so many illicit cigarettes, to write an open letter of support *"pour servir à qui de droit."* It ended with this endorsement: "Her precipitate departure from L'Hôtel-Dieu has caused all the staff of this establishment, Administrators, the Bursar, nuns and pensioners of all ages universal regret."

Louisa Lowe's timely intervention had saved Georgina from spending what might have been the rest of her life in Brandenburg House. The rest she had done for herself. Mrs. Lowe was soon to find that the cause of lunacy law reform could not have two champions, and the women fell out in rather an acrimonious way. There was always much that was straightforwardly dislikable about Georgina. She was not always as honest or as generous as the situation demanded, and she could be ungrateful. These are common enough human characteristics. But though she had experienced a profound shock in the mad doctors' episode, she had come out of it with the conviction, not that she was in need of help, but that she had somehow received an almighty blessing. Events had made her a Jeanne d'Arc. Her mind had latched onto the key point:

A wife has no recourse against her husband for an attempt on
her liberty such as I've experienced. She cannot bring a complaint

against him for conspiracy, defamation, imprisonment, assault and battery in a civil court. It's not *her* rights that are safeguarded. The reputation of a woman is the *thing* of her husband: if it pleases the husband to ruin her, he is the master and she has no legal right to complain. Against any other man or woman, who has not sworn an oath before God to honour and protect her, she has her remedy. Against her husband, nothing of the kind.

Mrs. Lowe was also a wronged woman, of course, and the Lunacy Law Reform Society was set up expressly to help just one aspect of married women's legal inequality. But to Georgina's tastes, Mrs. Lowe's methods were distressingly pedestrian. That was not what was wanted at all. Lunacy reform required a heroine. It required grand opera. By the time May was out, the direction the last part of Georgina's life would take had been set. From now on, if men—Harry, Dal, "that boiled lobster Neal," the revolting Menier, and anyone else that crossed her path—wanted a fight, they would get it.

Only a fortnight after Georgina's flight with Mrs. Lowe, Harry wrote to Dal, indicating his capitulation:

> My dear Treherne,
> I asked you last night for time to reflect on the arrangements you have made with my wife, begging me out of consideration to yourself and above all giving way to the urgent supplications of your mother "to give my wife yet again one more chance"; and so stop measures I believe it to be my duty to undertake in order to protect my wife; and which I still believe should have been taken. For as long as matters go along as they should, I consent to abandoning my pursuit of her and things can continue as they have done formerly.

Georgina had won back the house and an allowance of £1,000 a year. The terms of surrender were probably dictated to Harry by Mr. Neal, who had pressed Dal to secure a signed agreement from Georgina to behave herself in future. The solicitor knew that this paper and its conditions as to her future conduct were almost worthless. The last paragraph of the letter contains an understandable note of chagrin coming from Harry direct: "Believe me, nobody will rejoice more than me to see these conditions fulfilled, but I beg you to believe that I have only adopted this way of going about things out of deference to the urgent desires of yourself and your mother."

The conspirators had fallen out, and there was a flurry of correspondence in which Georgina's mother in particular tried to bat away the accusation that she had pressed Harry to have her daughter committed. The truth was that she had done nothing to dissuade him, and had it all not been so horribly botched, she would have seen Georgina go into a private asylum without a qualm. Her protestations of horror at what had happened and her insistence that she was innocent of any complicity in it were mealymouthed. Harry now saw the perfidy of the Trehernes in full. He and he alone was going to have to carry the can for what had happened. This time he had lost the battle and the war. If he was not prepared to fight again on the same ground—and he wasn't—then life for Harry Weldon in the future was going to be pure hell. He knew better than any of them what Georgina was capable of when it came to revenge.

It was not in his wife to let bygones be bygones, or to take time to digest what had happened. The Gounod clique was already conflated in her mind with the Menier clique. Now, thrown into the same geometrical stew, circles within circles, was the Weldon clique—Harry, her mother, and Dal. The three conspiracies interlocked. At the very time that Dr. Edmunds pronounced her mentally capable of managing her own affairs, she was agitating that the appointment of St. John Wontner to defend her interests in the Menier trial was somehow engineered by Forbes Winslow. In vain did Wontner point out that for thirty years or more his firm, along with Lewis and Lewis, had been the doyens of criminal law practice in London. He was there to help—indeed he had been appointed by the Treasury Solicitor expressly to make sure she came to no harm. Instead of being grateful, she was incredibly rude to the poor man. He lacked vision. His position was compromised. He completely failed to grasp the bones of the case.

She spelled it out to him, as to a child. Gounod was at the back of Menier, Harry at the back of Forbes Winslow. There was nothing that could not be ascribed to the fell designs of these three cliques. Who had threatened her with the St.-Lazare in Paris? Gounod. Who had done his bidding? Menier. How had Menier been encouraged and secretly funded? Harry. Who had egged Harry on with her allegations of hereditary madness? Her mother. Who was her mother's creature in the attempt to get her committed? De Bathe. And why had Harry supported de Bathe in this scandalous way? Because he had at one time wanted to marry Mary de Bathe. On and on, random pieces of jigsaw jammed together to make a picture.

It was useless for Wontner to try to narrow the subject to a case of theft. Nor could he employ what normally worked in such cases—a man's guiding hand to a beautiful lady. She swept that aside with contempt. They had tried to call her mad and she had defied them. Now would come revenge, now would come retribution of a biblical proportion. When she at last got hold of de Bathe on his return from Baden-Baden, she faced down him and his dizzy wife in their own drawing room. At first the general denied any participation in the plot, but at last she drew from him the miserable confession that he, too, had signed the committal order. She told him what she intended all her enemies to hear. "I said 'General de Bathe, you will repent this.' I turned to her and said 'You will both repent this.' "

The first casualty in her campaign to vindicate herself was her family. Her mother was struck with terror by the bitterness Georgina exhibited on that subject:

A father and mother bring you into the world for their own pleasure and not at all with the intention of rendering the least service to those who deserve it. They are obeying the laws of procreation. They owe their offspring nothing. In nature every animal chases away its young as soon as it can look after itself. The little ones only love their mother for what they can get out of her . . . In human nature, to the contrary, a child will love and cherish its parents or those who have brought it up only so long as it's possible to retain the least illusion about them . . . but then, oh yes indeed, *then*, when its eyes are opened—goodbye! I don't deny that happy

families exist, but they are extremely rare. For all the rest, it's
hypocrisy, banalities, Panurgism and "what will people say?"

Menier was sent to trial at the Old Bailey in September. The case was
heard by Sir Thomas Chambers, one of the first in which he sat as recorder,
and it easily outdid the Gounod trial for absurdity, monumentally irrelevant
testimony, and farce. Much did Georgina care: here was an opportunity to
outline the conspiracies ranged against her, of which theft was but a tiny
part. Try as he might, Wontner could not keep her to the point, and the judge
professed himself astonished at the violence of her language. After a chaotic
three days, the jury found for her, but the idea that Menier should spend five
years of his life breaking stones did not appeal to them. To the guilty verdict
they added a recommendation for mercy, clearly indicating that they
thought Menier and Georgina were far better known to each other than had
come out in open court. The innuendo was unmistakable.

The publicity surrounding the trial continued long after it was over. The
London *Figaro* commissioned weekly installments of Georgina's autobiography, which forced an embattled and disheartened Harry and an alarmed de
Bathe to bring down a criminal prosecution for libel on the head of its editor and publisher. So much the better! Let it all come out! Forbes Winslow
was sharply criticized in the pages of the *British Medical Journal* for his part
in the affair; Frederick Flowers weighed in with a thoughtful legal opinion
on the case. Now, wherever lunacy law reform meetings were organized,
Georgina easily usurped Mrs. Lowe as the star attraction. Soon enough, she
broke away with an initiative of her own:

> Mrs. Weldon invites all persons—lovers of justice—to attend
> her AT HOMES. Evening dress is not *de rigueur,* and every class of
> person is WELCOME. Mrs. Weldon gives these Lectures on the prin-
> ciple that "a drop of water will wear away a stone." Although her
> room can hold but 250 persons, still she hopes that her limited pub-
> lic may unite with her in doing all they can towards LUNACY LAW
> REFORM and the showing up of the practices of MAD DOCTORS.

Every Tuesday and Wednesday she gave these at-homes, at which she read from her own pamphlets and ended by singing from Gounod's *Biondina*. Many lost and lonely people took up her invitation. She was a gifted raconteuse, and her towering indignation at the stupidity of the establishment was exactly what her audience wished to hear. Nobody of any consequence came, but those who were potential victims of the system—and those over whom the shadow of the law had already fallen—fell in love with her courage and ferocious energy. They had the additional thrill of listening to their heroine in the very house where she had bested the mad doctors and exposed them for what they were. There was no admission fee to these meetings, but at the end of the evening a collection was taken up. Those that gave had sat through a unique testimony brilliantly staged. They went away uplifted.

Publicity, as she had always said, brought fame. Publicity was like fire, dangerous and unbiddable. She could easily afford to ignore anonymous letters like this, which once may have caused her hurt: "My dear, fools are like poets, they are not made but born. I know, I was born so. And I recognise a full-blooded member of the family in you."

The man who wrote this was a loser. He couldn't, as she could, understand the crackling urgency of publicity, its flamelike fascination for the weak and the fearful. And in its wake came something much more valuable, a phoenix glory not given to everybody. Natural-born fool or not, she was famous now. In October, when she sang at a Promenade Concert at Covent Garden, the house rose to its feet in acclamation. The whole house, as one person. She stood onstage, heart pounding, eyes glittering in triumph, a little short woman who had made her own luck, listening to the cheers ring around the auditorium, bows clattering on the orchestral strings. Trying to take it all in, she realized with a wild leap of the heart that she was being pressed to an encore. In the past, Sullivan had conducted at the Promenades: when had that ever happened to him?

Rivière

≈ 1 ≈

*G*eorgina had been engaged for the Promenades by a small-time impresario named Jules Rivière. He was more of a showman than a musician, an astute Frenchman whose background was in selling stoves. What he did not know about music he made up for with nerves of steel and an unerring instinct for the popular. In a way he was like Georgina herself—nobody believed in the value of publicity more than he. When she received her standing ovation, he knew it was as much a consequence of her summer of notoriety as her rendition of "The Sands of Dee." When the brief season ended, he engaged her for a second short series of concerts in Brighton and the same thing happened—she drew audiences much larger than were warranted musically. Rivière realized he had that most precious of journalistic commodities on his hands—a good human interest story. People came to see her out of curiosity, and if they rose to their feet after her recital, it was because she had surprised and perhaps even shamed them a little. That clear voice, the unaffected diction and unfussy stage presence: whatever madness was, it was not this. As the audience filed out from the theater, many sought out lunacy law reform leaflets from a booth provided in the foyer. Poor Mrs. Weldon had attracted, for the moment, the ultimate Victorian approbation—she was now poor *dear* Mrs. Weldon. Rivière admired her willingness to be exploited.

"I'll do my best to get accused of murder!" she told him breezily. "What brings money and crowds are people accused of crime. If only Peace could be resuscitated and whistle 'Pop Goes the Weasel' in a comb at the Promenade Concerts, you would have 10,000—what do I say?—100,000 nightly who would pay 2s. with pleasure and delight."

It was unusual for the impresario to have an artiste grasp the fundamentals of concert promotion in this way. Before he knew what was happening to him, he had agreed to a deal much wider in scope. He would create a permanent choir for her. The billings would read "Mrs. Weldon's Concerts, conducted by M. Rivière." Though his middle name was Prudence, the impresario had fallen for her. He was among the last of the older men in her life, and though he was careful to say how happily married he was, there was all the same something intoxicating about her. At the very outset of their correspondence, she playfully dubbed him "the General." "With a Lieutenant like you, a General ought to be victorious," he murmured. Dinners and tête-à-têtes followed.

Georgina was soon trying to force on him a choir of 250, which happened to be the number of seats in the rehearsal room at Tavistock House. They would be paid by the allocation to each of £10 of free tickets to the next Promenade season. Too late, Rivière felt the first ground tremors of the earthquake beneath his feet. He objected that what the theater world calls "papering the house" like this was completely uneconomic—he was giving away £2,500 of potential income—as well as being impractical. He reminded Georgina that in the Promenades the orchestra pit was boarded over and the musicians seated onstage. In the space left, a choir of thirty would be spectacle enough. Anyway, he very much doubted that for the grander vision she was touting there existed that many good-looking young women— and looks were as important as musical talent. "The fellows who pay their shillings like to see fine girls," he explained to his new partner. Georgina scolded him for being cautious and unimaginative, and used as an example of her drawing power her glorious part in the Gounod Choir. He brushed this aside with admirable candor. "I am popular, it is true. But Gounod was the lion of the day. I went to see him at St. James's Hall. I would not go to see Rivière."

Something else troubled him, a more delicate matter. Angele was back. Left with the wreckage of the orphanage, she had disposed of some of the children in Paris. Others had gone to Gisors, some to Rouen. With Menier locked away, Angele felt safe enough to come to London, fall on her knees, and beg forgiveness from Georgina. It had not been too difficult (though it must have been excruciatingly embarrassing) for her to wheedle her way into Georgina's bed again. Rivière, who knew his Paris probably better than he did London, could see at once who and what Angele was. He did not like her and he let it show. What he wanted from Georgina, though he had to embroider a little to describe it, was the pure article—an eccentric and over-weening egotist eager to be exploited. What he didn't want, what the public might not yet be ready for, was rumor that the put-upon heroine of the courts had a woman as her lover—not just any woman, either, but the wife of her despoiler. When he had taken Georgina down to Brighton to sing, she had been received and feted, among others, by Lady Downshire, wife to the second Marquis, and by the political and diplomatic de Bunsens. This was exactly what Rivière wanted to see. His artiste drew crowds because she was a lady, or as much of a lady as the general public could tolerate. He did not doubt she could sing, but if Rivière had found a blind girl on crutches, a hot-tentot, or a dog who could sing as well, he would have booked them. She was a novelty act, and he had supposed she perfectly well understood this.

At the first rehearsal for the new choir, only twenty people turned up. Rivière was not in the least dismayed. He could always find ten attractive girls to make up the numbers. Georgina ignored him and, egged on by An-gele, spent her own money on advertising extensively. As with all her plans, appetite was everything. She did not need Rivière to tell her how to go about her business—evading the mad doctors, it was clear to her now, had been no more than a conduit to the real fame that beckoned. The public was clamoring for her and would soon wish for no one else. Meanwhile, one did not take all London by storm with a choir of thirty! What was needed was a choir to rival all others, ready to reduce to rubble the most bitterly defended redoubts of the musical establishment where snobbery and ignorance lay entrenched.

What began as collaboration was now a fight for supremacy. She sold her Watts portrait to raise money, sent other items into pawn, and three times evaded the debt collectors. She found that being notorious was costing her rather more in time and money than she had bargained for—the law was drawing her in like quicksand. (She once walked through the door of her new partner's office declaring, "I have been to three police courts today and blown up two magistrates." Such talk did nothing to calm him.) "Do not spend your money on advertisements," he advised her sardonically, "or you will have 5,000 one of these days, and then you will have to get a Weldon Hall built in Regent's Park." She thought this very poor stuff: by August 1879 she had enrolled 350 singers.

Of one, the principal tenor, who had been gifted to her by the Rivière management, she wrote vengefully, "He knows nothing. He has not an idea of learning; he deserves to be beaten instead of paid. I laugh outright at them when they ask to be paid. Paid for what?" This sentiment and the atmosphere at rehearsals were very familiar to veterans of the Gounod Choir. These were amateur singers with their heads in the clouds, quite as hungry for fame as she was, but put to considerably more trouble. For her it was but a step upstairs from the famous library to the hallowed music room she had created for "the old man." Her choir made its way there by omnibus and on foot, to be greeted at the door by the mystery Frenchwoman attached to the household and ushered up to rehearsals that were sometimes no more than lengthy progress reports on legal proceedings. Like the Gounodists, they were promised the moon but asked to pay for it out of their own pockets. Signor Orazio Valentino, the tenor, smoldered miserably. Some of the sopranos Rivière sent along—"the pretty girls"—were much more notable for their chests than for their lungs. She described them pithily as "washed out figurantes."

It was part of the newspaper interest surrounding her that she remained in possession of Tavistock House, and she was very careful to insist in public that all she wanted was the restitution of conjugal rights and the chance to make a home for her beloved Harry. Rivière's visits gave him a quite contrary impression. The centerpiece of arrangements was not the absent husband, but the very visible and increasingly interfering Angele. The house was a shrine, the purpose of which was to venerate Georgina of the Miracles.

On August 16 she took the choir to the huge and echoing Crystal Palace and gave the first of three Saturday concerts under the baton of her new artistic collaborator, the suave and smiling M. Rivière. Included in the program was a woefully bad work by Urich, who had been summoned from Paris. She had only been dissuaded with difficulty from giving a solo spot to Herr Saemundsen, "the only Laplander in London." She herself was the star attraction. The *Morning Post* commented, "Mrs. Weldon was greeted with a perfect ovation, and her singing of the Sacred Song from Gounod's *Ruth* was so rapturously encored as to render its repetition necessary, albeit the special merit of the performance may be difficult to chronicle."

Much did she care: the key words in this were "a perfect ovation." Rivière was more sanguine, for some of the rapture of the evening had been provided by the choir itself, who acted as a kind of onstage claque. It was also completely against his musical policy to encore work—for her to accept such an invitation without first consulting him at the rostrum was an insult to his authority as conductor. It was no use her telling him his nose had been put out of joint. As he pointed out, her personal triumph had not stopped receipts for the concert from being disastrous. He regretted not taking closer artistic control of the venture. Even the venue was wrong—a choir of 350 was an achievement, but in the place it was heard, it was no more than a single pea swilled around a colander. She wrote:

> My General,
> I am going to write you a letter that will make you laugh. First let me tell you you are an IMBECILE. All these charming creatures to whom you listen, and who worry you, are dusters and dirty toerags. Listen to your own ears! Who is the pet? Who gets the tri-

umph? Who got all the applause last Saturday night? Me!!! I am only too much in the right, my General. I know what I am about.

Rivière was beginning to think otherwise. He had hired a choir and reaped confusion. It was obvious to him now that Georgina did not have it in her to think in terms of modest, attainable objectives. All the flimflam that had preceded the event, her tantrums, her startlingly vindictive way with the weaker choristers, her overweening certainty about what constituted musical taste (as, for example, commissioning such dire work from the unknown and shadowy Urich), made it clear she was not, in the sense he understood the word, a professional. "You speak in your letter of the applause which was bestowed on you: but this is precisely one of those things which causes me difficulties at the Crystal Palace. The Directors find that the applause prodigally bestowed on you by your Choir is in bad taste, and fear that it may cause a counter demonstration on the part of the public."

Two further concerts were poorly attended and went completely unnoticed by the music press. She did not realize how grave a situation this was for Rivière, because she supposed he had nothing else to do but think of her. In her mind she was, if not his sole crowd pleaser, then the principal one. The facts were otherwise. The Promenade Concerts were only a few weeks away, and his main concern was how to shoehorn the disastrous Weldon Choir into a schedule that included not one but seven military bands and half a dozen popular recitalists. She was bad at reading other people's feelings and may have missed the underlying threat in this remark: "I let pass the concerts at the Crystal Palace, without wishing to speak to you or torment you with the future."

Angele was clever where Georgina was not. Once she had read these words, she could see what was likely to happen. There was a solution. In the early days of his dealings with Georgina, the impresario had confessed to certain liaisons, certain ancient sexual adventures unknown to his wife. In fact, he admitted wryly, there were another two households in France that bore his name and children who could look to him as their father. There had also been one or more business deals that had gone wrong in the world of stoves. He may have judged that these confessions would be forgotten or forgiven in the delicious moments of flirtation he shared with her. He may even have thought she was not listening too carefully, because whatever he said was immediately capped with an arch little confession of her own—this was business conducted over candlelight and wine, with eye glances and the occasional touch of fingertips. Ah, but they were two of a kind, *la merle blanche* and himself! He did not know his adversary, nor had he properly judged the brutal pragmatism of her friend Madame Menier. In September Angele went to Paris to dig the dirt on the imprudent Jules Prudence Rivière.

It was Georgina's pattern relationship with older men—first the flattering interest, which may have disguised a real need to find a father figure she could trust, and then the attempt to mold him, make him obedient to her whim. Watts had passed this way, as well as Sir Henry Thompson and, most spectacularly, Gounod. In each case, when the man rebelled, he was made to pay for what she considered his betrayal. Her own father had been the first and Rivière was the last of the series. There is no doubt that he was opportunistic and self-seeking; he was also far more sanguine than she about the nature of the business they were trying to conduct. Furthermore, they were risking his money. Rivière was used to singers eating from his hand, eking out a livelihood in what had already become a crowded marketplace. He was not accustomed to having terms dictated to him.

On September 24, after another heated argument with the reduced choir chosen for the Covent Garden concerts, he lost patience and sacked all thirty of them. He accepted that he was in breach of contract, but he had suffered all he was going to. To his disgust, Georgina at once presented him with *le dossier Rivière* put together by Angele. He was stunned to read in it exact details of his undischarged bankruptcy and a description of him as a "trigamist." "It would, perhaps, be advisable to converse on this subject," Georgina suggested. It was blackmail of the crudest kind. After the few days given to him to reflect on matters, Rivière capitulated—"he came to rehearsal, looking like a sheep led to slaughter." With the lack of realism she had so often shown in the past, Georgina considered this a winning stroke. Rivière, for all his mustaches and macassar oil, was just another tradesman. He must do as he was told. The choir members were enraptured. One moment they had been looking at the ignominy of having to tell their friends they would not, after all, be appearing at Covent Garden. Then, by what means they knew not, all was saved. Art had triumphed.

There is no doubt Georgina was idolized by many of the choir. Some of them were attracted to her because of the spiritualist connection. Some were scrapings from the bottom of the barrel, rejects from other choirs or untrained aspirants who fancied a fling at choral work. Georgina began to grow suspicious of one such in particular. In the basses was a man named Fisher. No one had ever seen him sing. He turned up regularly enough, held the score open at more or less the right page, but made no effort to open his mouth. She was easily persuaded that he was a police agent installed by the management of the Royal Albert Hall (that old story) and paid in some way by Sullivan. Behind Sullivan was Harry. The more she pondered, the deeper and more obvious the conspiracy. Ernest Gye was the original leasor of Covent Garden, and who was Gye but a Garrick member and chum to Harry? Gye *père* was a drinking crony of de Bathe's, his son sublet the Garden to the Gatti brothers, who were nothing but pastry cooks, and they in turn had leased to Rivière, who, she was now in a position to disclose, was a failed bankrupt and serial adulterer. It all hung together—what she had seen as her salvation was yet another attempt to do her in. Maybe Wontner was involved in some way. If Wontner, then surely Menier, no matter that he was doing time in Coldharbour Lane. At the back of it all was Gounod with his inveterate jealousy. Once again, this was war!

She marked out the battle lines by quadrupling the choir demanded by Rivière for the Covent Garden concerts. He had advertised "a grand orchestra of a hundred musicians." Georgina made sure the choir exceeded this number, filling the stage and hardly giving room to the strings to bow. Packed shoulder-to-shoulder, they swayed and heaved, sweating most cruelly, their eyes alight with the big moment of their amateur lives. A critic commented acidly that he formed a bad opinion of their musical talents after the first bar, but here the choir shared something of Georgina's attitude. The critics could go to hell. They swung into Urich's "Amarilla, a South African Melody," the band hanging on to their music stands for dear life, Rivière swallowing his mustache in rage. He had in his program Emma Thursby, a young American soprano at the outset of her distinguished career and, for him, an expensive engagement. He had Signor Carrion from Her Majesty's Opera. The key to his whole promotion was variety and a certain Gallic wit. What he did not need was a Benefit Season for Mrs. Georgina Weldon. At one performance she managed to cram 160 choristers onto the stage, eyeing him triumphantly and daring him to do anything about it.

The crunch came on Balaclava Night, a rather dusty but popular tribute to the heroes of the Crimea. The choir was banished altogether from the stage for the excellent reason that Rivière had assembled his seven military bands in full fig, instruments burnished, ready to do justice to the theme "The British Army." An actor by the name of Swinbourne was engaged to recite "The Charge of the Light Brigade." Surely, even Mrs. Weldon could see that this was a special occasion. Unfortunately, she could not. She took a box with Angele and several of her more adoring ladies at her side, dressed in their choir costume, and besought the plaudits of the crowd. These were not slow in coming. As reward she scattered leaflets into the stalls. This was worse than the coarsest music hall. The acting manager of the theater was dispatched to remonstrate with her: she began to sing. Copies of a publication called the *Medium,* which carried an appealing photogravure of her, were flung over the wall of the box and snatched up by some promenaders. Others were scandalized. Balaclava and the destruction of the Light Brigade were subjects not to be abused in this way. Hayes, the front-of-house manager, explained in vain that Covent Garden was "a temple of music." Georgina, with the silly petulance of which she was always capable, accused him of being drunk.

The whole incident probably lasted only a few minutes and the actual program was barely interrupted, but it was more than the Gattis or Rivière could tolerate. On October 28 the contract with Mrs. Weldon's choir was terminated for a second time. This time there was to be no going back. Rivière and Hayes made it absolutely clear that no member of the choir would be admitted to the theater under any pretext.

The following night, Georgina, Angele, and a younger woman named Michou presented themselves at the theater, with tickets purchased in Mme Michou's name. Georgina was, of course, recognized, and at the door to the first-tier box she had booked, she found Hayes, Mr. Sydney, representing the Gattis, and Inspector Cruse of the Metropolitan Police. Sydney, who was Irish, had already had his temper provoked by leaflets being distributed to the crowd outside, outlining with Georgina's usual attention to detail the wrongs that had been visited on her by the management. He was having none of that and said so. He must now ask her to leave. By way of reply, she tipped his hat from his head and Sydney fell back, crying, "By Jove, she has given me a black eye!" The three women were bustled halfway downstairs, sat down and refused to budge, and were carried down the last steps by policemen summoned for the task. Georgina lost a bracelet that was wrenched from her wrist in the struggle and had her veil torn. The altercation was carried on outside, Georgina demanding that Cruse arrest her. "Lock me up! I wish you to do it!" He declined.

Georgina was, however, soon enough back at Bow Street, defending a civil action for assault brought by Sydney. Angele, who had not been harmed by anyone, pinched and pummeled her own upper arms until they were black-and-blue, got a doctor's certificate, and sued the Irishman in her turn. The choir sued Rivière, Rivière sued the choir. Then the two women settled down at Tavistock House headquarters to libel the impresario with the information gathered in Paris by Angele about his bigamous marriages, his bastard children, and his previous business dealings. They did this in a systematic way, calculated to bring a response. On December 9 Georgina was served with a writ for criminal libel.

O n May 24, 1880, on the morning of her forty-third birthday, Sir Thomas Chambers sentenced Georgina to four months' imprisonment as a common felon. She was taken from the court past suddenly indifferent defense counsel and driven by closed van to Newgate. That afternoon Neal, the solicitor, went to Tavistock House and evicted the hysterical Angele, after a four-hour siege.

Georgina served thirty-seven days of her sentence. The women warders liked her, the governor was polite but unfeeling. The medical examination she underwent was perfunctory and of course insulting. She reserved her biggest contempt for the chaplain. Prison life was ruled by regulation, some of it pettifogging in the extreme, so that she was forbidden, for example, writing materials. She worked in the sewing room, at night sang in her cell and recited poetry. She resisted the chaplain's attempts to make her see the error of her ways—the poor man did not grasp that she was above the law, as it was represented by English justice. Nor did she find the higher truths he might have to offer attractive.

She passed her time in Newgate without the slightest remorse and seemed not to be in any way fazed by imprisonment—it was another form of theater, in which she, by her own lights, acted out the principal role. She wore the prison uniform with pride. Many prisoners of conscience had preceded her at Newgate, and in that sense she was in noble company. She had the knack not every first offender has of seeing out her time in quiet dignity, and though a woman was hung during her stay, that was a secondary event, played off stage. This image of an exemplary prisoner was illusory, however: by now her head was crammed with dates and facts, a small encyclopedia of grudges. There were plenty of others in prison like her, who could recite in excruciating detail times and places, lost witnesses and false affidavits, maddening bad luck. For the first time she was solely in the company of the unjustly accused, and the idea pleased her. "I wonder women can endure men," she commented, after listening to their stories.

Newgate was the experience of asylum without the accompanying terror—everyone would leave one day. In her own case she knew that on the outside Angele was running distractedly from office to office, petitioning the Home Office and writing to the Speaker of the House of Commons. James Salsbury, an elderly member of the choir, was another ally. He kept a health food shop and vegetarian restaurant (probably the first in London) at 23 Oxford Street and, more useful still, was the proprietor of a newspaper called the *Herald of Health*. Never a door closed without another opening.

Georgina was released at the end of June, to be greeted by a welcoming crowd outside the gates. She estimated it to be twenty thousand strong. Two versions exist of her release. In one, Angele arrived to collect her in a closed carriage, and the governor had her bundled away before a demonstration could commence. The details are entertaining:

> My solicitor, who was a first class idiot and had been brainwashed by the opposing side, and who doubted the coup I was meditating [of causing a quasi-political demonstration] which would have been so easy to accomplish, hired a coach, did the Good Samaritan and got la Menier to accompany him with the little Duprat children. Once in front of the gates, seeing the crowd, she wanted to get out and greet me. The old fox stopped her. The Governor had told her that if she left the coach he wouldn't release me at all. She believed him: or did she believe him? God knows . . . I was released, I was flabbergasted, there was cheering: where were Blackie and the kids? There? In the coach! I threw myself forward to embrace them; someone pushed me in by my backside, the door slammed, the coachman whipped up his horses at a great gallop and I was left shouting stop! stop! I've been tricked . . .

In the second version of events, which she reserved for the platform of lunacy law reform meetings and rallies, the crowd embraced her, she was pelted with flowers and fruit, dragged in her carriage to the Old Bailey, where speeches were made in her honor, and then driven to Hyde Park, where she addressed the cheering multitudes at Speaker's Corner. She certainly went to see her mother at Stratford Street later that day. Louisa Treherne, at last stirred to be where the action was, counseled her yet again to seek a reconciliation with Harry. Or, if they could not live together, to accept what terms he might offer for a legal separation.

Money was not the immediate issue, though it may have seemed so to her mother. Georgina had lost Tavistock House forever. Her personal effects, including her musical scores and the chronofile she was building of her life, along with some furniture that was hers and not Harry's, had gone into storage at Shoolbred's in Tottenham Court Road. The house itself was bolted and barred—she learned it was being put on the market at £1,700. This had grave implications for the future of the orphanage, though just where everyone was was difficult to establish from Angele's wobbly narrative of what had happened after she left France.

For the present, Georgina had more notoriety than ever before and just after her release made a triumphant appearance at the Central Hall, Bishopsgate, dressed in her prison uniform. But the audience for this sort of thing was narrow and generally confined to what were called "progressive" elements of society. Mr. Salsbury of the vegetarian restaurant, who pleaded with her to let him help, was a self-styled utopian. She was falling among strangers here. Louisa Lowe was the model social reformer from the progressive ranks—cautious, diligent, and possessed of a patience Georgina soon found grating. It was not her job and in no way her style to campaign for others. The only instance of social injustice she recognized was her own. It might irritate the Lunacy Law Reform Society and The People's Cross to realize this, but she was being honest with them. It had been her head in the lion's mouth and not theirs.

Everyone interested in social reform found out sooner or later in their dealings with Georgina that she made an impassioned and reckless captain but a very bad foot soldier. Those who ate at Salsbury's restaurant did so under this banner:

The Novelty of the Nineteenth Century!
The ALPHA, First London Food Reform Restaurant &
Vegetarian Dining Rooms—No Fish! No Flesh! No Fowl!
No Intoxicants! No Tobacco!

As diners practiced their virtue, there were to hand pamphlets on almost every aspect of "rational being." They might, for example, browse the writings of a Mr. Nicholls and his wife, who between them had written a hundred works on "sanitary and social science," all published from the same address as where they sat. Some of the women patrons were members of the Rational Dress Society and wore simple straight skirts and plain blouses. Their figures were uncorseted, leading them to be mocked in the street but respected in the Alpha as harbingers of a new and more right-thinking age. Others, though they were not spiritualists, could find much to commend in the systematic investigations of the psychic world by such men as Sir William Crookes, the distinguished chemist, or F. W. H. Myers, an eminently respectable school inspector. Vegetarians ate Salsbury's lettuce and raw cabbage but also pored anxiously over statistics that seemed to show a correlation between industrial output and diet. In comparisons made between the French and British economies, it was often asserted that the latter's superiority had much to do with the boiled beef and carrots of the British workingman, as well as his penchant for beer over wine. These claims needed refuting. For many freethinkers, the comfort of being in the right when so many were in the wrong was greatly enhanced by the steady tone of the arguments set forth. The appeal was to the mind.

The defense counsel in the Tichborne Claimant case, Maurice Edward Kenealy, was a habitué of the Alpha restaurant. He was fond of quoting the toast of a country gentleman: "May every lawyer shoot a parson and be hanged for it." It was not exactly the antiestablishment sentiment with which Georgina herself entered the fray. Nor did she have any of the practical philanthropy of a man like Dr. Edmunds, who had so promptly given her a clean bill of mental health after the visit of the mad doctors. She liked to describe Edmunds, a neighbor of hers in Bloomsbury, as an atheist and thus a free spirit, without apparently knowing that he helped found the Ladies

Medical Society, to enable women to qualify as midwives. Just as Georgina had never met the criminal mind before the Meniers came into her life, so now she was among strangers with the freethinking allies who rallied to her cause.

Her mother's repeated advice was to give up fighting altogether. Georgina demurred. To do that, her life would be forever afterward the story of a woman who had defied her husband and lost. She knew very well that Harry did not want her back, yet was all that had happened to her really just the story of a bad marriage? Did her failure have something to do with being a misunderstood artiste, or was it the awful commonplace of being an inadequate wife? Her mother thought the latter and so did the insufferably priggish Dal. She did not know what Harry himself thought—he made no attempt to contact her except through the unfortunate Neal—but she believed (and she may have been right) that he was, if pushed, likely to be more generous about her than many of her critics. He had married exactly the wrong woman. Nevertheless, he had supported her ambitions for as long as he could and longer than most men of his generation would have attempted. He did not love her now, but where was the story in that? Many men did not love their wives. She supposed he must like her a little and even admire her. She had put him in the box he was in, but it could not be his intention to see her snuffed out altogether. Deep down, she knew Harry as well as he knew her. Although she was forty-three and heavy with prison food, tired and in poor voice, she was not ready to give up. Nor, much as Angele would like it, was she the kind of woman to live in semiretirement at some foreign hotel, eking out her days with whist and idle conversation. She had seen all that as a child in Florence.

She took rooms in Burton Crescent, which overlooked Tavistock House. Her two cats were still to be seen through the railings. She conceived a plan to exhume the bones of the dogs buried under the mulberry tree. Even the kindly officers of Hunter Street might jib at her breaking and entering a property with the intention of digging up two dead dogs. The problem at all points was the law. She owed the solicitor who acted for her in the Rivière case £280, which she knew he had not a hope of recovering. Neal controlled Schoolbred's, where all her letters and diaries were cached. On the sole occasion she had been permitted to inspect the depository, she found a crucifix given to her in Florence. One of Christ's arms had broken off. This struck her as a special omen, but there were a hundred other small daily irritations. Her mother called at 54 Burton Crescent and finding her not at home, wandered away again: Georgina explained in rage that she lived at number 45. Louisa returned and left a cake and some chocolates on the doorstep. Her reason for not knocking was that she did not have a card she could send up. (Another of Louisa's more endearing habits was to send letters she forgot to stamp, which drove Georgina into paroxysms.) Harry could not be found anywhere, and Neal refused to answer for his whereabouts.

This was a situation that could not endure. Georgina engaged a new solicitor, named Leaver, and instructed him to serve an order on Harry demanding restitution of conjugal rights. In September she quit London abruptly for Gisors, taking Angele and Bichette with her.

The nuns had done the best they could with the remnants of the orphanage. The unlucky Dagobert never reached Gisors, but many of the others did and were fostered with local families. Rosie Strube received instruction and was accepted into the Catholic Church. Beryl took her place as the nun's blue-eyed girl. One of the boys, Georgina does not say which, received a prize, she does not say for what. M. Robine, the lay administrator, greeted her like a long-lost friend and persuaded her to relax and, if not forget her troubles, at least enjoy the peace and tranquillity of an autumnal Gisors. She played cards with him in the evenings and tried to explain the conundrum of the Tichborne Claimant. In practical terms, the problem of the orphans was being gently prized from her hands. M. Robine and his staff did not see them as the advance guard of a new system of music education, but as children. They were gradually assimilated into the community, a process already started when Georgina rejoined them.

Robine sensed she would not stay long, one indication of which was the flurry of unstamped letters that arrived from England. In November Dal wrote, an unexpected and alarming event. He had bad news. Harry had wriggled for three months before the order for restitution of conjugal rights was successfully served on him. He refused it. The refusal was a legal ploy, and the situation was now quite straightforward. Harry had used his only defense. A husband could refuse restitution of conjugal rights on one ground only, adultery on the part of his wife. Georgina was genuinely horrified to hear that her husband intended to cite Sir Henry Thompson of Wimpole Street for adultery.

At first she denied everything. Her brother wanted her to come to London and meet him. This she refused to do. Nor would she give up the name of her solicitor. Dal persisted. He had seen a letter written to the Moth in her handwriting on which learned counsel engaged by Harry had given an opinion. Though no more than a few sheets of paper already sixteen years old, the letter provided sufficient evidence for Harry to have a good chance of winning his action. In citing the distinguished surgeon for divorce, he would disgrace and humiliate one of the most gifted and interesting men in London. The only possible way out of the impasse was for Georgina to withdraw the order and accept whatever terms for a legal separation Harry imposed. It was blackmail. "I seize the opportunity to abuse you of an idea you seem to have," Dal wrote,

> that I am afraid to appear in public and that consequently I want to hush up the whole affair. I have no such fear. I have worked and I am working entirely in what I believe to be your own interest and the best for you in all circumstances. You seem to think I am in the habit of seeing Weldon. I have only seen him once when he came in company with Mr. Jevons to make known his intentions (having been advised to do so by his counsel) I being head of the family . . . I ended the conversation by saying to them what I tell you, that I consider the Restitution of Conjugal Rights, after all that has taken place, *absurd*, unless he were a consenting party: but that I have felt, and I feel now that you have the right to claim a judicial separation with an allowance sufficient for the present and in the future.

Harry's response was to offer her, through Dal, an allowance of £500 during his lifetime, and it brought forth a blistering reply from Georgina:

Your common sense should have led you to show Weldon and Jevons the door as soon as they spoke with such insolence, demonstrating they took you for an innocent, making you swallow such rubbish . . . after the *infamies* M.W. has shown himself capable of towards a wife who has always been so devoted to him, something he himself has told you . . . I have no more patience with your lack of discernment or sense of dignity, nor am I happy at the conduct of Mr. Leaver, to whom I shall make my own observations. Nor more interventions for the love of God, except those that I myself suggest! I really do have reason to say that "the family is the enemy of what nature you are given when you come into the world."

Poor Mama! I do not think she has ever had bad intentions towards me, but, egged on by others, no one has done me more harm than her. There are instances where she has utterly failed in her duty towards me. She should have come to live with me at Tavistock after the mad doctors affair, as I begged her to do. Others were far too interested in keeping her with them for her to be able to respond to my appeal: I have been treated unworthily by you all. As for my *exhibitions at police courts:* give me the pleasure of citing a single instance where I have been wrong or out of order. I'm not asking you to furnish a list—it would not need more than one example. It should be possible to do that, surely, without you having to write or

me to read a book . . . Of what great statesman does this letter make
you think? None less than Gladstone. I sincerely hope that's so.

Georgina wrote these words to her brother just before Christmas of
1880 as the conclusion to an enormously long letter in which all the old accusations of bad faith are gone over again and again. The truth was she by
no means had Gladstone's talent for marshaling an argument. What she had
to say to Dal was more or less repeated in a pamphlet printed for her by Salsbury addressed to the new owners of Tavistock House. It was entitled *An
Urgent Appeal to the Israelite Men and Women, Patrons and Patronesses of a
School for Jews*. Nothing in the pamphlet was of the slightest practical value
to them, nor did it have any interest to the public at large, unless it was to
confirm their worst suspicions: she was becoming a one-note author, and
exile in Gisors was making her worse.

It was a sad thing, but everything that was going to happen to her in life
had already happened. She knew that. Nothing and no one new would ever
come along as exciting as Gounod or as dangerous as the mad doctors incident. Gisors was fine, but it was the kind of calm retired folk are thrust into.
Doing nothing when nothing is happening is no relaxation. She insisted on
rising at six and, after a cold bath, made at least the pretense of washing the
convent floors as a small act of religious obedience. She fed the chickens and
tended the rabbits. She filled her day with small duties, went to bed early—
and found she could not sleep. The same old tune was going round and
round in her head. She wished to justify herself, but the means she chose—
defamation of others and the most obscure projections of conspiracy (for
example, that Sir Thomas Chambers, who had heard the Menier trial, was
also M.P. for Marylebone, in which constituency many of her worst detrac-
tors also resided)—did her case nothing but harm. The good sisters needed
her money and acted toward her with unfailing common sense but were
completely unable to assuage her grief. The comic singer Arthur Blunt
thought it worth his while to come to Gisors in hope of debauching her
under the guise of cheering her up. He was sent packing.

Angele was even more restless. If this was to be the end—stalemate in the courts and a life eked out in Gisors watching the children grow up, take communion, and a year or so later marry some unwary farmhand—then where was the pleasure in that? It was not much different from the dreary life she had led in Clermont Ferrand and from which she had fled only to ruin herself. Her husband had vanished, vowing never to speak to her again (he was actually locked up in the Bicetre prison in Paris for an unrelated fraud, along with his equally scheming and devious brother Eugène). The nuns bored her, and she had heard the fine detail of the last two years of Georgina's tribulations until she was ready to scream. Georgina might have the constitution of a horse, but she also had an elephant's memory. Angele was far more easily downhearted than Georgina: failure made her ill. Seldom a week passed without the interment of some ancient old Gisorard, and the bells seemed to be tolling for her. Her youth, her looks, her years of promise, were as spent as Georgina's, and what had she to look forward to in the future? Nothing but arguments. She was no more capable of settling down to the life of *une bonne femme* than her lover. There was no cottage with roses over the door, no puttering exile in some forsaken village or other, there or anywhere else in Europe.

To the dismay of the sisters, she persuaded Georgina to let her take five of the children out of the convent and move back to London. The means existed—Salsbury's house at Brixton was at their disposal, and he was anxious to resume contact with his fellow utopian. In every other respect it was a crazy idea.

I should have been ashamed to confess to anyone that I was weak enough to take a house for her and five children when all that was managed so well at Gisors. I have a weird character. It's true! When a matter of principle is at stake, I'm steel! Adamantine! Otherwise I have a *deplorable* feebleness of character. People have told me about her "if she isn't happy, she sets about making life miserable for others. Fancy you needing to mess with such a woman!" They are telling the truth. My little friend Salsbury told me the same thing but . . . *she didn't want to let me go!* There's the truth of it and to get some peace and not have her on my back any longer, I pleaded the case so well that my friend did as I did. He gave in.

Angele left for England with the remaining five orphan girls in May 1881, leaving Georgina to celebrate her forty-fourth birthday alone in Gisors. Salsbury gave her the keys to the Brixton house and inquired anxiously after Georgina. Angele was curt and ungracious. She hired a maid and someone to teach the children, a young Frenchwoman named Eugénie Morand. Then, to Salsbury's dismay, she left for Clermont Ferrand, on the pretext that her father was ill. Though she undoubtedly loved Georgina, she could not help abusing her simplicity. It was not Angele who was the darling of the Alpha restaurant, nor had anyone there ever heaped sympathy on *her* head for a disastrous marriage and the general cruelty of men. In the confusion of the last three years Bichette had been left in Paris—as it turned out, for good. Angele's interest in her had evaporated. Nor did she act now out of love for any of the other children. Georgina was right about her motive: she brought the last of the orphans back to England as a demonstration of her power over her lover and left for Clermont Ferrand for the same reason.

It would have taken a novelist to unravel the exact relationship between these two women. There was no doubting they were intimate in a way that far exceeded that of mistress and servant, or a lady and her companion, although they generally preserved the outward forms of such arrangements. Whatever was or had been sexual in their behavior was never apparent, though it was obvious to people who knew them at all well that these were two women in thrall to each other. They squabbled, they sobbed bitter tears of reproach, they kissed and made up: in appearance, two short and dumpy women with volcanic tempers who dressed almost identically and had the same fine disregard for conventional morality. Like man and wife, they shared a secret history which they guarded with smiles and frowns, handholding and kisses, as well as dark moods and spectacular fits of sulking. It was not in Georgina to flaunt her deepest emotional desires any more than it was Angele's way to reveal her own crippled dependency on money as the substitute for love. Georgina wanted fame; Angele craved for the sheer ordi-

nariness of a bourgeois existence. Nevertheless they were—and were seen to
be—a couple. They were together because they could not bear to be apart.

Harry was not above using the bond that existed between them. A few
days after Angele left for England, Georgina received news that he was trying to get the divorce hearing heard *in camera*. "I'll move heaven and earth
to put a stop to that little game," she wrote to her mother on May 28. When
the letter was finally published, she glossed it with this note:

> Mr. Weldon had made his solicitors and lawyers really believe
> I was given over to a vice of which one cannot speak—although not
> a matrimonial offence recognised by the law. The lawyers acted in
> good faith, as did the judge, but you must understand very clearly
> that Mr. Weldon, who knew the truth, well appreciated that he was
> able to play the role of a generous man who would rather suffer
> himself than reveal the true wickedness, the real mania of someone
> he loved so much . . .

On June 7 she came back to England, staying with Salsbury in Oxford
Street. It was some small consolation that shortly after she arrived, she heard
that Dal was bitten by a dog and laid up in bed for a fortnight. She may also
have had trouble concealing her satisfaction at the news that Emily's husband, Bill, had sent in his resignation to the duke of Newcastle and was planning to move south and buy a restaurant. "The fortunes of the Trehernes
have never been at a lower ebb than this year," Louisa wailed. She discussed
waistlines with her daughter, who was trying to slim. Georgina had inherited the Dalrymple stomach, and Louisa advised her to conceal it artfully behind shawls, as she herself did. It was all trivial. The courts were on
vacation, the weather was unpleasantly close and warm, the bank and some
of her creditors were pressing—after only a few weeks Georgina retreated
across the Channel once again.

In December, while Georgina was right in the middle of deciding how
to avoid being represented as a vicious and heartless lesbian, the bomb that
had been ticking since 1863 finally went off. She rushed home to England
and wrote to her mother, straight from the ferry:

While I am very tired with my travels today, I must write to you, since I have been very shaken up to learn by the purest of chances that Mr. Weldon has a son (who it seems resembles him like two drops of water) who's about thirteen years old, and with his mother is often to be found with Mr. Weldon on board a *Houseboat* at *Maple-Durham*! I am in a fury!!! She, it seems is wonderfully turned out—and she's a dressmaker . . . Now we see the reason why he abandoned me at Muhlberg the winter of 1869–70. Remember how I was tormented on that rat's behalf? I've got your letters. Have you got mine, expressing my love and anxiety on his behalf? Yours did their best to reassure me. It makes me furious, all the more because he knows how much I would have been happy to have a baby to raise. I told him that no matter what bastard he were to have, I would be happy to raise it.

It was a terrible confession to have made, wrenched out of her by real anguish.

No sooner had she sent this letter than she received one from Angele's mother. Old M. Helluy had died in November, and Mme Helluy, who was far, far from the source of all these alarms and excursions, wrote a piteous and semiliterate letter asking for help. It was almost certainly dictated by Angele. As she always did, Georgina replied promptly. Her letter was courteous and kindly. She invited Mère Helluy to come and live under her roof in London, forgetting for the moment she did not have one.

In three days the deepest parts of her had been laid bare, both the hidden grief of being childless, a thing she never spoke about to others and which neither friends nor enemies took into account; and the streak of generosity and willingness that ran through all her actions. Mère Helluy had no more means of coming to London than she had of emigrating to Tahiti, and what she wanted was a bit of the money that Angele assured her was there for the taking; but that was not the point. Georgina believed without thinking about it that she could, and had the old lady come, would have tried to do her best for her. Not for very long, perhaps, and almost certainly without a happy outcome, but heartfelt.

It was Christmastime in Oxford Street, with brass bands playing at street corners and a distressing number of peddlers selling children's toys. In a fit of despair Georgina went out and bought a hat for £25, of embroidered velvet with a plume of ostrich feathers. She justified the expense by explaining she must have something suitable for the divorce court proceedings that could not much longer be delayed. In her heart she was competing with the elegant and sophisticated Annie Lowe wrapping presents for her son, somewhere in that dream of domestic bliss from which fate and Harry Weldon had excluded her forever.

The Courts

1

*I*n the new year a sulky Angele returned from Clermont Ferrand alone and resumed disgruntled occupancy of 33 Loughborough Road, Brixton. The children were noisy and obstreperous and Georgina seldom there. Angele consoled herself by taking Eugénie Morand, the orphans' tutor, drinking with her at the London Aquarium—a pickup place for lonely men and women. Life was turning her sour. She had some solace from being in sole charge of a house for the first time in her life, and while the neighbors may have found the children a trial, they could not help admiring Angele's way with lace and chenille. On fine days, Georgina's canaries sang in cages in the garden, which was much more scrupulously tended than the one belonging to Tavistock House. Harry's money, passed on via Georgina, was bringing out the stifled bourgeoise in the Frenchwoman. The days of running after her crazy Englishwoman were all but over, and Georgina was more like a lodger than a lover nowadays. Still mar-

ried to Menier, Angele hardly expected to see him again, or any of her confederates from Montmartre. There was nothing for her in Clermont Ferrand
except a grieving mother. She was stalled. Many of her neighbors in Loughborough Road were materially worse off, but was it really her destiny to sit
listening to the trams and waiting for the story to take a new twist? She
amused herself by practicing Georgina's handwriting.

In July 1882 Harry suddenly gave everything a new impetus. Georgina
was served with a summons to show cause why the respondent should not be
at liberty to withdraw his defense and submit to a decree for the restitution
of conjugal rights. She had to read it several times to confirm the sense, but
at last she was persuaded: Harry had given up the fight. It was rumored he
was suicidal and in failing health, and it may also have been that threatening
to ruin the reputation of Sir Henry Thompson by dragging his name
through the divorce courts was more than his Garrick friends could
stomach.

A week after being summonsed Georgina appeared before Sir James
Hannen, president of the Probate, Divorce and Admiralty Division, and
was asked by counsel, "Have you committed adultery?" "Certainly not,"
she replied, "it is an infamous lie and Mr. Weldon knows it." It was all that
was required of her in law, and Hannen and the jury gave her the triumph
she had been denied for four years. She wrote Harry a four-thousand-word
letter in which she demanded conjugality with a facetiousness that barely
disguises her contempt.

How can you suppose I can wish to live anywhere but under
your roof? There, at least, I am safe. If anything happened to me
there, the suspicion would fall on you and you would risk being
hanged. You would not like that. Remark, if you have not before,
how like your skull and chin are to Lefroy's [a notorious murderer].
Your voice, Lamson's soft and pleasant voice. It is not my fault, my
poor old man, if you have these instincts. The most elementary
rules of phrenology will teach you and show you I have the most
perfectly shaped head. I can no more help being good than you can
help being bad.

She might have done better by discussing with him what to do about Annie Lowe and under what roof they would resume relationships. There was the question of the house in Brixton: was Angele now to be director of the orphanage, which Georgina persisted in calling it, though her practical involvement in it had dwindled to nothing? If she dumped Angele, was Harry to find some sort of pension for the Frenchwoman? These were practical and immediate questions, though she did not fully realize that it was one thing to get a court to say they must live together and quite another to make it happen. She could not command it, and the lawyers were (though she did not know it yet) uneasy at the ruling. It could not be good law to be able to bring a husband to prison for failing to cohabit with his wife—though until now it had not seemed strange to punish a woman in this way. Harry had not attended the court hearing and he ignored her victory letter. After a pause, he let it be known through Neal that rather than submit to the findings of the court in deed as well as word, he would sell up and leave the country. Even though he had risen in the ranks of the Heralds—he was by now Windsor Herald as well as treasurer of the College—he would give it all up and flee.

In August an even more glittering triumph was in prospect. The Birmingham Musical Festival Committee had at last decided to offer the first performance of *The Redemption*, the work Gounod had tried to dedicate to the Queen in 1873 with such disastrous results. Georgina felt a special empathy with this oratorio, having been present at its gestation. She had heard some of its gloomy chords echo down the stairs at Tavistock House and discussed the work with its composer on many an evening. It was with tremendous excitement that she learned the Birmingham festival had tempted Gounod back to England to conduct the first public performance. In April she had gone in secret to Paris to attend the first night of what proved to be his last opera, *Le Tribut de Zamora*. For the occasion, she wore an enormous medal given her from an unlikely source—a French society for "the improvement of morals." With this as her breastplate, she found the libretto of the opera—the sale of virgins by auction—a disgusting subject and Gounod disheveled and elderly. She made no attempt to speak to "the old man" and sent him no flowers or tributes. Nevertheless, though she attended the theater incognito, she was sufficiently vain to feel certain she had been recog-

nized with sympathy by many in the distinguished audience, which included
Gambetta and the President of France. It was a golden moment, and now
she had a chance to repeat it on home soil. Gounod, who had embraced her
country only to desert it, should now see her in the stalls at Birmingham, not
as a humiliated mistress, but as a person of consequence.

She arrived in Birmingham to find the hotel of her choice full—full, or,
as she immediately suspected, the management was lying in its teeth. She
walked to the Town Hall and hung about outside, listening to the work being
rehearsed, too nervous to go in. Inside, Gounod was not less tense. He knew
she had been in the audience for *Le Tribut de Zamora*, and *Redemption* held
as many memories of Tavistock House for him as it did for her. It was in-
conceivable that she would stay away. If Georgina is to be believed, he had
also received certain anonymous letters claiming she was coming not merely
to enjoy the show, but with a loaded revolver in her purse. Angele's handwriting practice had not been in vain.

Meanwhile, the whole of Birmingham was talking of nothing else but
Gounod's visit. It was said that the festival veteran Sir Julius Benedict, who
was premiering a cantata called *Graziella*, the last work of a life now sev-
enty-seven years old, was infuriated by the public indifference in the city to
any topic but Gounod. There was almost a frenzy of anticipation in the city.
The chairman of the festival was the lord mayor of Birmingham and also
the proprietor of the *Birmingham Post*. The publicity attending the premiere
of *Redemption* was enormous. It was reported in the *Post* how Cardinal
Newman had begged permission to visit rehearsals of this mammoth work,
for which the festival committee had paid a record sum. Readers learned that
the musical score ran to 560 pages, the subject matter ranging from the Creation to the Crucifixion. No first night had been waited for with more impa-
tience since the days when Mendelssohn first performed as an organ recitalist
and conducted *St. Paul* in the year of Georgina's birth. In the circumstances,
it would have been more surprising if Georgina had *not* gone to Birmingham.

On August 30 she set off for the Town Hall with her ticket and a copy
of the score under her arm. Some way from the entrance, she was met by a
festival steward and an inspector of police. They gave her a note from the

management saying she would not be admitted, and when she tried to push past them, she was restrained. It was Rivière and Covent Garden all over again. The audience filed past in their thousands, the doors were solemnly closed, and what was widely considered the summation of the oratorio tradition, a work worthy to be compared to the great Handel himself, took place without her. It received a rapturous reception. For Gounod it set the seal on an illustrious career and was a total vindication of his English sojourn. *Redemption*, though hardly ever performed nowadays, was taken up with an almost hysterical enthusiasm. It was no surprise that Benedict had been outfaced: no composer could have stood comparison with the Frenchman, for whom the festival was a complete and unqualified succès fou. As the last bars spilled out from the auditorium onto the streets outside, carried by a choir of 400 and an orchestra of 180, Georgina was still squabbling tearfully with the festival staff and trying to get the police to make an arrest for assault. She was given the name of a local solicitor and told to be on her way.

At the end of the work, Gounod was carried back to his hotel in the full triumph of his achievement, his hands patting away the plaudits in mock modesty. He was probably never told what had happened to his little singing bird, his dearest friend, his English muse, nor did he inquire. Henry Littleton was waiting at the door to his suite to congratulate him. By one of those ironies that help define professional art, he had placed the rights of this work with the old enemy, Novello's. He may once have threatened to go to prison rather than pay Littleton his piddling damages, but things were different now. The newly elected grand officer of the Legion of Honour shook hands on a deal that was to net him many thousands of pounds. He could afford to dismiss the promoter with a wave of his hand and go in search of a good wine and as many pretty girls as wished to worship him. Georgina returned to London by late train.

Twelve days later she purchased a copy of the Married Woman's Property Act of 1882, studied it with the greatest care and interest, and realized she had at her disposal the means of revenge, not only on l'Abbé Gounod and his sickening hypocrisy but on all the others who had ever crossed or double-crossed her. It was like being given the keys to a palace. Under the provisions of the act, the fiction of unity that had dogged the legal interpretation of married life was at an end. She was now in law a *femme sole* with freedom to bring a civil action in her own name. The keys unlocked one door after another—behind which cowered the Birmingham Festival Committee to be sure, but many others. She had told de Bathe that he would repent of his actions, and now she had the means. It was dizzying. There was almost no one beyond her grasp—the four mad doctors, Rivière, and of course Gounod. Tucked away in her closely indexed correspondence was a letter by the maestro asking her to itemize his bill for the time spent in Tavistock House; and her extensive account by way of reply. She had not received a penny from him; now he would be brought to his knees before the majesty of the law, as interpreted not by some fusty clown in a horsehair wig, but by Georgina Weldon, plaintiff in person.

*R*evenge, say the Italians, is a dish best eaten cold. Before the act that gave her power to plead her own case in civil actions, Georgina's appearances in court had been as witness or defendant. She was well known within the legal profession for being a wrecker, with only the sketchiest understanding of how trials were conducted, an ignorant woman with an overinflated idea of herself. She was good for fees. Those who had dealings with her and went on later to deride her in their clubs had overlooked one thing. She might know nothing of the law, but she most certainly had a histrionic ability that if it were ever trained would be a formidable weapon. All she needed was the knowledge with which to back it up.

A few months after she first read the Married Woman's Property Act, she met a man after her own heart, an elderly solicitor named William Chaffers. Some time earlier, Mr. Chaffers had been aggrieved to notice that a titled gentleman had secured tickets to the royal enclosure at Ascot for a lady of loose morals. This would not do, and he wrote to the Lord Chamberlain to say so. The lady proved to be the wife of the knight in question—a fact Chaffers may well have known. He was prosecuted for attempted blackmail. However, on the morning that the wife was to be called to give evidence about the respectability of her origins, she fled the country and the case collapsed. Chaffers's victory was short-lived: though innocent as charged, he was struck off for his impudence and had since eked out a miserable and understandably embittered existence. This was exactly the sort of boon companion Georgina needed. Chaffers taught her the language of law and how to prepare a plea.

In September writs were served on Neal, Winslow, Rudderforth, Rivière, the editors of the *Daily Chronicle* and the London *Figaro,* Semple, de Bathe, and finally Harry. "Now I must look out the other ruffians," she commented grimly.

The writs had been issued from premises in Red Lion Court at the head of Fleet Street, more or less opposite the Inner Temple, where Morgan had sauntered in the days of his youth. They struck their recipients dumb with amazement. Harry had been served in the Garrick, his solicitor Neal at the office. When they conferred, it was clear she proposed to mount an all-out attack on the mad doctors episode, with the incident on the stairs at Covent Garden as a side dish. The provisions of the 1882 act gave her the powers, and no other woman in England had acted so swiftly upon them. To call it alarming was an understatement. Neither Harry nor any of the others gave a damn for her plaint against Rivière, though Neal was at a loss to see what possible action she could bring there: she had been found guilty of criminal libel and gone to jail for it. The events surrounding the four doctors, Harry, and de Bathe were a different matter. While the affair was now five years old and though the public had a short memory, the notoriety surrounding Mrs. Weldon's "escape" had not gone unnoticed by learned judges. The doctors involved were quite horrified at the thought of being dragged through the courts. Winslow in particular had most to lose.

These first writs were served by a willing if timid clerk named Lever, but there soon appeared someone much more to Georgina's tastes, the drunken, argumentative, and—as it was to prove—unstoppable Captain William Harcourt. Nothing about him was as it seemed. He was not born Harcourt, but Johnston. He never was captain. Gazetted ensign in 1853 just in time to be sent to the Crimea, he found himself before Sebastopol. Quite as weary of the siege as his generals, he exchanged uniforms with a dead Russian and simply walked into the town, where he had "a jolly good time." He marched out of one gate with Menshikov's army as the French and British arrived through another. His later career included a total of twelve years of hard labor and any amount of tall stories. Georgina describes him presenting himself for employment: "a poor thin miserable creature, smelling fearfully strong of beer, stale onions and tobacco, with a suspicion of kipper and bloater." He was taken on at once.

In the little firm she set up in Red Lion Court, the elderly and high-minded Chaffers deviled away in one corner, Georgina rehearsed her legal phraseology at an ink-spattered desk, and Captain Harcourt lounged at the door, ready to dart away at a moment's notice to serve another writ. She found the life entrancing. Chaffers was only there as consultant, for in all the suits she brought forward, she intended to be the plaintiff in person acting *in forma pauperis,* words she was beginning to relish. F. C. Phillips wrote a biographical sketch of her as she was in these Red Lion days:

> In the first room was a grille, behind which, when not serving writs and other processes at his own personal risk, used to sit Mrs. Weldon's secretary, Mr. Harcourt. Mrs. Weldon herself used to transact business in the outer room amid a chaos of ink bottles, stumps of pens, papers and memoranda, legal and otherwise. The inner room was her sanctum, and here she made tea and received her visitors.

Phillips was impressed by her and made note of her short hair, vivacious features, and "eyes strangely brilliant and piercing." He was conscious of her reputation as an escaped lunatic, a thing he scoffed as quite impossible to believe. All the same:

That she was strangely unlike most other women was evident at once. Her manner no doubt was feminine; one could understand in a moment the power she claimed to exercise over children and animals; but with all this there was a strange masculine thread in her character. She behaved like a woman, but she thought and expressed herself as a man, and would and could beyond question make herself extremely disagreeable if she chose to do so . . .

By the end of her first year she had, with Captain Harcourt's energetic assistance, served notice of her first twenty-five actions, which are worth tabulating. They read:

Weldon v. Weldon

Weldon v. de Bathe

Weldon v. Neal (two cases)

Weldon v. Lloyd

Weldon v. Bates

Weldon v. Semple

Weldon v. Rudderforth

Weldon v. Johnson (Figaro)

Weldon v. Winn

Weldon v. Misu

Weldon v. Misu (second case)

Weldon v. Maddock

Weldon v. Jaffray (Birmingham Music Festival)

Weldon v. Sylvester

Weldon v. Moncrieff

Weldon v. Winslow

Weldon v. Winslow (second case)

Weldon v. Weldon (second case)

Weldon v. Gounod

Weldon v. Lloyd (second case)

Weldon v. Rivière (second case)

Weldon v. Budd and Brodie

Weldon v. Stevens

Weldon v. Wontner

In all but three of these cases she represented herself. *Social Salvation,* the *Herald of Health,* the *True Cross,* and all the other little publications for which she had written, all the esoteric knowledge she had been offered from cranks and do-gooders, even the unfailing accuracy of predictions from the Other Side she had received, could now go hang. This wasn't litigation; it was war. It was blitzkrieg.

eorgina recruited one more assistant, Bernard de Bear, a young shorthand writer. Full transcripts of court proceedings were no more widely studied then than they are now, and most people happily took their view of the law from reports published in newspapers— the greater the crime, the more lurid the reporting. Georgina had no trust in what she called "press gush." Hadn't journalists inserted remarks in the Menier trial, attributing words to defense counsel that she was quite sure he never uttered? This would not do for her, always suspicious that some wrong would accure if *any* record were not complete and entire. De Bear was the answer. In giving him the job of reporting her verbatim and demanding from him scrupulous accuracy, she was unknowingly fostering the future principal of the Pitman School of Shorthand. Chaffers to prepare, Harcourt to serve, de Bear to report; nevertheless, the bulk of the work fell upon her. Her enormous energies, her appetite for the impossible challenge, were at long last given shape and focus. The first flurry of actions was merely the beginning. Altogether, from 1883 until the end of the century, she brought over a hundred cases before the courts, pleas heard by learned judges up to and including the Lord Chief Justice, but also footling affairs brought before magistrates' and sessions courts—wherever she could attack her enemies. The sheer scale of these labors was enough to make her famous, irrespective of the results.

The press was not slow to pick up her story. On quiet news days editors would demand in print, "What is Mrs. Weldon up to?," and often the question was answered within the week. In one sense the press invented her—she was in the public eye, a metaphor she by no means found displeasing. As with music, so with journalism: she remained to the end completely naive. She did not and could not distinguish between being newsworthy because of some exceptional talent and being the construct of the newspaper industry. When she was told by a news clipping bureau that she garnered more column inches than many a cabinet minister, it seemed to her a straightforward demonstration of her own superiority, without realizing she was a victim of news values quite as much as their beneficiary.

Her old enemy A'Beckett drew her cartoon in *Punch*, in which she walked a tightrope looking childishly plump and overinnocent, with the minatory caption "Be careful you don't fall, Mrs. Weldon." The implied suggestion that she would fall soon enough was not shared by the wider public. This was a unique instance of a woman clearing her name and reputation with a fearlessness and determination that seemed somehow modern. After such a long journey she had come into step with the mood of the age. If the laws of England were at last offering women a modicum of independence, here was one that seized it with both hands. In the period of her greatest activity, 1883–88, the General Post Office had no trouble at all in delivering letters from all over the world addressed simply to Mrs. Weldon, London.

> Mrs. Weldon is a woman of great natural talents, much increased by conscientious and untiring cultivation, and she has specially addressed herself to the art of singing in which she has few equals and very few superiors. But she is also a very energetic lady, entirely unshackled by conventional ideas. Mrs. Weldon is certainly not as other women are for she has a most indomitable courage, a marvellous energy, and an incredible activity and industry . . .

This description by "Jehu Junior," a pseudonymous newspaper biographer, was cheap puffing journalism, but it reflected popular opinion. For five years or more, hardly a month passed without her presence in one or another court. If the detail was sometimes hard to follow, the broad-brush concept was simple: this was a woman whose good character was the point at issue. She was determined to reinstate it by using the law as her megaphone and the royal courts of justice as an amplifying chamber. Whatever the lawyers might think about that, the general public was on her side. The first journalist to call her Don Quixote struck a chord. Yet in addition to tilting at windmills she also set her lance at the establishment. Part of her popularity came from the desire newspaper readers had to see the world of frock coats and top hats humbled.

"We pay for a Government. We have it! We pay for law. We have it! Fancy paying for substance and receiving—what? Jokes! Chaff! Witticisms on the part of Judges and Magistrates. Bounce! Bluff! Bullying on the part of Barristers." When she spoke like that, she was touching an exposed nerve.

For generations the common experience of those unlucky enough to fall foul of the civil law was how laggardly and cripplingly expensive it was. "Pettifogging" sounds like an adjective flung off by Dickens, but has a much longer ancestry than that. For three centuries perception of the law had been colored by stories of delay, chicanery, and expense. At the same time (and partly as a consequence) newspaper law reports about other people's miseries were a piquant form of theater. For many Victorians they also acted as a kind of social forum. When *Weldon v. de Bathe* was reported by the *Times*, on the same page was a much more extensive report of a case in which a widow sued a life assurance company for payment of a policy of £2,000. What made the case so interesting was that it turned on the deceased man's drinking habits, which it was held he may have falsely represented when taking out the policy and which may have contributed to his death. Much of the evidence was provided by staff and members of the Sunderland Conservative Club, where the policyholder had been a member. The particular point of interest in this case was implied rather than stated. Mr. Lotinga was a Jew.

Weldon v. de Bathe may have taken second billing in the *Times* in that day's law reports, but there was a sequel to it that indicates the general and uneasy interest her suits aroused. Georgina won the case. In doing so she uncovered a piece of law that made the jurors sit up and take notice. It emerged during her questioning of de Bathe that someone who signed an order for committal to an asylum had no power under the law to revoke it. One of the jurors, a Mr. Walter Holcombe, wrote to the *Times* after the trial had concluded:

> The argument that "the person who had signed an order under the statute for the reception of a supposed lunatic had no power to get the party out again" was the most powerful weapon my fellow-jurors had against me in my almost singlehanded fight for what I considered their extravagant idea of the damages to be awarded; and which, had I not taken a firm stand, would have been largely in excess of the substantial sum agreed upon.

Holcombe's letter missed the point. This was not a story about the scale of damages. The jury had heard in evidence a piece of law that seemed to the majority of them completely unjust but that had lain undisturbed since the lunacy laws were first framed. It had taken Georgina Weldon to bring it out into the light.

All the high-profile cases that followed one another down the decades, in addition to their human interest, had the effect of theatrically relighting the fabric of society. An instance of how the law raised matters of general social interest was the conviction of Colonel Valentine Baker for indecent assault in 1875. Baker was one of the most dashing and intelligent cavalry officers in the army when he came to court. He was a Crimean veteran and assistant adjutant general. On conviction for an indecent assault in a railway carriage upon a woman of good character, he asked to be allowed the honorable way out by resigning his commission. Both the Duke of Cambridge and Prince Edward attempted to intercede on his behalf with the Queen. Victoria refused and he was paraded, stripped of his insignia of rank, and had his sword broken. Much was made of the fact that during the trial, out of courtesy to the young woman who brought the charge, Baker refused to question any part of her evidence. By so doing, he ensured his own destruction. This was gentlemanly and ungentlemanly conduct all in the same story.

Everybody (especially Georgina) had an opinion about the Tichborne Claimant. Maurice Kenealy, the Claimant's disgraced and disbarred counsel, went on to publish a scurrilous newspaper about the history of the trial called the *Englishman*. It was edited from grimy rooms in Fleur de Lys Court, a few steps away from Georgina's office. The first number sold a staggering 100,000 copies. With a face value of 2d, this first edition changed hands for as much as half a crown a copy. In only a few years' time, in 1888, the whole country would be convulsed by the Whitechapel murders. It was a story about Jack the Ripper and unsolved crime, but it was also an indictment about the way some people lived. Mrs. Weldon's adventures in court fed this same curiosity. They were high entertainment—the circus attraction of the tightrope walker—but in the actions she brought against Harry, de Bathe, and the mad doctors she added very significantly to the weight of public concern surrounding the operations of the lunacy laws.

In the Semple trial, heard before Mr. Justice Hawkins in July 1884, she subpoenaed Lord Shaftesbury, the chief commissioner of lunacy. Shaftesbury's reputation as a philanthropist and evangelistic social reformer was unimpeachable—he had interested himself in the plight of lunatics since 1828. Now in the last years of his life, almost as old as the century and laden with honor, he came to the Queen's Bench in aid of the strange Mrs. Weldon, a woman he had little sympathy with socially. It was a brilliant coup on her part. Both he and the trial judge exhibited signs of the greatest unease as the evidence unfolded—it has to be remembered that Shaftesbury was being questioned by the very woman who in only slightly different circumstances would have been confined in an asylum without him, as chief commissioner, ever knowing about it.

The judge heard evidence from Shaftesbury that licensed madhouses were conducted on principles of profit. When defense counsel stood up to object, he was waved down. "It is obvious, is it not? It is not to be supposed that anybody will keep a lunatic asylum except for profit."

"Sir Henry Hawkins then asked Shaftesbury, on a point of clarification, whether it was the practice of asylum keepers to send out their own agents and servants to arrest persons as lunatics. Shaftesbury could see where this was leading. Hawkins asked the key question. "Surely it can't be contended that a *doctor* has a right to arrest me, or make an order for my reception into his lunatic asylum just as though he were a policeman arresting me for some offence?"

Before Shaftesbury could reply, Georgina interrupted him. "Ought the *proprietor* to get medical men to give the certificates?"

The chief commissioner for lunacy glanced at Hawkins. Speaking to him rather than to the plaintiff, he replied somberly, "We should look with great suspicion upon such a course."

The public interest aspect could not have been clearer to the jury. What had been uncovered here was bad law. They responded accordingly, giving Georgina damages of £1,000.

As she became better practiced, the knockabout style with which she started out was tempered by a firmer understanding of the law and a shrewd grasp of its personalities. Appearing before the master of the rolls, Lord Esher, she argued a verdict given by Vice-Chancellor Bacon on the grounds that he was too old. (He was in his eighties.) Esher replied, "The last time you were here you complained that your case had been heard by my brother Bowen, and that he could not do justice to you on account of his youth. What age do you require a judge to be?" Plaintiff: "Your age, my lord." It was the kind of swift and easy retort that endeared her to the bench.

Her cross-examining of witnesses was often prolix and in some cases spiteful; nor did she always avoid digging holes for herself. In the Winslow case, defense counsel, a Mr. Clarke, tried to savage her.

Q: You thought the only course of action was to libel people all round?

A: Yes.

Q: Did you send to Dr. Winslow all you wrote against him?

A: Quite everything. (Laughter)

At the end of Clarke's cross-examination, Lord Huddleston directed her gently as follows: "Mrs. Weldon, the position is this: the cross-examination is finished and you have the right to re-examine yourself."

She replied loftily, "He has not asked me anything."

As well as inexperience it was an example of her notorious petulance, and Huddleston was disappointed, because she had just admitted libel and he wished to give her opportunity to defend herself. She had come to the law with more than a little contempt for lawyers and seemed not to understand that judges had once been barristers. It sometimes made her look stupid. Yet her memory was phenomenal, and she was gradually learning how to score points.

Three days later in the same trial she managed to extract from an exquisitely embarrassed Dr. Winn, in an examination about the nature of her certifiable delusions, the admission that in his medical opinion one of the worst of them was that if she had charge of the management of the Albert Hall she could make it pay. This was more impressive. Huddleston heard the evidence with extreme patience and courtesy but in the end nonsuited her. However, in his summing-up he expressed surprise at the workings of the lunacy acts as they had been shown in Georgina's case. Though the actions of the defendants were legal, the law was unsatisfactory. This—and the calling of Lord Shaftesbury as witness in the Semple case—had in the end far more repercussion than who said what to whom.

Not every judge was so well disposed to Georgina, and not all the actions she brought were worth the effort she put into them. The one thing she did not experience was ridicule. Inside the court and out, she was treated with increasing respect. In two areas she scored major successes. The first of these was in *Weldon v. Weldon,* where she attempted to make Harry honor in full the restitution of conjugality. This case caused lawyers some anxieties. As the law stood, the only means of restoring Georgina's rights was by "attachment," which was granted with great reluctance by the president of the Probate, Divorce and Admiralty Division in 1883. The meaning of this was that if Harry still refused to comply with the order against him and cohabit with his wife, he must now go to jail for contempt. The House of Commons took sufficient note of the legal interest in this case to amend the Matrimonial Causes Act of 1884 by abolishing attachment. It was instantly dubbed the Weldon Relief Act, but had far greater consequences for women than for men. Lord Esher, master of the rolls, commented that "the passing of the Act of Parliament which took away the power of attachment in such cases is the strongest possible evidence to show that the legislature had no idea that a power would remain in the husband to imprison the wife for himself; and this tends to show that it is not and never was the law of England that the husband had such a right." It did not matter that in the Weldon case the wife had come close to imprisoning the husband. As Lord Esher indicated, she had uncovered bad law. She had also significantly added to women's rights.

ollowing Maurice Kenealy's example, Georgina published her own paper, *Social Salvation*, a cut-and-paste job on recent newspaper reports of legal injustice, spiked with republished extracts from her earlier pamphlets, advertisements for her forthcoming concerts, and a youthful-looking portrait of her on the back page. On September 15, 1883, the *Daily Chronicle* reported a strange story from the South Coast:

> Considerable anxiety prevailed throughout the whole of yesterday in consequence of nothing being heard of the fate of the balloon "Colonel" which made, with Captain Simmons and Mr. Small, a local photographer, an ascent from that place on Thursday. They landed at Cap de la Hogue at midnight, having given people on the ground reassurance with a printed bill which read *Read The Englishman, founded by Dr. Kenealy, 2d weekly. Read Social Salvation 1/2d monthly, Printed published and sold by Mrs. Weldon.*

Readers were left to guess how these pamphlets came to be in the balloon. However, Captain Simmons was wrestling at the controls of Menier's self-steering invention, which the aeronaut had purchased from Georgina and which showed an exasperating desire to return to its maker.

It was fun to publish the paper, despite the crudity of its production technique and its indifferent sales. It added another arrow to her quiver. But it was not the center of her attention, any more than the concerts she still gave at the Charles Street Chapel in Mayfair or, less romantically, Goswell Road in Clerkenwell. The big battles had to be fought in court, and once Harry had been disposed of, her second most important target was Gounod. The mad doctors paid in full for their impudence and temerity and the part they played in turning her out of Tavistock House. Gounod, however, was a special case. He stood with Harry as an instance of that earlier betrayal she had suffered in the days when the three of them were like brothers and sister. He could never be forgiven his cowardly flight or the subsequent repudiations he made of her once safely back in Paris.

"His letters to me in 1871 . . . besides the numberless conversations we had on the subject gave me the right to believe I had found in him an experienced ally, a robust friend and *an honest lodger*, but as subsequent events have proved, I found but rejection and deception." These words were written in an article for the *Cosmopolitan* which she reprinted in a pamphlet of 1875. That was at a time when nobody had paid her much mind because she had no powers to set things right. If she complained too hard, she would be put down as an example of a type, the hysterical bad loser. Eleven years on, things were very different. She had in her hands now a weapon she fully intended to use. After conferring with Chaffers and checking her legal powers she summoned Captain Harcourt from his lounging post by the door to her office and sent him to Paris to serve a writ on the composer. It was a brilliant stratagem, only too quick to take effect.

After the runaway success of *Redemption* in Birmingham the Queen expressed a desire that the composer should return to England and conduct a new work in the royal presence. There was as it happened something suitable ready to hand—Gounod had composed an oratorio in similar elevated vein entitled *Mors et Vita*. It was nevertheless his painful duty to decline Her Majesty's invitation. The writ Harcourt served made it certain that if he ever set foot in England again, he would be taken up for debt. Though he pleaded with Georgina through intermediaries, she was adamant. His flight from London, the obstacles she believed he had put in her way when she was Valerie de Lotz, and the humiliation she suffered at the Birmingham festival went too deep. Justice must be served!

In personal terms, it was the second of her great victories. Despite entreaties from Littleton, who was making a pleasing amount of money for him in royalties, Gounod never again came to England to conduct. Georgina won both the actions she brought against him, and though she would never collect a single penny in damages, she had scotched the libels drawn down on her by Wolff and the French press.

The news from the mad doctors was equally satisfactory. By the time of the second Winslow trial, Winslow himself was ruined and since he could not afford to engage counsel, was forced to represent himself. He made a miserable job of it.

She was less lucky with Rivière. In the first action she brought against him, the impresario spent £1,600 on lawyers, only to lose the case for a piffling £50 in damages. Rivière had moved from deriding to hating her, an emotion she returned with interest. Her attacks on him intensified. In March 1885 she found herself in the Central Criminal Court defending a crown prosecution on a charge of criminal libel. Everything in the 2,500-word indictment had to do with words she had published since the first case. Rivière now risked his entire wealth to take revenge. No fewer than three leading counsels were ranged against her, including the man she came to fear most among the legal profession, Montagu Williams, Q.C.

Right from the outset, the venom between the two parties was apparent. In cross-examination of Rivière she asked, "You have never trained a choir?"

"No."

"You, not being a musician, you don't know how to."

"What! I beg your pardon. My lord, I can't stand this! I can't be abused in this court. I have been conducting concerts for twenty-five years in this country and I think I am recognised."

"Have you ever given a lesson?"

"I don't give lessons. What for should I give lessons?"

"Have you ever trained a choir?"

"I have never trained a choir."

"You just beat with a stick?"

Sometimes abuse like this found favor with the jury. Here it did not. Her defense in the second Rivière case was her worst performance, and there is no doubt that Montagu Williams did his best to draw out and emphasize the egoist in her. In one exchange he forced this retort from a nettled Georgina: "I have taught little children and now I teach grown up people if I can. Judges can sometimes get a lesson from me."

Williams struck back instantly. "Mrs. Weldon, you teach children, you teach men and you may teach judges, but don't try to teach me."

Nor was the jury impressed by the evidence of Captain Harcourt. "I am in consumption and blind and only want St. Vitus Dance to make me a perfect specimen," he declared, mistaking the mood of the jury. (A little later he was removed from the court for saucing the judge.)

Montagu Williams was two years older than Georgina and, like her, a late starter. He had been a soldier and an actor before taking up the law and had dabbled in journalism and the theater since. The jury had endured a very long and spitefully conducted trial about matters so small, so exact in detail, and very often so far from the point that it became itchy. Williams simplified it all for them in a devastating closing statement:

> Here is the whole cause of it. I will tell you what has been the cause from first to last of all this invective—egregious vanity and an insatiable thirst for notoriety. And that is what led to all this. Why, gentlemen, it was patent from every letter that she read. "Why do you give Madame So and So a hundred pounds a week and not to me? I am the person. I am the great musical star. I am the person who is making your fortune." And because she was not a musical attraction; because she did not bring money into Covent Garden; because she utterly failed; and Mr. Rivière was obliged to remonstrate with her as to the shortcomings of this choir; the history of this black spot, the very origin of all this, was egregious vanity.

She could not hold that Williams was some fusty lawyer who had never lived in the world: he put into his jury address the indignation that comes from experience of theaters and stars and agents. Speaking in a dramatically hoarse voice—he was in fact suffering from cancer of the throat—he managed to compress all the usual prolixity of a Mrs. Weldon trial into one damning word: vanity. When it was her turn to address a closing statement to the jury, she made it one of the shortest of her career.

I am not a young woman, gentlemen of the jury: I have not got a career to look forward to; if I could only get my character into my hands again, it would be to pursue that which I devoted myself to in my youth, sitting quietly at home in my chair, teaching little children. Of course a verdict against me, gentlemen, would be my ruin—you see they have three barristers—the costs would be something tremendous and I could never pay them. They might send me to prison for a year, and there I suppose I might die, because perhaps none of you have been in prison, but I have, and I know how hard it is. I was in the best prison here, but I have never been quit of gout since then. I was half starved, but I was not worse treated than other people are. They were kind women there, but they dared not show it. I was very cold all the time though it was in summer, and the hardships of prison are what nobody can imagine till they have been put there . . . I won't say any more because I feel I have tired you; and therefore I leave myself entirely in your hands, never believing you will find me guilty and condemn me as a common felon.

After twenty minutes' deliberation, the jury found her guilty, and she was sentenced to six months without hard labor. She was taken first to Millbank and then five days later to Holloway.

*B*eautiful place. I have such a nice room." Holloway was then a prison for both men and women serving short sentences. The governor was the courteous and sympathetic Colonel Milman, whose uncle had been "the great dean" of St. Paul's, Henry Hart Milman. She spent another of her birthdays in jail—her forty-eighth—and the governor gave her a musk plant as a present. She kept goldfish and a newt she fed on minced beef. She was even allowed to collaborate with another prisoner in writing a play. She was a very high-profile inmate. On one occasion Milman called her to his office so that she could be served with a writ for costs against her. Only a little while later he was happy to send her with Miss Jackman, the matron, to the Middlesex Sheriff's Court for judgment in the Gounod case.

The Queen's Bench had already awarded her £1,640 for her services to Gounod as amanuensis and the costs of his stay at Tavistock House. The issue now was costs in the part Gounod had taken in the libels made by Wolff and others. The jury was out for a quarter of an hour and returned to award her £10,000. It was a joyous moment, and it drew a line under the emotional and turbulent years she had given to Gounod during his London exile. She never saw a penny of the money, nor did she expect to. Instead she commented breezily, "I shall be able to bother him for the rest of his life."

This was a way of breaking up the tedium of a jail sentence not given to many. She was extremely popular with the warders and delighted them by directing from her prison cell a sensationalist newspaper story of a cockatoo trapped by its chain on the steeple of a church she could see through the bars of her window. A man named Charles Balshaw got the bird down in front of a wildly enthusiastic crowd drummed up by the press.

Before she left, she and Milman exchanged photographs, hers inscribed

"To my dear Governor, in grateful memory of my six months in Holloway." To forestall a demonstration, Milman sent her home fifteen hours before she was due to be released. She was not to be cheated of her martyr's crown and returned the next day in a barouche and four. Accompanied by hundreds of supporters, she drove down into Piccadilly, where the horses were taken out of their shafts and a jubilant crowd dragged the carriage to Speaker's Corner. It is said the people gathered there exceeded seventeen thousand.

There were in the sea of faces that stared up at her as she waved and smiled those whose interests in the occasion were quite narrow and specific. Her case had highlighted the need for a court of criminal appeal, and it had been a committee of political activists who had carried her down from Holloway and organized her triumphant reception. But such huge numbers indicated a more general enthusiasm. This was the apotheosis of her legal career and something even more valuable to her. She was loved. Eccentric or not, however foolhardy and exasperating she might be, there could be no question that she had won from the city a spontaneous demonstration not given to many Londoners. Plump and excitable Mrs. Weldon, in her silk dress and jacket and her borrowed white bonnet, was for a day the most famous woman in England. The monkey had vanquished the crocodiles.

Not everybody there that day knew or cared that the president of the Mrs. Weldon Release Committee, pumping her hand and praying silence for her speeches, was none other than her old adversary Dr. Forbes Winslow. For her it was a specially rich detail and a fine irony for her to savor. She had brought them all low—Harry and Gounod and now the mad doctors. Five years of press publicity, five years of doing things her way without regard for the dull proprieties of her mother or the remonstrances of her cowardly brother, had ripped like a bullet through asylumdom as well as the inequitable marital status of women. She could shake hands with Winslow with triumph in her eyes. Much of the credit for this changed public awareness was hers. Everyone present knew it.

Finale

1

r. Semple christened his child Georgina Angele. Forbes Winslow wrote her a comic song and offered to appear onstage with her to perform it. At Peckham Rye one day a spontaneously generated crowd estimated in thousands threatened to overturn her carriage with their fervor. Leslie Ward—the cartoonist "Spy"—added her to his famous caricature gallery of legal personalities. She toured the provinces for a year with a play called *Not Alone*—a bad play, an awful play, but one that gave people who knew her only through newspaper reports a chance to see her in the flesh. (Some of her stoutest supporters had been provincial press editors only too pleased to belabor the London establishment with such a handy stick.) She trod the boards of the music halls, dressed as Buzfuz and singing extracts from *Biondina*. There was not a radical platform at which she was not an honored guest and principal speaker. Henry Irving and Ellen Terry sent her tickets to the theater. She was invited to debates in the House of Lords. In 1887, when the Queen astonished her subjects by hurling herself into the Jubilee celebrations with a vivacity and energy they had not seen for years, every London omnibus carried a portrait of Mrs. Weldon with this legend: "Though I am 50 I have the complexion of a girl of 17—thanks to Pears Soap."

Georgina Weldon had the fame she so much desired as a child and for which Victoria's accession had been the guiding star. In one way she had finally triumphed over the oppressions of her lunatic father, just as Victoria had overcome, with an almost girlish surprise at the consequences, the long years of seclusion following Albert's death. Eighteen years separated them in age, but here they were—Victoria's image on the postage stamps, Georgina's on the buses.

The Queen was about to enter her most serene decade. More and more great-grandchildren were given to her, until the total numbered thirty-seven. Her popularity was established beyond all doubt. During her reign, seven attempts had been made on her life, but henceforth it was unthinkable that anyone should wish to hurt or harm her. As with Georgina, the newspapers printed the legend, and Victoria became a kind of public property. Benign old age suited her. She was no more enamored of London than she had ever been, but then London had changed, enough to assert a sovereignty of its own. The great houses, the preeminence of a few families, all the aristocratic privilege of Victoria's youth, had declined and was on the verge of disappearing altogether. One of the duties of the Jubilee that the Queen accepted with pleasure was to drive to Mile End Road and open the People's Palace. It has its symbolism, that journey to the East End. As well as the new People's Palace, both General Booth and Dr. Barnardo had premises in Mile End Road.

Georgina was older than either of these two philanthropists, but in the heyday of her popularity her name was far better known, measured by column inches in the papers. There were a dozen things she might have done to capitalize on it. She might have developed her orphanage ideas in a more practical setting. She had enough connections to radical and philanthropic groups to follow Victoria down to Stepney, where she met General Booth. In fact, she had the honor of sharing with him a shower of mud and stones and horse droppings flung by people who could not care less about social salvation. Booth was personally kind and encouraging, but she was put off by the hymns he sang. She dismissed them as "comic music-hall religious songs" and seriously misjudged her man. About the citizens of Stepney she said, "If they want to throw mud and stones, let them throw at the Judges, the Magistrates, the M.P.s, the Ministers." That had a fine radical ring to it, but Georgina was no more the revolutionary than she was a salvationist.

She seems never to have met Barnardo, whose duty of care to orphans was so much more sophisticated than her own, resembling more the clearheadedness of the Gisors sisters than her own confused fantasies. Another avenue open to her was to have taken a role in more general law reform. She campaigned in a small way for the freethinker Charles Bradlaugh in his effort to take his seat in the House of Commons. Her personal life had, she discovered, much in common with Annie Besant's. But Mrs. Besant's mind was sharper and clearer by far, and as a plaintiff in person (in the famous obscenity trial of 1877) she had shown a grasp of legal argument beyond anything Georgina accomplished. Writing in the *National Reformer* in 1887, Annie Besant observed: "The closest of human ties may be the noblest or the basest of relationships; fully and graciously given, it crowns friendship with its last perfection. Life has nothing fairer for its favourites than friendship kissed into the passion of love." This was language Georgina could not match. No one can be taken to task for what they cannot do: they cannot be taller, or younger. The question is whether she could have done more with the opportunities dropped in her lap by an adoring press and public.

Experience swiftly taught her she was no playwright, and the entertainment she gave at the North London Colosseum or Shoreditch Music Hall was offered in defiant ignorance of what was popular in the halls. As a novelty act she had a short career, if an uproarious one. Working-class audiences soon enough gave her the bird. She had a few engagements to sing elsewhere, but the Rivière case had slammed the door forever on music as a profession. No impresario of any note would touch her, and in any case she was fifty. The wave she rode after her release from Holloway curled, broke, and was dissipated. Little by little, week by week, the frenzy of interest ebbed away. Now the headlines in bold—What is Mrs. Weldon up to?—become ironic. She had peaked. When everything is interesting, nothing gets done. She wanted fame more than anything else in the world, and when for a few short seasons she had it, she let it fall from her hands.

The orphanage had shrunk to the two youngest children, of whom Sapho-Katie was the last to leave. Angele was tired of living in Brixton and persuaded Georgina to give the house in Loughborough Road back to Salsbury and take up the lease on a more imposing property at 58 Gower Street. She represented the move as being a more economical way of using the allowance that Harry was required by law to pay Georgina. At the last minute, Angele suggested that the lease be in her name, the better to protect it against distraint if things went wrong in the courts. Georgina agreed to this with only half her mind on the subject. She was busy preparing to tour her play when the move from Brixton was made, and she was staggered to find on her return that neither Sapho-Katie nor Pauline, the other orphanage veteran, had survived it. Pauline had been packed off to an aunt and Sapho-Katie sent to Canada "to be the companion of another little girl of the same age." In their place, Angele had adopted the two girls of her brother-in-law, Jean Helluy. "One thing after another," Georgina complained. "I don't know how my brains could endure so many sorrows [chagrins], so many deceptions and disappointments." With this single absentminded farewell, Sapho-Katie, the girl who had always been her favorite among the orphans, the child "who could converse in three languages" when she was two, was dismissed from the story.

In Gower Street Angele maintained a household more than sufficient for the task and lived better than she had ever dreamed possible. With the children gone, the need for Eugénie Morand would seem to have ended also. She stayed on. In addition, Angele kept up three servants. What was ineradicable in her was the kind of avarice that sometimes besets the poor. Hunger becomes greed, greed becomes theft. She simply could not let the opportunity pass of taking what was there to take. Once, in the beginning, the two women had quarreled over the price of a pair of gloves. Now Angele bought furniture, amassed her bibelots, dressed in the height of fashion, abused the financial trust Georgina had placed in her. Left alone for days and weeks on end while Georgina deviled in Red Lion Court or rushed from hearing to hearing, what was there for her to do except to be the householder, the long-suffering wife? From the point of view of the greengrocer, the coalman, and all the rest of the tradesmen, she was the fixed point and Georgina the occasional visitor.

There was a homemaker at the heart of Angele, a gift Georgina discounted too readily and of which she might have made much better use. It was true the Frenchwoman drank too much, flew into hysterical rages too often, pretended to romance a solicitor's clerk she met (using the same wiles on him as Georgina always found successful, the helpless wight who turns out to be a witch). The psychological balance shifted, and the emotional dependency on her lover that Angele started out with finally came to an end. Ten years with Georgina had robbed them both of their youth and in Angele's case her dreams and illusions. She, who so loved Georgina, despite the chasm of difference between them, of language as well as class and life experience, was drawn insensibly into becoming the last great enemy.

eorgina's old friend Edward Maitland and Mrs. Anna Kingsford had come home from France, she to work in a medical practice in Kensington, he to write and study. They joined the Theosophical Society together and, disenchanted with that, founded in 1885 the Hermetic Society, more mystical than spiritualist and based on the teachings of Hermes Trismegistus. Georgina was never capable of such sustained abstract intellectual effort. Though she was vice-president of the Magna-Chartists, a reforming social movement founded by Kenealy, her interest in it was strictly limited to the publicizing of her own legal history. She was not a woman of ideas, as so many around her were becoming. She could not draw together all the threads of social reform, nor did she have the inclination. If she went out at night to address some meeting, it was always about herself, never about the broader issues. She read very little and was easily flummoxed by art—she got her information on that from back copies of the *Athenaeum* which her mother sent up from Hampshire whenever she could remember. She did chase money, but not in order to use it purposefully. For example, having learned that her mother had made a will, she tried to persuade Louisa to make her an early gift of her portion. (If Louisa was ambivalent about this, it was because she had no intention of giving Georgina more than the merest token.)

What Georgina wanted out of any social transaction was what she considered her moral due, and this she was not always able to identify with any precision. Nor was she prepared to get along with other people in what might be called a good-natured way, winning some, losing some. To lose was not to have your worth recognized. The law was a ready-to-hand substitute for real life, for the disobliging and unsatisfactory nature of day-to-day existence. With it she had won great battles, but even then she was not always vindicated as she wished. The most titanically absurd of her legal wrangles was beginning against her own lawyer in the Menier trial, St. John Wontner. She pursued him and his firm through the courts all the way down to 1901, when the evidence being disputed was a quarter century old. Her friends (like the faithful Salsbury) waited for her to move on, find new challenges. She never did. She was nobody's lieutenant and followed no flag but her own.

In most lives, people live in a settled place. They give and receive hospitality and in this way build up a network of friends and confidants. They take pleasure in small things, like food and drink, or the best choice of curtain material, the progress of a particular shrub in the garden. They read. They follow the doings of the famous. The seasons of the year announce themselves by sunlight falling across a lawn or flooding a room that is otherwise dark. The passage of time is marked by the growth of children—their own or others. In other words, they are overwhelmed (or comforted) by sheer ordinariness. This never happened to Georgina. There is no evidence that—with one exception—she ever met her nephews and nieces. Hers is a story without

Christmases. For nearly fifteen years she had not taken a vacation. All these benefits were enjoyed by the rest of the Trehernes, who might have been dull but were secure in the world of little things.

Her fiftieth birthday could not go on being celebrated forever. Angele was away from home, Georgina could not be completely certain where. She wrote the Frenchwoman an enormously long letter outlining all her faults, ending with an ultimatum. She should come home to Gower Street or be forever banished. It was imperious but it was the last of her mistakes. Angele did come home nine days later. She pointed out, with the sort of cold savagery that Georgina herself employed in the courts when the occasion demanded, that the house was in her name and that if her lover, now her former lover, did not leave it at once, she would go to solicitors, seek an order, and have her evicted.

Perhaps it came as a relief. Once, Mrs. Weldon would have rushed to the law herself and whatever the cost, however rocky the road ahead, found some way to drag Mme Menier through the courts. She had done it for everyone else who crossed her or betrayed her: why not Angele? It is an indication of what Angele meant to her that she did not. She accepted that it was over between them with a kind of exhausted grace. She conferred wearily with Harcourt (who offered to go to Bloomsbury and shoot the lady), wound up in the office in Red Lion Court, and arranged for her goods and chattels to go temporarily into storage. She wrote in her diary: "It quite breaks my heart to leave my garden, my window boxes, my little green room and everything. I hope I can keep the dogs and I must try to keep my darling monkeys. My little birds, too. How sad to leave them. I must take a few."

There were more than two dozen budgerigars that could not make the journey with her. Her papers and correspondence filled twenty-seven tea chests, which were removed to storage as though her life had been lived in nothing but an office. It was a dramatically dry-eyed parting and, as always happened with her, once a thing had been decided, swift. She never saw Angele again.

On September 23, 1888, she went to Charing Cross and assembled on the platform her two pugs, the monkey Tittileelee, and several cages of birds. Her own luggage was modest by comparison. As she waited to board

the train, she reflected it was the twenty-eighth anniversary of her miscarriage. It was also the death by exhaustion of the personality she had raised
and nurtured in the baby's place. Of that Georgina Weldon, there was nothing more to say. She wrote:

> I'd given myself until my fiftieth year to get together the sum I
> would need to raise and educate 50 children; and as late as 1885 I
> thought every incident, every adventure would end for me in tri-
> umphant success. When 1887 and my fiftieth birthday arrived,
> something broke inside me. Since then, my powers have noticeably
> declined. I had never been robust. The doctors said there was noth-
> ing wrong with me, but I felt exhausted.

The whistle blew, the last door slammed, and like Gounod, with tears
streaming down her face, she said good-bye to her past. A day later she presented herself at Gisors and was given a room on the second floor. She engaged a maid, calmed herself, put on the work uniform that the sisters wore
(to their undying shock), inspected the garden; and then slowly, laboriously,
began to compose the judicial memoirs on which this book is based.

*H*arry survived Georgina's onslaught. He rose inexorably in
the College of Arms and as Norroy supervised the cere-
monies surrounding the interment of Gladstone in Westminster Abbey in 1898. He was acting Garter king of arms for the funeral of
Victoria and the accession of Edward VII. In time he brought Annie Lowe
ashore from the houseboat at Windsor to a cottage at Shiplake in Oxford-

shire. They lived in separate houses—hers was called Hope Cottage. In 1915, as soon as he decently could after Georgina's death, he married Mrs. Lowe. Soon after, he was given his Grand Cross of the Royal Victorian Order. He died in 1923.

Angele left England four or five years after Georgina and settled in Levallois-Perret, a suburb of Paris. There she set up as a piano teacher and a small-town fabulist, much in the manner of her former lover, claiming, among other things, an intimate friendship with the director of the Paris Opéra. He wrote to tell her to stop the nonsense. One afternoon a young girl serving in a post office in another banlieue of the city was startled to be addressed by a portly and elderly customer, her eyes streaming with tears. "Don't you recognise me?" the woman sobbed. "It's me—Auntie!" Bichette backed away in terror, calling for the postmaster to summon the police.

Angele died in November 1898, leaving a generous amount of furniture to her nephews and nieces (but not Bichette). In the will she left five hundred francs for the poor, to be distributed by the newspaper *L'Aurore*. Someone in the reporter's room confused her with the widow of the chocolate manufacturer Menier and composed a fulsome paragraph of thanks to a distinguished citizen of France noted for her many charitable acts.

Angele survived her husband by six years. Anarcharsis Menier died in January 1892. He had come from a village outside Bordeaux and as a young man was anxious to make his fortune on the grand scale. After two terms of imprisonment, one in London, one in Paris, and the utter failure to dream up an investment swindle worthy of their talents, he and his brothers (ever on the lookout for the coming thing) started selling steam baths and respirators at Bois-Colombes, twelve kilometers from Paris. The various Appareils Menier that came from their "laboratories" won a bronze medal at a hygiene exhibition in Dijon, the town where Georgina's *Mémoires* were eventually published.

Louisa Treherne died in 1894. The woman who had been taken to Florence for her health and whose letters seldom omit mention of her various ailments, lived to be eighty-three. Late in life her will had been altered, and save for an unimportant minor legacy, Georgina did not benefit from it. It led, of course, to an acrimonious contest in the courts.

Dal had astonished everyone by meeting and marrying a merry widow in 1883, at the very bottom of his fortunes. A brasserie in which he had invested in Muhlberg went bust, and by chance and a generous helping of luck of the sort not often vouchsafed to a Treherne, he managed to find his consolation prize in life. The lady was the young and beautiful widow Countess Wald- stein, possessed of huge and lawyer-infested estates in Bohemia. His stepson Hugo inherited what was left of the great Dux estates in 1894, including the house in which Casanova had been the librarian. The countess gave Dal a son of his own, Phillip, who wrote the first biography of his aunt in 1923.

Of the orphans who survived Georgina's experiments in music educa- tion, nothing is known. In Paris, Gisors, Rouen, London, and somewhere in Canada, their descendants are walking about today in complete ignorance of what splendor and misery there was in being one of "Grannie's" children. If Freddie *was* buried under the mulberry tree in Tavistock Square, as Georgina hinted but could never bring herself fully to admit, his grave is marked today by the headquarters of the British Medical Association, which occupies the site. Mireille's tiny bones are lost or scattered in Argeuil. In the whole orphan- age, only the peripheral figures of the Rawlings brothers made even the tiniest mark in history. Two of them became small-time music-hall impresarios.

George Werranrath, whom Harry suspected of adultery, went to New York in 1876 and became the principal tenor of the Brooklyn Cathedral Choir. He married and in August 1883 his wife gave him a son, Reinhart. The father taught the son to sing, and in time Reinhart Werranrath appeared with Caruso at the Metropolitan Opera House, playing Silvio in *Pagliacci* and the part of Valentin in Gounod's *Faust*. He died in 1953, not before leav- ing a permanent record of his baritone voice on discs cut with the Victor Opera Quartet.

As for Georgina, once in Gisors, she quickly recovered her composure and admitted to herself that the time she had on her hands was never really going to be spent in reflection and contemplation. The greatest part of her possessions on earth was her vast collection of legal papers. When they fol- lowed her across the Channel (after the inconvenience of a London dock strike), she at once set to work indexing them. Slowly but surely, they fell into place, and the deed boxes in which she stored them lined the walls of her room. In the sifting process new injustices were revealed and new lines of inquiry opened up. No detail was too small to be overlooked. The *Mémoires* are stuffed full of tales of the hunt for missing documents, dismay at willfully destroyed letters or joy when others were miraculously recovered. Her whole daily routine was dictated by this obsessive exactitude. Never a day passed when she did not study and annotate, combing through ten years of turbulent history.

It soon occurred to her that her labors merited a book. But what kind of a book should it be? Over the years, she had written half a dozen small pamphlets published at her own expense, and it was these that seemed to her to be the model for the work she contemplated. Sitting at her desk in the hospice, looking down the short road that led to the market, she slowly came to see the theme as an exposé of the English system of justice, nominally addressed to the French (who were going about their business buying potatoes in sublime ignorance of its value to them). The post office was at the end of the road. Unless it was in response to a letter of hers, there was seldom any news from England. No one visited from London, and her journeys to Paris were few and far between. As she pondered what to write, the loneliness of her life overcame her. Without a real friend in whom to confide and constantly playing the mysterious milady with the hospice staff, she chose exactly the wrong book to write. She compounded the error by deciding to write it in French. This required the translation of hundreds of thousands of words and drove her even further within herself. Once, she thought she would be lost without Tavistock House to keep her dream alive. Now it was her room in the hospice, smelling of moldering paper and cigarettes, that drew her back out of the sunlight and the vegetable gardens which she had more or less taken as her own.

When the *Mémoires* came to be printed, they were furnished in the French fashion with a *table des matières* for each volume. The synopsis of the first eight pages of volume III gives an indication of the way the book was assembled:

2. La Menier "accomplishes the sacrifice" of leaving Bichette with Marie Helluy. Her return, 28 June 1877. Mme Paul Julien.

Loans and advances. French system of pawnbroking. 3. La Menier jealous. Watch sold to M. Landrec. 4. La Menier throws suspicion on Rosie of stealing it. 5. The big wardrobes from The Minories. Extracts from my journal. Menier an egg seller and Director of the *Liberté Coloniale*, 27 June 1877. 6. Scenes from La Menier. The *mattress*. Marie Helluy arrives with Bichette, 30 July 1877. 7. La Menier proposes placing the children at Argeuil. Endless uproar. 8. Terrible row with La Menier 10 August. Version of this same row with Marie Helluy . . .

The appendix to each volume has as full a collection of letters as she could furnish bearing on the matters under discussion. While her mother lived, Georgina pestered her unmercifully to find all the family correspondence and return it to Gisors. She tried to make the record complete and in the process incriminated herself without apparently realizing it. It is in a letter to Louisa that she at last mentions how she may have struck orphan Freddie once too often. In another section she publishes an open letter she sent to the editors of every London newspaper at the time of *Weldon v. Weldon*. It is a prime example of the dangers in her method. In order to get her conjugal rights restored, the single question she had to answer at the hearing was whether she had committed adultery. In a formula devised by her counsel and Harry's she had only to say one word about that: "No." Instead she named Sir Henry Thompson, Cadwalladwr Waddy, and George Werranrath as persons with whom she had been accused of sleeping. The judge who heard the case was incensed.

"If you hadn't repeated them, those names would have remained unknown."

"But I wanted them known, because people have said—"

"I wouldn't have let you into the witness box if I had known you were going to repeat those names."

"I know *that* alright," Georgina replied.

Thompson and his wife were still alive when the *Mémoires* were published. It caused Georgina no qualms if these revelations caused them pain, any more than it did to apostrophize judges and lawyers still living as "dirty old monkeys," "old goats," "redfaced old lobsters." She explains that no London editor would pick up the story of her imprudent behavior with Sir Henry Thompson, though all the provincial papers did. To her mother she wrote:

> The case has been completely hushed up and there has been a universal conspiracy of silence. Not a name has been reproduced in the [London] papers. That reticence can only have one reason in the eyes of the world, above all when one knows what happened, and what my own mother and my own brother have had to say . . . Your letters, and I suppose those of Dal, Emily and Bill have been the secret weapons Mr. Weldon has used against me and are the secret weapons I can see everywhere . . . They are private letters that have ruined me *publically*. Your private protestations to me are absolutely useless. They want me to believe that you don't have the intention of doing me harm, but it's impossible to understand your full intentions or your goal. You don't know what you want, nor what you want to say. As for Dal, Zizi and Bill, that's another matter. They're harming me just for the pleasure of putting a spoke in my wheels. *And* [she adds in an acid footnote] as a way of doing me out of my inheritance.

Dal, Emily (Zizi), and Emily's husband were all still living when this letter was finally published. It soon becomes clear to the English reader that one reason for writing in French and publishing in France was to give her the freedom to libel people with impunity. She admits this. "I said to my publisher, Darantière, that as what I was writing was defamation to a superlative degree, I would like to prepare a document for him by which I would undertake to keep his own liability completely safeguarded."

Darantière was understandably alarmed, and not much reassured, when she refused to sign the standard disclaimer he sent her and instead substituted one of her own. In the event of a prosecution, she offered to pay all his costs. The price was that he should publish it all, without attempting to edit it or withdraw it. She added artlessly, "I have already been caught out in

England. I guaranteed all the costs of an editor who printed my truths in his paper *(Regina v. Mortimer)*. De Bathe and my husband had the impudence to threaten criminal proceedings against him; and this coward, instead of continuing publication and establishing the truth, was either bribed or stupid enough to back down and got three months in prison."

Only some of the letters she published reveal a more intimate and domestic side to her. They are few and far between, but they come like islands in an ocean of unrelenting fact. She wrote to her mother:

> If I was like Benedict, who can do without sleep . . . but I must have my nine hours, during which I sleep like a nest of dormice, or like my little canary who sleeps no matter what the noise, even though the little rascal refuses to be put to bed before half past eight. He is completely tame and generally flies free. I am horribly afraid of losing him. I tamed him myself and I am, it goes without saying, completely tyrannised and made an idiot of by him. And there's an argument for Dr. Winslow!

By far the longest letter she allowed into print is the one most damaging to her reputation. It is the hysterical paen of hate she wrote to Angele as a form of ultimatum shortly before being flung out of Gower Street. The letter comprises 117 numbered paragraphs and uncovers aspects of their life together that no one completely sane would have contemplated publishing. In it we learn that Eugénie, the governess appointed by Angele to look after the two remaining orphans in Brixton, had two sisters, and Georgina accuses her lover of debauching all three of them. The servants were drawn into the hell that Angele seems to have created, being told things about the past they should never have had to listen to, asked to inform on their mistress, squabbling among themselves. The actor who played opposite Georgina in the play based on her life, *Not Alone,* was a young man named Clifford.

> They all knew about your intrigues with Clifford, and everybody except me knew that Clifford was sometimes hidden in the house for three hours without being able to escape (me being the

stumbling block) that Eva kept watch for you, that she was supposed
to warn you of my approach by ringing a little bell or making a
cough, and the day I did find you on Clifford's knee (an old woman
like you, on the knee of a vulgar actor) and Eva followed me, you
gave her a good mouthful because she hadn't rung hard enough, the
fact being that you were licking your lips so hard you couldn't hear
anything. How you must have mocked me when I said "If it hadn't
been for my presence of mind that child would have seen something" . . . Eugénie, as you know very well, caught you in your che-
mise—naked—in your bedroom with Clifford. And you made her
come in! And then made Clifford leave, who tried to put his arms
round her as he went. "No," she said, pushing him away, "save the
dirty business for Madame." After he was made to go, you said to
Eugénie "Have you noticed the effect, the power I have on men?
Did you see how pale Clifford was? White as a sheet!"

The letter runs to forty printed pages and stops at nothing—Angele's
thefts, her deceptions, her sexual preferences, the whole life between them
laid bare. There are paragraphs devoted to how Angele inflated the cost of
hats or purchased without Georgina's consent eau de cologne, pillows,
handbags, soap. And there are paragraphs that make the heart stand still:
"Aren't you ashamed to tell these young girls such things? Isn't it infamous
and ignoble enough that you told the story of Antonio, giving them to understand that I was much older instead of a child of four or five and saying:
That will give you an idea of what she is by natural inclination. And then:
She likes to pass for this or that—think about it, a husband who used to take
her up the rear and she liked it!"
  The publication of this letter points up the basic structural fault of the
Mémoires. The longer Georgina went on, translating, assembling, glossing,
the more she lost touch with what she was trying to achieve. The letter to
Angele serves no practical purpose by being included and adds nothing to
the story she was trying to unfold of the injustices of the English legal system. One reads it in the same way one might listen in horrified silence to a
drunk at a party. There is a nightmare quality in it, like hearing someone de-

stroy herself for no good reason, when a moment's reflection would have stopped her mouth. Since the greater part of the whole six volumes sets out to prove that Mrs. Georgina Weldon was not mad, the pain of material like this is all the greater. From a letter to her mother written in 1881, again included for no good reason:

> You've told me I have not appreciated Mr. Weldon in the right way. As if I didn't know that only too well!!! He has shown now what he has for guts. One of his old teachers, the Reverend W. O'Reilly told Madame Menier he was capable of no matter what cowardly or ignoble act. When he was only sixteen, he seduced one of his mother's housemaids and chased after her without pity and of course he was never suspected of it. The poor girl got pregnant. He threw live cats down the lavatory—always denying it, it goes without saying.

There are dozens of such gratuitous "truths" strewn recklessly, as, for example, that she did not sleep with Harry after they moved to London because he suffered from the pox; that Dal was an alcoholic; that her mother was weak in the head. She did not have it in her to write with any literary merit, but the colossal effort she put into the manuscript to make it a complete account was self-defeating. It was the dossier method run amok, and in the end it undid her. In life, as in the law itself, there are some things best left unsaid. Before he left London forever, Dal had written to her:

> Plenty of people, and I too, accept that you've been treated abominably, everyone's ready to admit that; but also, that you've lacked judgement or have been very badly advised. To make comparisons between yourself and Patti doesn't serve any good purpose. It's her success and not her immorality that makes her what she is. You too, you've had your success, a great moral success, for in spite of all your vicissitudes, you've kept your honour and your name intact.
>
> Moreover, you must be considered a real benefactress to hu-

manity, for thanks to you and the bloody exposure made of their iniquities, the lunacy laws will certainly be much improved. Of that there's not the shadow of a doubt. Equally, you have succeeded in unmasking plenty of other abuses—but it is exactly because of your success in this direction that you've made so many enemies . . . You have set against you a numerous and powerful class of the population.

It was about as generous a statement as Dal was capable of, and it has the ring of truth about it. Maybe for that very reason she glossed the letter in a footnote: "The reader will think perhaps that my brother is pulling my leg: but no! He declaims like Solon and everything he says is completely contrary to the facts."

Gounod died in October 1893 at his second home in St.-Cloud. In his last years he was frail and going blind, and toward the end his doctors forbade him to work. Instead, he rejoiced in playing l'Abbé Gounod, the silver-haired old patriarch, replete with honors and a friend to humanity. Almost to the end he would travel every Saturday to attend the Institut, carrying in his pocket the exact amount of money necessary, counted out into his palm by an ever-watchful Anna. One day he hailed a cab at the St.-Lazare station, and at the end of the journey the cabman said, "Monsieur Gounod, I'm proud to have driven the composer of *Faust*." Gounod patted away the compliment with good-humored wit. "My friend," he said gently. "You've a fine turn of speed. You would have made a good conductor."

The little vanities of old age sat well with him. He liked to muse aloud on art and religion, safe in the belief that his epoch had done him the honor his life in music deserved. Like a good priest, the personal agonies his work had cost him were smoothed away until what was left was the goodness, the light within. He was very rich. When he said things like "God loves those whom He admits into suffering," his listeners in their thirties and forties took it to be a noble and pious reflection that had nothing to do with the material circumstances of his life.

The end came with a fine operatic pathos. On October 15, while Anna and her daughter played dominoes at his back, Gounod sat at his desk smoking his faithful clay pipe. He was looking over the score of his *Requiem*. When Anna looked around to say something to him, the pipe was still burning, but Gounod's head had fallen forward onto the table beside it. He lingered for two days, a crucifix clenched in his fist, before dying at half past six in the morning of October 17.

There was a state funeral in the Madeleine in Paris ten days later. After that, the coffin was taken to Auteuil, where it was interred in the family vault. The French newspapers received indignant letters from an unknown woman in Gisors, reprehending Madame Gounod for not insisting her husband be laid to rest in the Panthéon. Georgina managed to stop herself from attending the funeral. She wrote in her diary, "Poor old man—how I did love him and how hard all hope died." It was a telling remark. Was the hope that he should snatch her up from a failed marriage and share his genius with her? If so, hadn't he offered to do that when he suggested he accept the post of director of the Conservatoire and bring her to Paris with him in 1872? In the end, Gounod can be forgiven for misunderstanding the depth of her feelings toward him. She was saying something to her diary that she had never really expressed to him or indeed to any other man. To love was to give, and it was not in her to be so vulnerable as that.

She had kept up her interest in spiritualism, and now that Gounod was on the Other Side, Charlotte, Georgina's maid, suddenly discovered psychic powers. With the help of her boyfriend she arranged séances in which the shade of the great composer came to Gisors to tease and chide. What Charlotte knew about Gounod was mostly gathered from her mistress's conversation; and what she knew about spiritualism was borrowed from the shocked hearsay of her parents. Accordingly, Gounod's ghostly visits to the hospice were sometimes more like cheap stage illusions. Cups bounced off the table, and chairs were mysteriously flung against the wall. Every word the spirit Gounod uttered was written down afterward in all its banality. His tone was generally forgiving and he liked to josh his old admirer. But Georgina was disappointed. Where was the genius in him, the messiah of new music she had done so much to promote? He was talking to her like the shade of a jovial butcher or a man who had gone to his grave as a hearty but short-tempered baker. He was talking in fact like a Gisorard.

This was a fault he learned to correct. He began to write to her in regular alexandrines, of the sort written by Hugo and studied by children in school. His themes narrowed. What he wanted to express in this spirit-poetry was the evils of the justice system as experienced by honest litigants. Now what he said was received with enthusiasm, all the more so because Charlotte produced these couplets when she was in deep trance and so could not be accused of deception. It was automatic writing! Charlotte sat at the desk with her eyes rolled back in her head and took down by dictation what Gounod had to say as Georgina looked on, spellbound. Her boyfriend hovered nervously in the corner, willing the girl not to get it too wrong. When she let the pen fall saying she was exhausted, it was often no more than the truth. Then, helped by the money Georgina had paid for the séances, Charlotte left with her young man for London. Gounod left with her.

Georgina seldom went outside the walls of the hospice in these years, and her pleasures and appetites grew simpler. Ever since her first imprisonment in Newgate she had suffered from what she diagnosed as gout but was probably arthritis. Her hands slowly seized up. By the time of her sixtieth birthday, her unremitting labors on the hospice gardens had paid such dividends that she could to some degree sit back and enjoy the fruits. Her undergardener, Petit Pierre, was one of the hospice inmates, an old and slow-witted simpleton who was devoted to her. The greenhouse she designed with doors on rollers was a great success, and she had grown interested in bees. She had hives built and she corresponded with local apiarists. If she was sometimes lethargic and could no longer command Petit Pierre to fetch water from the stream or rake up leaves with quite the vigor she once had, it was only understandable. She was growing old.

The Dreyfus Affair interested her (and would have done so more had she known of the part played in the family's search for justice by a Normandy psychic, Léonie, who helped Mathieu Dreyfus to understand what had really happened to his brother). Georgina was naturally a Dreyfusard, and there were other stories in the French press that she followed keenly, always of injustice done in the name of the law. Crimes against women particularly interested her, such as the false imprisonment at home of a girl by her own family in the city of Poitiers, a famous case. The local magistrate in Gisors was a man named Delatin, and she sometimes went to court to listen to him. She admired his suavity and imperturbable good humor. Slowly, inexorably, life caught up with her. Petit Pierre died, Delatin was transferred to Le Havre.

In 1890 Dal's boy, Phillip, came to see his notorious aunt. She drew a tactful veil over what she thought of his father and complimented the young man for having learned from Dal the art of writing a letter. She explained:

> A circle of Dante's *Inferno* should be set aside for people who neglect to answer letters. You will find it is the busy people in this world who are the best correspondents; it is also a question of proper method. Owing to the telephone the letter will become as obsolete as the snuff-box in times to come. One has only to compare the correspondence in memoirs of the eighteenth and part of the nineteenth centuries to realise the gradual decay in correspondence.

Phillip Treherne adored her. She never mentions in the *Mémoires* how, late on, she found a new lease on life, teaching herself Braille and going from time to time to Paris to read and sing to a music school for the blind. Her nephew tells us that story. Georgina made a huge impression on him, and they corresponded regularly for as long as she lived. She went to his wedding, he was present at her funeral.

This serious and bookish young man also made her a wonderful gift, something that came about from a chance meeting he had in Paris. One evening in 1898, he was sitting at a café table in the rue Scribe when a shabbily dressed but striking-looking man came and sat down nearby. Phillip Treherne recognized him as the disgraced and ruined Oscar Wilde. He introduced himself, and they talked pleasantly of books and literary figures until midnight. Three days later Phillip went to Gisors and told his aunt of this encounter. He wanted her advice. Wilde had invited him to visit his rooms in the Hôtel d'Alsace. Georgina was cautious:

> It's distressing to think that this unhappy man, so gifted with real talent, has been lost entirely by his own fault. But I think he's been cured of his deplorable instincts. My pals in the Law Courts have assured me he has completely repented and that he has said he doesn't know how he could have been such a boor [brute] and such an idiot. If he's sincere, I think you might reply to his invitation. I'll find that out for you. Ever since these friends at the Law Courts told me all this, I have really wanted to write him a word of sympathy. But I didn't have his address. Since he's given it to you, I have it, I'll write to him, and I'll soon know if he repents. If that's not so, I counsel you not to accept his invitation.

She did not keep a copy of the letter she wrote to Wilde. The one remark she *could* remember of her sympathy toward a fellow martyr was this: "I can't tell you how happy I would be to think that you have repented of your insane and unnatural conduct." Wilde replied at once, and his letter is worth quoting in full:

> My dear Mrs. Weldon,
> So Phillip Treherne is your nephew. I wondered if he was kith and kin with the lady whom friends of mine remember as the beautiful Miss Treherne and whom the world will always remember as Mrs. Weldon. But we talked of books and art and the idea passed from my mind. How cultivated he is, and so well bred in his gravity and courteous ways. I enjoyed meeting him very much and hope he will do well. For the moment he has perhaps too much appreciation of the work of others to realise his own creative energy.

Yes, I think that, aided by splendid personalities like Michael Davitt and John Burns, I have been able to strike a heavy and fatal blow at the monstrous prison system of English justice. There will be no more starvation, nor sleeplessness, nor endless silence, nor eternal solitude, nor brutal flogging. The system has been exposed and so doomed. But it is difficult to teach the English either pity or humanity. They learn slowly. Next, the power of the judges (an entirely ignorant set of men—ignorant, that is, of what they are doing), their power to inflict most barbarous sentences on those that are brought before them must be limited. At present a judge will send a man to two years hard labour or five years penal servitude, not knowing that all such sentences are sentences of death. It is the lack of imagination in the Anglo-Saxon race that makes the race so stupidly, harshly cruel. Those who are bringing about prison reform in Parliament are Celts to a man, for every Celt has inborn imagination.

For myself, of course, the aim of life is to realise one's own personality, one's own nature, and now as before it is through Art that I realise what is in me, and I hope soon to begin a new play; but poverty with its degrading preoccupations with money, the loss of many friends, the deprivation of my children by a most unjust law administered by a most unjust judge, the terrible effect of years of silence, solitude and ill-treatment—all these have of course killed to a large extent, if not entirely, the great joy in living I once had. However, I must try, so the details of Prison Reform will have to be worked out by others. I put the fly in motion but I cannot turn the wheels. It is enough for me that the thing is coming—so that what I suffered will not be suffered by others. That makes me happy.

One word more. Your letter gave me pleasure. Charity is not a sentimental emotion; it is the only method by which the soul can attain to any knowledge—to any wisdom. Very sincerely yours, O.W.

Wilde was ill and had only two more years to live when he wrote this. It says wonders for his forbearance that he did not comment on Georgina's desire that he should exhibit remorse for what he was. Nor did he mention that he would have perhaps avoided his own prosecution if he had not made the fatal mistake of bringing a suit against the Marquis of Queensberry for criminal libel. Wilde's experience of the courts and the dangers of challenging the establishment was brief and chastening indeed. In February of 1895 he was the acclaimed author of that glittering new play *The Importance of Being Earnest*. On May 25 of the same year he began serving two years' hard labor at Reading Gaol. In the circumstances his letter to Georgina Weldon was extraordinarily gracious. Repentant or not, he wrote her the most sympathetic commendation she ever received.

5

Work on the *Mémoires* came to an abrupt end at Christmas, 1901. The last words she wrote are tacked carelessly onto a lengthy section about papers lost or withheld twenty years earlier and the profound lack of interest shown in their recovery by the director of public prosecutions. The very last sentences of her monumental labors act like a switch thrown on a machine that might otherwise have run on forever.

> If I had been able to produce this document in the trial against Neal, it would have been impossible for the judges to non-suit me. The jury would have awarded me heavy damages that my cowardly robber of a husband (up to his back teeth in perjury) would have been obliged to pay. And I, at the age I am now, would at least have the needs of my old age provided for. I hope that everyone who reads this work—even those of whom I have spoken most se-

verely—will admit that out of consideration to them I could not speak too frankly. They will regret having being led astray by the secret dossiers on me and they will thank me for having taken so much trouble to give the public the fruit of my experiences, which cannot miss being the most useful of the nineteenth century.

Darantière's anxieties about legal proceedings may have been partly responsible for the peculiar abruptness of this ending. The remnants of the Menier gang—Eugène Menier, Marie Helluy, and Victoria Claisse—had got wind of the work and, cheated of any money from Angele's will, were making one last attempt to fleece Georgina by threatening to sue her for defamation. In England she was involved in a similarly bitter squabble with Emily over Louisa's will. Beset with irritations on all sides, summoned to appear before the Procurator General in Paris, she arranged to have the copies of her great work sent from Dijon by freight train to Gisors. It was time to throw herself on the mercy of the public. Crippled with arthritis, hugely heavy with twelve years of institutional cooking, but still possessed of an amazing soprano voice, she crossed the Channel for the last time and went home to London, taking the cartons of books with her. Though the work was nominally addressed to the French, she was determined to publish it first in England. She did not want her English public to think she lacked the relish for a fight.

The *Mémoires* were never commercially published in the sense that most books are, and it is small surprise that they did not sell. Those copies she sent for review were studiously ignored, and the general reader in France and England remained (and remains) hardly aware of the book's existence. The few friends in England who read the work were scandalized on three counts. The minuteness of the detail and the many digressions she had been drawn into made her six volumes extremely difficult to read. The willful defamation of people still living was impossible to countenance, even among her loyalest allies. But most of all, what she had written that was spiteful to others or just too self-incriminating about herself contradicted the desire her closest friends had to remember her courage and discount all her other shortcomings. She had done wonderful things, and the world that knew her best wished to cherish the myth of Mrs. Weldon, "the modern Portia," rather than have the unvarnished truth. Those who welcomed her home and looked on her so benignly wished to see reflected in their eyes a calm and dignified old lady. It was a popular misconception in the press that she had long ago retired altogether and that the purpose of her sojourn in France had been to cultivate orchids. To have come home with this monster was a terrible embarrassment.

Her opinions were curiously out of joint with the times. She held that men in prison should be whipped once a month to keep them up to the task of repentance (though here she may have been speaking particularly of Frenchmen). When she came home, all London was talking about the Boer War. Her more liberal friends were pro-Boer on the grounds that a big country was oppressing a minority but she would have none of that. "I am in a fury with the Government," she wrote to Phillip Treherne, "for keeping all those dirty Boer prisoners in the concentration camp. Draining, ruining the country because a few ignorant Yahoos whose only merit is to shoot, slaughter and sjambok since they first learned to walk choose to keep on a useless, murderous warfare, dressing up in our khaki, murdering, massacring bewildered boys who do not know if they have to do with friend or foe."

Her answer was to issue an ultimatum to the Boers: stop now or face complete annihilation. Her views on suffrage were similarly out of step with the times. Emmeline Pankhurst's husband had drafted the Married Woman's Property Act of 1882, from which all Georgina's court actions flowed. Though she never acknowledged it, she owed the Pankhurst family a vote of loyalty. She was in the audience at the Albert Hall in 1906 when Christabel Pankhurst addressed the Women's Social and Political Union rally but was considerably put out not to be asked to speak. She was unaware that the politics of feminism had grown beyond individual acts of heroism, nor did she ever grasp that the WSPU was brought into being for the benefit of all women, of all classes, everywhere.

Christabel Pankhurst was twenty-six when Georgina sat in the audience listening to her. It may have struck the older woman that nobody that young could speak with any real authority. But Miss Pankhurst had a first-class degree in law and a complete willingness to subsume her own desires and ambitions to a greater good, something Georgina never really acquired. In 1908 the two Pankhurst sisters and their mother organized a rally in Hyde Park that drew half a million people. Measured against this, Georgina's story was a relic of the past. She was an eccentric old woman with but one tale to tell.

She remained estranged from her family to the end. What cosseting she got was from friends like Ellen Terry, her faithful Lise Grey, Bernard de Bear, and Phillip Treherne and his wife. When she first came home, she was astonished to find Captain Harcourt still alive and still as impudent as ever. He was planning to emigrate to Canada but was momentarily strapped for the £25 fare. She could not keep herself away from the courts completely and tried to sue the authors of two biographies of Gounod for libel. It was a lost cause. She herself had written the epitaph for all that. "Old man gone and I fast going. His music is thought nothing of now." All that was embers now, and try as she might, she could not fan the flames. Before he died, Gounod wrote down a sentiment she would have understood and might have taken to herself. "I feel as young as I was at the age of twenty," he said. "What ages in us is the dwelling. The tenant doesn't."

About the time of her seventieth birthday, she moved to Brighton, where fifty years earlier she had thrown away her chance of marrying Merthyr Guest in favor of the penniless and indolent Hussar, Harry Weldon. Guest had married a daughter of the Duke of Westminster and died with assets of £177,000. As for Harry, the chance meeting at Lady Sudeley's ball had changed his life, not always in ways that reflected credit on him. The acting king of arms kept well out of her way and though he may have read the *Mémoires* made no comment on them.

Brighton was breezy and vulgar, but she liked it. She rose at six every morning and took a cold bath, read the papers (especially the law reports), and then tried to master the typewriter, tapping out letters to her nephew and trying to console Apsley's widow. Dal was also dead, and of all the Trehernes only she and Emily survived. Even so late in the day, the two sisters could not be reconciled. They agreed to hate each other. As for the *Mémoires*, they were all but forgotten, apart from the nuisance of what to do with the boxes in which they were stored. They had not crossed the bridge between the centuries, any more than she had herself. In a curious last act of defiance, in 1913 she summoned a photographer and had her portrait taken in bed, her eyes closed, her face composed in the image of death. The youthful cast of her features, which so many people had remarked over the years, the famous Pears complexion, all that had fled. Her cropped hair peeps out from under a nightcap, her cheeks have fallen away, and her nose rises like a beak. Her landlady, Mrs. Gunn, was sufficiently alarmed to phone Lise Grey in London, so strange was the job Georgina had asked the photographer to do. But Georgina knew exactly what she wanted from the image. The photograph is saying more powerfully than any words that its subject might as well be dead.

The end came on Monday, January 12, 1914. It was snowing in Sussex. Four days after her death, the body was taken to Mayfield, but not along the same roads that Harry had ridden out along on his horse Multum to ask for her hand in marriage. The coffin went by train, attended by the funeral director and a reporter from the *Brighton Gazette*. The paper had noticed her death in a short front-page column on January 14:

> Mrs. Georgina Weldon died on Sunday [*sic*] at Brighton. To the present generation the name may not be very familiar, but the lady who passed away quietly at a Brighton boarding house—she was in her seventy-seventh year—had in her time been a conspicuous figure in musical and legal circles, and was, for several years, the despair of Her Majesty's judges. In her prime she was of very attractive appearance, had a voice of great sweetness and flexibility, was a ready wit, and an accomplished woman.

The reporter who attended the interment contradicts Phillip Treherne, who was present and who says "we saw her laid to rest in the Dalrymple vault near the entrance of the fine old church of St. Dunstan's." Instead, the *Gazette* mentions how the vault that Morgan prepared for himself—and which was inside the church fabric—was opened after an interval of fifty-one years. The reporter was very struck by the good condition of the remains within and the extraordinary size of the provision. There were "thirty spaces, sufficient to accommodate forty coffins." Though no one present remarked upon it, the vault was found to contain not one coffin, but three. Georgina was interred with her father, her baby sister Cordelia, who had been removed from Clapharn Parish Church at some time in the fifties, and another child, Gilbert Offley Thomas, born November 27, 1845, died June 29, 1846. This was not Morgan's child but almost certainly his brother's. What strange fate had brought him to be reburied in Sussex with an uncle the whole family detested is the last of the mysteries surrounding this unhappiest of families.

There was one final indignity to be posthumously endured by the dedicated searcher after truth. As Georgina joined her father, the man from the *Gazette* duly noted down: "The coffin was of polished oak with brass furniture and bore the inscription Georgina Weldon, born May 23, 1838, died January 11, 1914." Of the twelve digits in these dates, six were wrong.

It was bitterly cold in the church, though while the committal service was being read, a pale wintry sun came out. Only seven mourners were present to see her home: Phillip and Beator Treherne; Apsley's widow; Lise Grey and her brother; Mrs. Gunn, the boardinghouse keeper; and an old man named Tom Bridger who had once worked for Morgan and alone could say what kind of a prison Gate House had been in the days when the father had forbidden his most talented child permission even to sing in the choir of the church in which they now lay side by side.

On the previous Sunday, perhaps a more oblique but fitting epitaph to Georgina's life of triumphs and tribulations had taken place at the parish church of Aldrington, near Hove. At the end of the second collect, an unidentified woman stood and cried out, "God save Rachael Peach, Sylvia Pankhurst and all the women who are persecuted and suffer in prison for conscience's sake, and open the eyes of Thy Church, we beseech Thee, Amen."

Bibliography

The primary source for this book has been the six volumes of *Mémoires de Georgina Weldon: Justice (?) Anglaise*, self-published as from Gisors/34 Hart St., Bloomsbury, 1902. This huge and ramshackle work includes French translations of some but not all of the other pamphlets published by Georgina. It is especially rich in letters to and by her. English-language copies of the pamphlets, as well as the shortlived newspaper *Social Salvation*, can be found in the Bodleian Library, Oxford.

Her contemporaries had much less to say about her than might be imagined. Her nephew, Phillip Treherne, published an affectionate and uncritical portrait of her nine years after she died in *A Plaintiff in Person* (Heinemann, 1923). It is from this book that the letter from Oscar Wilde is quoted.

Georgina's only other biographer has been Edward Grierson, in his *Storm Bird: The Strange Life of Georgina Weldon* (Chatto and Windus, 1959). Grierson had access to the entire Weldon chronofile, and quotations from her diaries and journal in the present work can be traced to his genial and entertaining book.

A much less successful attempt to shoehorn her into nineteenth-century feminist history can be found in *City of Dreadful Night: A Narrative of Sexual Danger in Late Victorian London* by Judith Walkovitz (Virago, 1992).

One of the satisfactions in hunting for her ghost in the Tavistock House years has been the chance to read the wise and witty *Gounod* by James Harding (Allen and Unwin, 1973).

Other works that bear directly on the story are listed below:

Bancroft, Squire. *The Bancrofts*. Murray, 1909.

————*Empty Chairs*. Murray, 1925.

Bessborough, Earl of, ed. *Lady Charlotte Schreiber, Extracts from her Journals*. Murray, 1952.

Blunt, Wilfred. *England's Michelangelo*. Hamish Hamilton, 1975.

De HegerMann-Lindencrone. *In the Courts of Memory*. Harper & Brothers, 1912.

Doggett, Maeve E. *Marriage, Wifebeating and the Law in Victorian England*. University of South Carolina Press, 1993.

Du Maurier, Daphne, ed. *The Young George Du Maurier, Letters 1860–67*. Peter Davies, 1951.

Kennedy, A. L. *My Dear Duchess*. Murray, 1956.

Scull, Andrew, with Charlotte MacKenzie and Nicholas Hervey. *Masters of Bedlam*. Princeton University Press, 1996.

Weinreb, Ben, and Christopher Hibbert. *The London Encyclopedia*. MacMillan, 1983.

Weintraub, Stanley. *Victoria*. Murray, 1987.

Wilson, Guy Fleetwood. *Letters to Somebody*. Cassell, 1922.

Young, G. M. *Victorian England, Portrait of an Age*. OUP, 1936.

Index